THE FOOTPRINTS OF FAITH

EXPLORING THE FOUNDATION OF OUR FAITH IN THE LIFE OF ABRAHAM THE FATHER OF FAITH

DR. ABRAHAM PETERS

Best Selling Author - Awakening The Prophet In You : Understanding The Prophetic Ministry.

DR. ABRAHAM PETERS

Copyright © 2019 Dr. Abraham Peters – All rights reserved.

ISBN: **9781730935008**

No part of this book may be reproduced, stored in a retrieval system, or transmitted by any means—electronic, mechanical, photocopy, record, or otherwise—without written permission from the author.

All correspondence to: abrahampeters@rocketmail.com

PREFACE

Father Abraham is one of the most famous spiritual giants in the Bible. He is known to be the father of the faithful (Romans 4:11) and the friend of God (Isaiah 41:8; James 2:23). His life is so significant that Abraham has been mentioned more times in the New Testament than anyone in the Old Testament. His story covers a good portion of the book of Genesis. To this day, his impact is so big that three of the major religions today consider him as a significant religious figure. We can learn important lessons from the life of Abraham. His life is filled with so many accomplishments and failures that we should not fail to take note of. God's call is to all, as Abraham we must have tough faith for tough times. There will never be a time when the choice to choose faith in God will be easy. God always beckons us to have faith in Him, because faith in God will always conquer anything.

Father Abraham is a powerful figure for so many reasons. His faith was incredible. He literally left everything he knew to follow God in a direction he didn't understand. Despite his shortcomings, Abraham triumphed time and time again because he believed God would show up. He believed it so much that he was willing to bet his own life as well as the lives of his family. And in every situation, God did show up and Abraham's faith was proven true, he is just as ordinary human like me and you and everyone else but what made the difference is faith in God and he became extraordinary hero of faith.

Faith is firm relying, solid trust in GOD. And no matter what life brings our way, we must always activate our faith. Abraham is among the best known men of the Bible. There is not a single book in our scriptures written by Abraham and He did not speak any recorded prophesy. Yet, Abraham is known as the father of the Hebrew nation. It was through Abraham's seed that all nations on earth have been blessed (Genesis 12:3) and God even refers to this historic man of faith as His friend and a prophet (Genesis 20:7 & Isaiah 41:8).

When Abraham was told to leave his country, his people, and his father's household (Genesis 12:1), he obeyed, even though he had no idea where he was going (Hebrews 11:6). Though Abraham's wife had been barren their entire marriage, when the Lord told the patriarch his offspring would be as numerous as the stars in the sky, Abraham chose to believe God, despite his circumstances. Abraham's faith was credited to him as righteousness (Genesis 15:5-6).

Through the journey in the Footprints of Faith, you will watch the budding father of a nation question God's plans, take matters into his own hands, and, at times, compromise truth. Like us, Abraham and his wife, Sarah, made mistakes along their journey with God, but Abraham learned to trust God more fully from each misstep. Abraham became a great man of faith. Through his story, you too, will develop unwavering faith as you gain a greater understanding of the covenant God made with Abraham and his descendants. You will find a greater sense of peace and security. For as a believer in Christ, you are Abraham's spiritual descendant and an heir according to the promise (Galatians 3:29).

Believers can reach out in faith, take back what belongs to them, and begin to live in success, happiness, and liberty. The principle of calling things that are not as though they were is the spiritual principle through which everything physical becomes manifest. God created the light by calling for light when only darkness was there. Jesus used this same method, calling the lepers clean, and the dead to life, and peace to the storm. Abraham the father of faith believed God for resurrection even though he had never seen anyone resurrected before his faith in God was unwavering he did not staggered he trusted in God without any limitation. (Romans 4:20-24 and Hebrews 11:19) If you do not waver You will receive and have in your life exactly what you believe for and say.

All Jesus asked from us is Faith just as small like the mustard seed (Luke 17:6), great things start small. Abram became Abraham one day at a time. Through trials, tests of time, his faith was built on the victories of God in his life. And it was through learning and remembering that he grew into the patriarch we know him as today. That is why I want to share these twelve key lessons with you. I want us to live with BIG FAITH. And to get there we must start here, exactly where we are at today. I hope these insights inspire you to take small steps, to dig into God's Word, and to believe that you are already living in the extraordinary story God is writing. With these in mind, let us explore the life of Abraham and inculcate in our minds the vital lessons we must learn:

BE WILLING TO GIVE UP EVERYTHING KNOWN FOR GOD TO FOLLOW GOD INTO THE UNKNOWN.

Abraham is called the father of the faithful for good reasons. When God calls him to leave his homeland, the land where he grew up and where his family is, he immediately "went out, not knowing where he was going" (Hebrews 11:8). The test of his faith did not stop there. God asks him to offer his only begotten son. Can you imagine the torment, doubt, and fear that could have raced behind Abraham's mind? If you are a father, will you have the strength and courage to put your beloved son on an altar, kill him, burn him, and offer him to God?

God will never leave us empty. If He asks us to put something down, it is because He wants us to pick something better. Abraham is also a human, however, his faith is bigger than his doubts because he strongly believed that God is able to raise Isaac up, even from the dead (Hebrews 11:19). Abraham is fully convinced that what God had promised He is also able to perform. This is the type of faith that makes Christians unstoppable. Abraham has the faith that there is a reason behind everything that God asks him to do. His faith is so strong that he is willing to give up EVERYTHING for God. Abraham made a decision to give not just 50%, 70%, 80%, or 90% of his life but he decided to give 100% of his life to God. Abraham is ready to leave behind everything familiar to him. Even his own son, he is willing to offer to God.

The faith of Abraham is so impressive that Paul devoted a good portion of the Faith Chapter to Abraham. Like Abraham, we must have the willingness to devote our whole life and being to God. And do you know the best thing about surrendering everything to God? God will never leave us empty. If He asks us to put something down, it is because He wants us to pick something better. We may not always understand why God commands us to do something, but we can be 100% sure that it is for our own good (Psalms 84:11).

EVEN SPIRITUAL GIANTS ARE STILL HUMANS

There is no doubt that Abraham's faith is among the strongest in the Bible. However, as strong as his faith might have been, he is still human, subject to frailties and weaknesses. Abraham and Sarah were already old and they still didn't have a son. This was a big issue in their life and was considered to be shameful in their culture. Since Abraham didn't have a child, he had no proper heir for all his properties. When all hopes seem to fade, God promised Abraham and Sarah that they will have a son in their old age (Genesis 12:1-2, 13:16, 17:6). This promise has been mentioned to Abraham multiple times and Abraham believed God. Nevertheless, the fulfillment of the promise is not immediate. It took about 25 years before it was fulfilled. Because of this, Abraham and Sarah grew impatient and Sarah gave her handmaid, Hagar, to Abraham. Hagar eventually got pregnant and had a son named, Ishmael. This fatal mistake of Abraham had caused division within his family. When Isaac finally was born to Sarah, Ishmael and his mother were driven out from their place. Ishmael eventually became the father of the Arab nation, while Isaac became the father of the English-speaking nations and the Jews. This explains why Arab nations and the Western nations can't find a common ground to sustain long-lasting peace. After the death of Sarah, Abraham took concubines (Genesis 25:6), which is something that God does not approve. As expected, if you break the Law of God, it will break you. Abraham will soon suffer the consequences of his sinful actions. Although we can see that Abraham is not perfect, he is still considered as a friend of God. We can find comfort from his life that though we may commit mistakes and sin, God is always faithful to forgive us as long as we repent and change our ways.

MY STORY IS PART OF A MUCH BIGGER STORY. (GENESIS 11:27-32)

Abraham's story didn't just begin when God called him, or even when he was born. God had begun writing it long before Abraham was ever born and continued long after he was gone. The reason our stories matter is because they are part of something infinitely bigger.(Jeremiah 1:5)

DON'T GIVE UP ON GOD, WHEN GOD DOESN'T SEEM TO BE KEEPING HIS PROMISES ON TIME. GOD IS WORKING ON SOMETHING BIG AND HAS NOT FORGOTTEN ABOUT YOU. (GENESIS 13:14-18)

If the story is so big, then that means I'm pretty small and insignificant, right? Wrong – God doesn't work that way. The God we serve is a God of the details. He sees every piece and knows exactly why He needs it. Absolutely nothing and no one is insignificant in God's eyes.

IT'S OKAY TO ASK GOD, HOW CAN I KNOW? FAITH DOESN'T ALWAYS HAVE TO BE INVISIBLE. (GENESIS 15:7-21)

Every time God does something significant in my life I build an "altar." Sometimes they are simple, like a hundred-dollar bill or a note in my Bible. Other times they are more extensive like writing a book. These physical objects act as reminders. Whenever I see them, I am reminded of that time in my life when God stepped in and radically changed my situation. If altars were good enough for the patriarchs, I think they are definitely something we should implement.

TITHING LEADS TO PHYSICAL BLESSINGS

Did you know that the first mention of tithing is found in Genesis 13:20? It is the time after Abraham defeated possibly four kings to rescue his nephew, Lot. After defeating these kings, he gathered many spoils and gave a tithe to Melchizedek, who later became Jesus Christ (Hebrews 5:6-7). This automatically dispels the wrong assumption that tithing is only commanded to the Israelites since the Israelites haven't existed yet during the time of Abraham. The truth is that God commanded His people, both in the past and today, to give tithes and offering. Because of Abraham's obedience in the law of tithing and to the law of God as a whole, he was blessed and increased by God (Isaiah 51:2). He became a "mighty prince" (Genesis 23:6) and "very rich in livestock, in silver, and in gold" (Genesis 13:2). Needless to say, tithing opens the windows of Heaven and releases outpouring floodgate of blessings. We can read in Malachi 3:10-12.

OUR RELATIONSHIP WITH GOD AFFECTS EVERYONE AROUND US. (GENESIS 17:15-27)

Because Abraham had faith, his family had the courage to take steps of faith as well. Abraham influenced his wife, children, and descendants by his walk of faith in obedience to God. We have the same opportunity. Whether it's our family, friends or coworkers, every time we step out in faith, people see that. The greatest way to share the Gospel is to simply acting on God's call and let Him do the rest.

REMEMBERING GOD'S ACTIONS IN OUR PAST WILL HELP US FIGHT TODAY'S FEAR. (GENESIS 20:1-18)

If you have ever had to retake a test? Usually, you do much better the second time around because you know what to expect. Then why do we still fail so much in our own lives? We have a dangerously short-term memory when it comes to God's actions in our lives. Whether it's helping us fight temptation or watching Him provide, we tend to fall back into our old ways, way too easily. It's only when we take the time to remember how God has already helped us win before, that we can have the faith to win again.

OUR GOD DOESN'T RUN AWAY FROM MESSES. HE RUNS TOWARDS THEM. (GENESIS 21:8-21)

Abraham's life got messy at times. Between family drama, physical pain, and outer turmoil Abraham had his hands full. God wasn't turned off by what He saw. In fact, when situations get messy and out of control, that is when God rolls up His sleeves and dives right in. We have to learn to run towards God and not away from Him when we are neck deep in life's craziness. Our good Father God is always ready and able to help.

WE ARE ALWAYS PUTTING OUR FAITH IN SOMETHING. (ROMANS 4:16)

The truth is we put faith in things everyday. If you're sitting, you had faith the chair would hold you up. If you ate food today, you had faith that it wouldn't poison you. Our jobs, education, relationships, these are all objects of our faith. We hope that they will take care of us and protect us and when they don't, it feels as if our whole world is falling apart. God wants our faith to be in Him alone. Abraham succeeded by putting his faith in the right One. We can do the same. Abraham had an uncommon life and so can we. We serve the same God he did thousands of years ago and the best part is, God is still writing.

FAITH IS BOTH BELIEVING AND DOING

The Apostle Paul said, "Therefore we conclude that a man is justified by faith apart from the deeds of the law" (Romans 3:28). On the other hand, James said, "You see then that a man is justified by works, and not by faith only" (James 2:24). Did Paul and James contradict each other? A deep look at these passages will tell us that they did not. As a matter of fact, Paul and James were complementing each other. They were in agreement. Both Paul and James used Abraham to explain their point. Abraham both believed God but did not just let that belief remain in his mind. He acted upon his belief. Paul and James included in their letter that "Abraham believed God, and it was accounted to him for righteousness" (Romans 4:3 and James 2:23).

Abraham showed us that no one can earn salvation and it is equally true that salvation cannot be earned without works. The point of Paul is that no amount of work can earn us salvation. Most of the Jews in Paul's time are so self-righteous that they trusted on their work. They thought that their tradition and law-keeping will make them right with God. This is the kind of thinking that Paul wants to correct. Looking at the statement of James, he is dealing with Christians who have the "intellectual" faith. They are Christians who have the gift of God's knowledge and yet, that knowledge is never translated in their lives. They have faith but they lack action.

Faith is demonstrated through action. Believing is one thing but acting on that belief is completely different. Abraham exemplified what true and living faith is. Abraham's belief in God behooves him to act upon his belief. Abraham has faith and how would God know if he really has faith? Through his actions. Faith is both belief in God and doing his commandments. Abraham showed us that no one can earn salvation and it is equally true that salvation cannot be earned without works.

WHEN MAKING A DECISION, THINK GENERATIONALLY

Abraham is a man of decision. Whether we like it or not, we are all presented with different choices. Some are minor, while others are really significant. The story of Abraham showed us that every action leads to another. This is importantly true in Abraham's life and it is certainly true in our life today. Abraham made a decision that did not just affect his life but also the life of other people. The effects of his decision did not just affect his immediate lifetime but also down through the history of man.

The decision of Abraham to take into his own hands the fulfillment of God's promise caused a tremendously negative effect. One decision led to the creation of the different modern nations today. Because of his decision to obtain a son from Hagar, he started a domino effect that run through the ages. We now have that ripple effect of seeing the Middle East as a powder keg of strife and war. His descendants are always in conflict because of the family feud that had started with Ishmael and Isaac thousands of years ago.

The story of Abraham and his descendants show us that the decision we make can potentially affect everything around us. For this reason, before we commit a sin, we must also remember that sin can put a toll on us in a personal and national level. So many times we have seen people suffer not because of their own actions but because of the sin of other people. Sin can affect the person doing it and the people around him. In Abraham's case, his sin of adultery affected not just himself but also his family and descendants. So before making a decision or committing a sin, think about how it can affect not just yourself but also your loved ones. Think in a generational scale.

Abraham is known to be the father of the faithful. Whether you are a Jew or gentile, an Israelite or non-Israelite, you are part of Abraham's seed (Galatians 3:29) when you accept Jesus' sacrifice and follow God's commandments. Therefore, it is important for us to think about the life of Abraham. Learn the lessons from his life and like faith, let these lessons be evident in your life through righteous deeds and actions. Volumes of hundred of thousands books have been written by many on this great man of faith, surely many more will be written until we finally see him face to face at the bosom of Abraham in heaven (Luke 16:22) But here we can be partaker of the blessings of our Father Abraham (Galatians 3:14) Abraham was no coward, he's a great warrior who trained his servants and they fought unto victory to rescue Lot and others (Genesis 14:14) He was also a great intercessor a man of prayer who stood in the gap before the Lord praying interceding for Sodom and Gomorrah (Genesis 18:16-33) The life application for us today is a call to faith, love, integrity righteousness, generosity and prayer, that's how to walk in the footsteps of faith.

We can see that this patriarch Abraham was an exemplary individual, not so much in his piety or perfect life (he had his shortcomings), but because his life illustrates so many truths of the Christian life. God called Abraham out of the millions of people on the earth to be the object of His blessings. God used Abraham to play a pivotal role in the outworking of the story of redemption, culminating in the birth of Jesus. Abraham is a living example of faith and hope in the promises of God (Hebrews 11:8–10). Our lives should be so lived that, when we reach the end of our days, our faith, like Abraham's, will remain as an enduring legacy to others.

God made the eternal promises, to bless him and his descendants. After He miraculously heals Sarah's womb she gives birth to Isaac. This "father of the faithful" is blessed to meet with a Priest of the Most High God named Melchizedek, who is actually a pre-incarnate appearance of Jesus Christ. After visiting Abraham two angels save Lot and family before the destruction of Sodom. Lot's wife becomes a pillar of salt when, while fleeing, she turns to view God's judgment on Sodom and Gomorrah. His faith is tested when God commands him to sacrifice his only son Isaac. Now fasten your seat belt and get ready for a great flight, deep study in the Footprints of Faith as we journey with Abraham to explore this great patriarch and hero of faith.

TABLE OF CONTENTS

PREFACE..iv
PROLOGUE..1
Introduction Believe, Respond, Obey 36
   Single Minded Service 38
   Discover Our Roots 40
   Abraham's Children 42
   First Will And Testament 45
Chapter One Moving With God 46
   Continual Consistency 47
   Look To The Rock 48
   Abram Of Ur 50
   The Idols In Our Lives 50
   Move Out! 52
   Traveller's Journal 53
Chapter Two The Blessings Of God 54
   A Great Nation 55
   The Blessing of God 56
   Great Name 56
   To Be a Blessing 58
   Bless and Curse 60
   Blessings for All 61
   Our Prayer 62
   Traveller's Journal 62
      REFLECT 62

RECOMMIT	62
Chapter Three Following God's Way	63
Prayer	71
Traveller's Journal	72
REFLECT	72
RECOMMIT	72
Chapter Four Even Saints Make Mistakes	73
Problems in the Promised Land	74
The Intention of the Heart	78
E-G-Y-P-T- Spells Trouble	79
Affliction or Consequences?	81
Traveller's Journal	86
REFLECT	86
RECOMMIT	86
Chapter Five Choosing God.	87
The Road Not Taken	88
Problems of Prosperity	89
Territorial Terrain	90
Selecting Sodom	92
Abraham and Lot	94
Contemporary Commentary	99
Traveller's Journal	103
REFLECT	103
RECOMMIT	103
Chapter Six One Priest – One Sacrifice	104
The Order of Melchizedek	106
Only One Mediator	109

- A Kingdom of Priests 112
- Traveller's Journal 115
  - REFLECT 115
  - RECOMMIT 115
- Chapter Seven Promises Made – Promises Kept 116
  - The Promise Renewed 118
  - God's Land 120
  - Taking and Leaving the Land 122
  - The Hand of God in the Affairs of Men 124
  - Traveller's Journal 129
    - REFLECT 129
    - RECOMMIT 129
- Chapter Eight Receive The Gift 130
  - Traveller's Journal 139
    - REFLECT 139
    - RECOMMIT 139
- Chapter Nine Outer And Inner Signs Of Faith 140
  - Covenantal Requirements 143
  - External Sign, Inner Reality 146
  - Individual Faith 148
  - Traveller's Journal 151
    - REFLECT 151
    - RECOMMIT 151
- Chapter Ten Joined To God 152
  - An Intimate God 153
  - The Sign of the Covenant 156
  - The Name Above All Names 157

- Traveller's Journal 165
  - REFLECT 165
  - RECOMMIT 165
- Chapter Eleven Running Away Form God 166
  - Giving God a Hand 167
  - Hagar and the Angel of the Lord 169
  - The God Who Sees Me 171
  - Prayer 174
  - Traveller's Journal 174
    - REFLECT 174
    - RECOMMIT 175
- Chapter Twelve Backsliding 176
  - Traveller's Journal 185
    - REFLECT 185
    - RECOMMIT 186
- Chapter Thirteen Testing And Triumph 187
  - The Test 191
    - REFLECT 199
    - RECOMMIT 199
- Chapter Fourteen Sarah, Our Mother 200
  - God's Order 202
  - Sarah, our Mother 206
  - A Tribute of Tears 209
  - Prayer 213
  - Traveller's Journal 214
    - REFLECT 214
    - RECOMMIT 214

Chapter Fifteen The Trust Of A True Believer 215
   The Custom of the Day 218
   The Task for Which He was sent 220
   Yesterday, Today, Forever! 225
   Traveller's Journal 228
      REFLECT 228
      RECOMMIT 229
Chapter Sixteen The End Of The Journey 230
   A View of the Church 235
   The Legacy of Abraham 237
   Prayer 242
   Traveller's Journal 242
      REFLECT 242
      RECOMMIT 242
Epilogue 243
The List Of Kinds Of Faith Identified In The New Testament ... 253
A To Z Biblical References About The Life Of Abraham 256
Dedication 243
Acknowledgement 243
ABOUT THE AUTHOR DR.ABRAHAM PETERS 272

DR. ABRAHAM PETERS

PROLOGUE

The Footprints of Faith

What will be left of your life's work when you leave this earth? Will there be any "footprints" left in people's lives? Were they changed unto a greater zeal to earnestly seek and study and pray and live in such a way that God is glorified?

Your faith, my faith, is very little if we are not making a measurable impact daily on those around us. One preacher calls our modern-day Church one of "low impact, high maintenance" Christians. Perhaps this is not true of you. What I would ask is for you to pray and ask God to do ANYTHING necessary to facilitate the changes that He wants to make in your life. But, we must remember that we are not passive automatons that are shaped by the Lord and have no free will! God is not creating a race of robots, or slaves, if you will, but rather willing men, women, and children who know their God, and have freely yielded their lives for His use. Such men founded this great United States of America.

The Scripture reads: "Go ye therefore, and teach all nations, baptizing them in the name of the Father, and of the Son, and of the Holy Ghost: teaching them to observe all things whatsoever I have commanded you: and, lo, I am with you always, [even] unto the end of the world. Amen." Matthew 28:19

Go to someone! Meet them personally. Tell them what Jesus did to change your life. The Lord will work in you and through you and change you as you go. And THAT is the real change that yours truly can believe in.

Seven Footprints of Faith

How is your faith? How does your faith compare with the faith of Abraham, the father of the faithful?

THE FOOTPRINTS OF FAITH

Don't mess with the children. A little girl was talking to her teacher about whales. The teacher said, "It's physically impossible for a whale to swallow a human being because even though it was a very large mammal, its throat is too small." The little girl stated that Jonah was swallowed by a whale. She'd not done Apostolic Bible College (ABC), but that's beside the point. Irritated, the teacher said that the whale could not swallow a human being. It's physically impossible. The little girl said, "What I get to heaven, I will ask Jonah." The teacher asked, "What if Jonah went to hell?" The little girl replied, "Then you ask him."

A kindergarten teacher was observing her classroom of children while they were drawing. She would occasionally walk around to see each child's work. As she got to one little girl who was working diligently, she asked what the drawing was. The girl replied, "I'm drawing God." The teacher paused and said, "But no one knows what God looks like." Without missing a beat, or looking up from her drawing, the girl replied, "They will in a minute."

A Sunday School teacher was discussing the ten commandments with her five and six year olds. After explaining the commandment to honor thy father and thy mother, she asked, "Is there a commandment that teaches us how to treat our brothers and sisters?" Without missing a beat, one little boy, the oldest of the family, answered, "Thou shalt not kill." And a couple more. I like these.

One day a little girl was sitting and watching her mother do the dishes. Suddenly, she noticed that her mother had several strands of white hair sticking out in contrast to her brunette head. She looked at her mother and inquisitively asked, "Why are some of your hairs white, Mommy?"

Her mother replied, "Well, every time you do something bad, and you make me cry or unhappy, one of my hairs turns white." The little girl thought about this for a moment, and then said, "Mommy, how come ALL of Grandma's hairs are white?"

And finally, a story from a Catholic elementary school. The children were lined up in a cafeteria at a Catholic elementary school for lunch. At the head of the table there was a large pile of apples. The nun made a note, and she posted it on the apple tray. "Take only one. God is watching." Moving further along the lunch at the other end of the table, there was a large pile of chocolate chip cookies. A child had written a note. "Take all you want. God is watching the apples."

Well, children can sometimes be very charming and very believing and very much people who believe what they hear. Young people often are a good example of faith. The question I've got for you this morning is, "How is your faith?" How does your faith compare with the faith of Abraham, the father of the faithful? Probably, if we're all very honest about these things, and we think about our faith from time to time, we realize that our faith is not perfect. We have faith; we're people of faith, but our faith is not, perhaps, exactly the way we think it ought to be. Let's go to *Hebrews:11:1Now faith is the substance of things hoped for, the evidence of things not seen..* Probably many of you know how that scripture reads. It gives us a definition of faith, doesn't it? But let's begin with a definition of faith.

Hebrews:11:1Now faith is the substance of things hoped for, the evidence of things not seen. - We're told what faith is. Now faith is the substance of things hoped for, the evidence of things not seen. In other words, faith makes reality out of something that isn't yet. It's firm; it's substances; you can reach out, and you can touch it. You make it real because you know that it's going to be because God has promised it. It's substance. It's evidence.

How then does faith work in our lives, and how may we strengthen our faith? What if, maybe we should delete the word — if — when you and I feel weak in the faith from time to time. The title of the sermon is "Seven Footprints of Faith." The starting point, point number one in the seven footprints of faith is God said it; I believe it, and that's that. God said it; I believe it, and that's that. Simple, it may be, but it encapsulates something; it captures something.

And I'd like to begin with a story of a very wealthy man who was living very comfortably in a place where, well, you wanted to be, if you wanted to live comfortably and makes lots of money. His name was Abram, and he was living in a place that has been much in the news over the last few years, a little bit less in the news for the last few weeks. He was living in Iraq, in Ur of the Chaldeans, and you probably know what the map looks like there. He was living at the intersection of two big rivers. If you wanted to be wealthy and progress in life back in the ancient world, you had to be where the water was. People didn't get very far in life where there wasn't any water.

So, he lived in Ur of the Chaldeans by the Tigress and the Euphrates, especially the Euphrates River, when God began to deal with him. Let's go to Genesis 12. The story of Abraham is an amazing story, and it tells us an awful lot about what it's like to be a member of the Church of God and to be people of faith. This is a man of faith.

Genesis:12:1Now the LORD had said unto Abram, Get thee out of thy country, and from thy kindred, and from thy father's house, unto a land that I will shew thee: - God begins to deal with a man whose name has not yet been changed yet. His name is Abram. Now the (Lord) eternal (had) said to Abram: "Get out of your country, from your family and from your father's house, to a land that I will show you."...Abram is being told to go somewhere. He's being told to leave the part of the world where you can be comfy, where you can be wealthy, where you can have your family, he had an extended family, of course, a large number of people and servants and so on, and he's being told to go, well, somewhere. He didn't know where he's being told to go. He had no car. He had no GPS system; he had no maps. GO!

Verse 2 — "(I will) I'll make you a great nation; (I will) I'll bless you (and) I'll make your name great; and you shall be a blessing.

Verse 3 — "I will bless those who bless you, and I will curse (him) those who curse(s) you; and in you all the families of the earth shall be blessed." This is a starting point, we heard about a starting point involving John, the Baptist. This is very much a starting point in the Old Testament. Here is a man who is kind of a loner. Now I know he'd be surrounded by people, but God begins to deal with him individually and gives him a vision. He didn't have what you and I have at present right in front of him, a Bible or Bibles, lots of different translations. He had no church, no temple. He had a direct revelation from God, and it's difficult to imagine what went through Abram's mind when all of this happens. But we're given his response in Verse 4. Look at what he did. If he'd had a bumper sticker, that would have been the bumper sticker. God said it, I believe it, and that's that.

Verse 4 — So Abram departed as the (Lord) Eternal had spoken to him,...he left, got up and left by donkey and cart, no doubt, departing for a part of the world he didn't know where he was going. Simply trusting this God who'd made Himself known to him.

What was so special about Abram? He simply took God at His word, simply took God at His word, and if an Abraham is a prototype of people of faith, like you and me, then this tells us something. We are people who just take God at His word. When God says something, we believe it.

I was putting together one of my schedules of classes, one of the classes that we do at Apostolic Bible College (ABC). I was working on it, and in Foundations of Faith, we do a unit of study, which I really enjoy covering with the students. It's called the Proof of the Bible through the Fulfilled Promises. And in that particular section, what we do is we go through some of the promises in the Bible, promises of physical blessing, promises of healings, promises of protections, and we read the scriptures, and then I like to open it up and talk with the students and get from them some of the things that happened to them, or in their families, or people that they've known in the church, and there are so many stories, so many things that have happened, so many times that God has intervened in the lives of His people. We read it and we believe it. We're people of faith. It's really quite amazing. I kind of wish you all could sit in on some of that, but you know, we talk about these things among ourselves, don't we, on other occasions.

You know, we do that blessing of the children right after the Feast, and our kids really do keep the angels busy. Some of the stories of protection, and some of the things that have happened to little children in the church are absolutely amazing.

The point that I'm making here is that we're people of faith. We read what God does for us, and we take Him at His word. God says this is what He does; this is what He does. We're people of faith. We're not the great ones of the world; we're not the most educated; we're not the most prestigious, but we're people of faith, and it's amazing how many things have happened. And I contrast this with some of the people that I meet occasionally in the world, in the academic world and in the world of Biblical scholarship. Occasionally, I listen to the voices of Biblical scholars, and I hear a voice of cynicism. I hear voices of people who really don't believe in God the way that you and I do. Now that's not all Biblical scholars, but that is many Biblical scholars. They're cynics. They don't believe that this book that we have here is really the word of God, and then I contrast it with what I hear among God's people and what we cover in the Apostolic Bible College (ABC) classroom from time to time, and the contrast is so striking. It's really, really striking.

God said it; I believe it, and that's that. That's our starting point. When God says something, it's true. You can take it to the bank. Abram, when he departed, had to take it to the bank. Had to believe God because he left not knowing where he was going.

Point number two. Faith comes by hearing. We see in Genesis 12 that Abram received a vision. God made known His word to him in a vision. Genesis 15. Let's turn forward to Genesis 15 where God is still dealing with this man. The promises get reiterated many times in the book of Genesis. It's amazing how many times God tells him the same thing over and over again. Of course, I think you know, the promises kind of narrow, don't they, from Abraham to Isaac and then to Jacob, and you can follow it all the way through the book of Genesis. It's much the same wording.

Genesis:15:1After these things the word of the LORD came unto Abram in a vision, saying, Fear not, Abram: I am thy shield, and thy exceeding great reward.— And there's a repetition, but a slight rewording of the promise. After these things ...and we'll talk about Genesis 14 briefly. ...After these things the word of the (Lord) Eternal came to Abram in a vision, saying, "Don't be afraid, Abram. I am your shield, and your reward will be very great. (Your exceedingly great reward.) Actually, the wording in the New King James version sort of hides something here. There's a double promise in *Genesis:15:1After these things the word of the LORD came unto Abram in a vision, saying, Fear not, Abram: I am thy shield, and thy exceeding great reward..* Number One, the first part of the promise, Abram, I'm your shield. That was easy for Abram to understand. You know why? Because in Genesis 14, he had seen it. That was the occasion where he had to go out to war to rescue his nephew, Lot. And we'll come back to that briefly. And Lot found himself sort of embroiled in this big war between four kings and five. So, that was easy, because he'd already experienced it.

But a second part of the promise, "Your reward is going to be very great." I think that reads that way in the New International Version. God is here promising Abram a reward, an estate, a family. That's what's implied here, and you can see it clearly in Verse 2, which we'll read momentarily because Abram has difficulty believing it. Abram is being told here, you're going to have an estate; you're going to have offspring; you're going to have family. Now you know the story. They're too old. They're too old.

Verse 2, (But) Abram said, "Lord Eternal (God), what will You give me, seeing (I go) I'm childless, and the heir of my house is

Eliezer of Damascus?" One of the fascinating things about Abram, Abraham, is that he wrestles with this subject of faith. And his initial reaction — How am I going to have an estate? How am I going to have offspring when I have no children of my own?

Back in the ancient world back then, apparently, it was the custom for a wealthy family that was childless, where the parents were childless, they would name a steward, a servant, born in their home, who would be the one who would take over the estate when the patriarch and the matriarch were gone. Now, it's interesting, of course, Eliezer of Damascus, he's got God's name in his name, so he had probably, we don't read much about him, but he probably adopted the faith of Abram. But nevertheless, he wasn't physical offspring. He wasn't physical offspring of Abram.

Verse 3 — (Then) Abram said, "Look, You have given me no offspring; indeed one born in my house is my heir!" If he was born in God's house and he's got God's name imbedded in his name, he was presumably part of the community of faith.

Verse 4 — (And) behold, the word of the (Lord) Eternal came to him, saying, "This one shall not be your heir, but one who will come from your own body shall be your heir." We don't get an awful lot of internal thought. One of the interesting things about the Old Testament is that we're not always told what people are thinking. We're left to fill in the gaps for ourselves.

Verse 5 — Then He (God) brought him outside and He said, "Look now toward heaven, and count the stars if you are able to number them." And He said to him, "So shall your descendants be," And this man, Abram, comes outside, tilts his head upwards, looks at the stars, he could see a lot of them, this wasn't the big city; they weren't shrouded by smog, and he looked at the stars, and he said to himself, "You know, if God says I'm going to have offspring as numerous as these stars, I guess I'm going to have offspring as numerous as these stars." And then this very famous verse,

Verse 6 — And he, Abram, believed in the (Lord) Eternal, and He accounted it to him for righteousness. In spite of the fact that physically, this was impossible. He simply believed. Faith comes by hearing. God made known a promise to him, and he took Him at His word.

Romans 4 — Let's go forward into the New Testament. That statement in *Genesis:15:6And he believed in the LORD; and he counted it to him for righteousness.* is quoted several times in the New Testament. In Romans 4 where Paul is discussing a slightly different matter, actually, but he draws in this example of faith. Can you I imagine that, you know, Abram just walking outside and looking up. God said it; it must be true. Faith comes by hearing.

Romans:4:3For what saith the scripture? Abraham believed God, and it was counted unto him for righteousness. — (For) what does the scripture say: "Abraham believed God, and it was accounted to him for righteousness." Paul quotes this in the context of a discussion of works and grace. *Romans:4:19-22[19]And being not weak in faith, he considered not his own body now dead, when he was about an hundred years old, neither yet the deadness of Sarah's womb:[20]He staggered not at the promise of God through unbelief; but was strong in faith, giving glory to God;[21]And being fully persuaded that, what he had promised, he was able also to perform.[22]And therefore it was imputed to him for righteousness..*

Romans:4:19And being not weak in faith, he considered not his own body now dead, when he was about an hundred years old, neither yet the deadness of Sarah's womb: — And not being weak in faith, he did not consider his own body, already dead (since he was about a hundred years old), and the deadness of Sarah's womb.

Verse 20: He (did not) didn't waver at the promise of God through unbelief, but he was strengthened in faith, giving glory to God.

Verse 21 — and being fully convinced that what He had promised He was also able to perform.

Verse 22 — And therefore "It was accounted to him for righteousness." Abram knew he was dealing with someone who was different from the other gods. Back then, in Abram's time, they believed the gods were localized. They believed if you went to this particular area, there was this god there, Baal or Molech. You moved away and you got away from the sphere of influence of this other god. That gods were localized, and yet this God brings them outside, has them look upward at the stars and says, "Look, I'm this powerful."

And Abram said, "I guess it must be true. God told me." Faith comes by hearing.

You remember, by the way, you may remember there's an incident in the book of Numbers. You remember the Balak and Balaam events, where Balak, the king of Moab, brings Balaam, this sort of prophet for hire, and he tries to get him to curse Israel on his behalf. You remember those events, those things with the donkey, and all of those things that went on then. It's a very interesting thing that they did. We'd like to go back and check it. I'm not going to read it right now, but go back and read it sometime, and you'll see that Balak has Balaam, he tells him, "Please curse them."

And Balaam won't curse them, because God won't let him. And you know what they do. Notice what they do. They go from mountain top to mountain top. The reason they go from mountain top to mountain top is because Balak's belief was that if he could get Balaam to a different place, he'd be free of the influence of this God of Israel, and he'd be free to curse them. Of course, several times he's moving around and he never curses them.

But anyway, Abram knew he was dealing with a different kind of God, and that this God had told him something. Faith comes by hearing. We didn't finish the quote, did we?

Romans:10:17 So then faith cometh by hearing, and hearing by the word of God. - I think you probably know how it finishes. So then faith comes by hearing, and hearing by the word of God. And the amazing thing is that Abram had no word of God. How many translations have you got at home? You know, you talk to church members and you know, we sort of have "translation championships." "Well. I've got six translations at home.

"I've got ten translations at home".

"I've got twenty different translations and foreign language translations."

He didn't have any of that. He had no written word of God the way that you and I have it. He was just on his own, and God made Himself known. Now, you and I have God's word right in front of us, the Bible, and of course, faith does come by hearing. When we read God's word, when we're exposed to God's word, it builds our faith, hearing by the word of God.

So, of course, the lesson for us in the twentieth-first century is that we have to be reading the word of God on a regular basis. We've got to be studying the Bible, regularly, and I know, because it's tough for some of us, if we're not careful, we find that study of the Bible gets pushed out of our day. We're very busy, I know. But we all need to find some way, we need to find whatever works best for us, to put it into our lives and make sure that Bible study does not get pushed out, that Bible study is a regular part of our day. You know, if it works well for you at the beginning of the day, study the Bible in the beginning of the day. Some people are morning people, and they get out of bed bright and early and they study the Bible before they get their day underway. Others need that infusion of caffeine, don't they, before they can get their day underway, and the last thing of the day is the time that works best for them.

Sometimes, of course, faith lapses, it's because we're not spending enough time with the word of God. This word that we have in front of us is living, just like it was for Abram, and we've all had the experience of going through something, going through an experience in life, and looking for the answer to what we're going through, and trying to find the right way out, and sitting down with the Bible in our laps, and there it is. I think everybody in this room has had that experience. I certainly have.

There have been times in my life where I was going through things, and this amazing way that God's spirit does things, I turn to the right portion of the Bible, or somebody was up there preaching, and I heard or read what it was I needed. God speaks to us through this word. There've been many occasions when we've all experienced that.

Faith comes by hearing, and hearing by the word of God.

Point number three — Let's move forward. And now I'd like to move forward about one thousand years away from Abraham to demonstrate the point that faith builds on previous experience. Faith builds on previous experience. I want to go forward to a young man, not King David yet, he was a kid, I Samuel 17:34-37. Faith builds on previous experience.

You ever heard people say, "I didn't enjoy it when I went through it, but I'm glad I went through it. I'm glad it's behind me." We've probably all said that when we've gone through difficult times in life, and God has brought us through those difficult times. Why do people say, "I didn't enjoy it?" Well, probably because the experience wasn't fun. It wasn't enjoyable.

But why do we all say, "Well, I'm glad I went through it." Because we learned something from it. We learn what it's like to go through it, and we learned what God can do for us.

This young man, and he was just a kid, had a similar lesson in I Samuel 17:34. He was just a kid. He was freckle-faced, and everybody thought, "There's no way. How's this little kid going to go out against this giant? Goliath was huge, enormous. It describes the dimensions, and the dimensions are quite impressive. This guy was no ordinary guy. He was not a super heavy weight. He was more than a super heavy weight; he was enormous.

And along comes this little kid, and he doesn't have very much. He hadn't been working out in the gym; he was in good health, I'm sure, but he did have a couple of things going for him, courage and faith.

I Samuel 17:34 —(But) David said to Saul,...whom he's just encountering for one of the first occasions. Your servant used to keep ...Let's pick it up in verse 33. I want to read what Saul says to him in verse 33.

Verse 33 — Saul says to David...when David comes forward to volunteer...."You are not able to go against this Philistine to fight with him; (for) you're (you are) a youth,...you're a kid... and he a man of war from his youth....He's fought all kinds of people. Don't you know he's the Philistine champion? He probably killed lots of other champions of other nations.

I Samuel 17:34 —But David said to Saul, "Your servant used to keep his father's sheep, and when a lion or a bear came and took a lamb out of the flock,

Verse 35 — I went out after it and struck it, and delivered the lamb from its mouth...I wonder what David's mother would have said about him doing that. But, you know, that took real courage. Can you imagine doing that? It goes to pull this little baby lamb out of the mouth of the bear...and when it arose against me,...ever seen a bear angry? You imagine that huge great bear with its paws rising up against this little kid, David....I caught it by its beard, and struck and killed it...Now, that's not mentioned elsewhere in the scripture, but it surely happened, and David learned a lesson from that. He didn't do it just in foolhardiness. He did it trusting God that He would deliver him.

Verse 36 — "Your servant has killed both lion and bear; and this uncircumcised Philistine will be like one of them, seeing that (he has) he's defied the armies of the living God."

Verse 37 — Moreover David said, "The (Lord) Eternal, who delivered me from the paw of the lion and from the paw of the bear, He will deliver me from the hand of this Philistine."...So Saul agrees. (And Saul said to David,) "Go, and may the (Lord) Eternal be with you!" David is saying, "I know what God has done. I trust Him to do it again. I know what God has done. I trust Him to do it again."

As God leads us from the time that we're baptized as people of faith until the time that He makes us a part of His family in His kingdom, these are lessons that we build. Of course the same mechanism should be there for you and me. "I know what God has done. I know He'll do it again. I trust Him." That's the reason why we say, "I didn't' enjoy it when I went through it, but I'm glad I went through it. I'm glad I experienced it. "

Romans:1:17For therein is the righteousness of God revealed from faith to faith: as it is written, The just shall live by faith. — Talking about the process of salvation, the apostle Paul makes a similar comment. He says, "...in it the righteousness of God is revealed from faith to faith; as it is written, 'the just shall live by faith.'" God brought me through this before. I know He can do it again. It's like building blocks. We build a block of faith, and it becomes part of our character. So, hopefully, we don't have to go back and prove it again because we've experienced it. Because experience can sometimes be the best teacher. It becomes part of us. "I trust Him. I know what He can do." Faith builds on previous experience.

Point number four — Faith has moments of perplexity. I want you to note the word that I'm using here. The word is perplexity. I'm not talking about a breakdown of faith. I'm not talking about moments when God's people break faith with God. I'm talking about something that's happened to me and I dare say, it's happened to you when you've been through a real tough trial and you look at something and you say, "I know what God says, but I know what I'm going through and how do I reconcile the two?"

I want to go back to the life of Abraham, *Genesis:15:8And he said, LORD God, whereby shall I know that I shall inherit it?.* Because when you put the whole picture together, the life of Abraham and the life of Sarai exemplify this. Moments of perplexity. We're told he's the father of the faithful in the New Testament. But he had these moments when he was troubled inside, and his faith was challenged. His faith didn't collapse, but his faith was challenged.

Genesis:15:7And he said unto him, I am the LORD that brought thee out of Ur of the Chaldees, to give thee this land to inherit it. — Again, God has given him the promise in *Genesis:15:7And he said unto him, I am the LORD that brought thee out of Ur of the Chaldees, to give thee this land to inherit it.*, "I'm going to give you this land, I...brought you out of the land of Ur of the Chaldeans to give you this land to inherit it.

Verse 8 — And he said, "Lord God, how shall I know that I will inherit it?" Now didn't we just read back in Verse 6 Abraham believed God and he counted it to him for righteousness? Yes, we did. Didn't we read about Abraham going outside and looking up at the stars and saying, "God said it; it must be true." And yet, he asks for proof. And then there's kind of a covenant ceremony later on in Chapter 15. *Genesis:16:1-4[1]Now Sarai Abram's wife bare him no children: and she had an handmaid, an Egyptian, whose name was Hagar.[2]And Sarai said unto Abram, Behold now, the LORD hath restrained me from bearing: I pray thee, go in unto my maid; it may be that I may obtain children by her. And Abram hearkened to the voice of Sarai.[3]And Sarai Abram's wife took Hagar her maid the Egyptian, after Abram had dwelt ten years in the land of Canaan, and gave her to her husband Abram to be his wife.[4]And he went in unto Hagar, and she conceived: and when she saw that she had conceived, her mistress was despised in her eyes..*

Genesis:16:1Now Sarai Abram's wife bare him no children: and she had an handmaid, an Egyptian, whose name was Hagar. - It gets to be so interesting when we study the lives of Abraham and Sarai. We see them, how shall we put it, not as superman and superwoman, we see them as very human. Examples of faith, but human. Now Sarai, Abram's wife, had borne him no children. And she had an Egyptian maidservant whose name was Hagar.

Verse 2 — So Sarai said to Abram, "See now, the (Lord) Eternal has restrained me from bearing children. Please, go in to my maid; perhaps I shall obtain children by her." And Abram heeded the voice of Sarai. What? I thought we just read about Abraham being given a promise that he's going to have offspring. I thought he took God at His word. And here we've got this domestic situation, and I think that some of the commentaries bring out — this probably took place over a length of time. I would guess that Sarai nagged at him. You see back then, for woman not to have children was the ultimate indignity. A man married his wife to have children. Marriage was a different kind of an institution. Marriage was different back then in the ancient world from what it is today. The woman had to give children to her husband, and the husband had to provide for her. In a sense, it was much more practical.

So Sarai regards herself as having failed. She hasn't been able to provide children for her husband. And so I think she probably kept coming back at him. You know we've got this woman here, Hagar, she's young; she's fertile; she's sprightly; you know, why don't you take her and have children by her? And she probably nagged at him, and eventually Abram caves in. That's what's going on here in Verse 2, where he caves in finally.

Verse 3 — (Then) Sarai, Abram's wife, took Hagar her maid, the Eqyptian, and gave her to her husband Abram to be his wife, after Abram had dwelt for ten years in the land of Canaan. They've been there for quite some length of time, so I think this is kind of an encapsulation of something that had gone on in their household for some time.

Verse 4 — So he went in to Hagar, and she conceived. And when she saw that she had conceived, her mistress became despised in her eyes. And you can almost imagine Hagar looking down on Sarai. "I can have children, and you can't." And you've got this terrible situation that than breaks out within the family. And, of course, God had a purpose in the life of Ishmael as well. It was His purpose that Ishmael should be born, but later on, it's made very,

very plain it's through Isaac that God is going to work. God will bring the line, the promise line, the one leading down to Jesus Christ through Isaac, not through Ishmael.

But, we're faced with this paradoxical situation. Also, in Genesis 17. Let's read it in *Genesis:17:15-18[15]And God said unto Abraham, As for Sarai thy wife, thou shalt not call her name Sarai, but Sarah shall her name be.[16]And I will bless her, and give thee a son also of her: yea, I will bless her, and she shall be a mother of nations; kings of people shall be of her.[17]Then Abraham fell upon his face, and laughed, and said in his heart, Shall a child be born unto him that is an hundred years old? and shall Sarah, that is ninety years old, bear?[18]And Abraham said unto God, O that Ishmael might live before thee!.* It gets even more interesting. Faith, your faith, my faith, Abraham's faith is not made out of iron. It's not made out of iron. Look at *Genesis:17:15And God said unto Abraham, As for Sarai thy wife, thou shalt not call her name Sarai, but Sarah shall her name be.*, Abraham's name is now Abraham, father of many, not Abram, exalted father. We've got the circumcision covenant in Genesis 17, but then *Genesis:17:15And God said unto Abraham, As for Sarai thy wife, thou shalt not call her name Sarai, but Sarah shall her name be..*

Genesis:17:15And God said unto Abraham, As for Sarai thy wife, thou shalt not call her name Sarai, but Sarah shall her name be. - (Then) God said to Abraham, "As for Sarai your wife, you shall not call her name Sarai, but Sarah shall be her name. Sarah means princess; Sarai means My princess, apparently, very similar. Abraham's had a more meaningful name change.

Verse 16 — "And I will bless her and (also) give you a son by her; (then) and I will bless her, and she shall be a mother of nations;..." Now when God says she shall be a mother of nations, she shall be a mother of nations. I think probably it's easier for you and me, you know, on a Sabbath in the twenty-first century, to read this and say, "Well, yes, of course, I understand that you know. I know all the promises of God are going to be fulfilled. But it wasn't easy for her. And it wasn't easy for him. "....kings of peoples shall be from her."

Verse 17 — (Then) Abraham fell on his face and he laughed and he said in his heart, "Shall a child be born to a man who is one hundred years old? And shall Sarah, who is ninety years old bear a child? This is impossible. And he laughed. What's going on? Didn't we read that Abraham took Him at His word? That God counted to him as righteousness because he believed Him?

I won't ask for a show of hands. I imagine every one of us has had moments in life where somebody says something to us, and our emotional reaction, you get that bundle of nerves inside, and you can't find any other reaction than to laugh nervously. Sometimes laughter is a nervous release. And I wonder whether that's what's going on for Abraham here because he looks at his own body and he says, "It's impossible." And she's ninety years old. And so, what's happening? Let's read Verse 18.

Verse 18 — (And) Abraham said to God, "Oh, that Ishmael might live before You!"

Verse 19 —(Then) God said: "No, Sarah your wife shall bear you a son, and you shall call his name Isaac; I will establish My covenant with him (for) as an everlasting covenant, and with his dead descendants after him. We know the end of the story. We know God's word had to be fulfilled. Abraham is wrestling with this thing inside. He believes God, but he knows it's impossible, and he has this moment of nervous laughter. He's the father of the faithful. What's going on? Did his faith break down? Was it gone completely? *Genesis:18:11-12[11]Now Abraham and Sarah were old and well stricken in age; and it ceased to be with Sarah after the manner of women.[12]Therefore Sarah laughed within herself, saying, After I am waxed old shall I have pleasure, my lord being old also?.*

Genesis:18:11Now Abraham and Sarah were old and well stricken in age; and it ceased to be with Sarah after the manner of women.

—Look at Sarah now, same reaction. Now Abraham and Sarah were old, well advanced in age;...It's lovely the way the book of Genesis describes this. God inspired Moses who wrote this down.... and Sarah had passed the age of childbearing. As it says in the Hebrew, literally, the manner of women had ceased with Sarah. In other words, menopause is disappearing, you know, it's disappeared over the hill so to speak, and she knows. She knows it's simply too late. And then Verse 12.

Verse 12 — (Therefore) Then Sarah laughed....the same reaction. She laughed... within herself, saying, "After I have grown old, shall I have pleasure, my lord being old also?" And the commentaries bring out perhaps she might be referring to the pleasure of sexual relations with her husband, or perhaps the pleasure of bringing forth a child. It could be either or both.

Verse 13 — (And the Lord) God said to Abraham, "Why did Sarah laugh, saying, 'Shall I surely bear a child since I am old?'

Verse 14 — "Is anything too hard for the (Lord) Eternal? At the appointed time I will return to you,...She laughed, again, maybe the nervous laughter as she's got faith and doubt battling it out inside of her. But that's impossible.

Has God done the impossible in your life? Has God done the impossible in our lives? Will God do the impossible in our lives sometime in the future? And do you, I won't ask you for a show of hands, do you ever look at the impossible and say, "That's impossible," and then you've got within yourself, probably the same thing that's going on inside Abraham and inside of Sarah. Faith and a little bit of doubt. How can this be? I'm a person of faith. I'm a baptized member of the church of God, and yet, I have these moments of doubt that go through my mind.

Now, I've got a little bit of good news for you. That's natural. It happens to us all. We all have these moments where something happens in our life, and we have a moment of doubt inside of us, and we look inside the book and we say, "Look, I know what God says. I know how this has to come out. I know what He's done in my life before, BUT, and then we struggle. We have that dialectic going on inside of us — But that's impossible. We're not faith automatons, brethren. We're not faith automatons. Your faith is not made out of iron. You know what? You're in good company because Abraham's faith was not made out of iron either. He had something, perplexity. It wasn't a breakdown of faith. It was this moment when he was troubled inside.

What I think church members should understand, what we should all understand is that when we go through a moment like that where we look at a physical situation, where we look at a trial we're going through, and then we look at the promises, and we have this battle going on inside. We're not committing the unpardonable sin when we're troubled inside, when we have moments of perplexity. We're going to get to the outcome of this, briefly.

Remember the story of Queen Esther? Remember in the book of Esther, which is a very memorable, colorful story where this Jewish princess ends up in the Persian king's court, and she hides the fact that she's Jewish. And then there's this decree, extermination against the Jewish people throughout the Persian Empire. And her cousin, Mordecai, who's sort of pacing around outside, you know, like a mother hen, very worried about his young cousin, Esther, inside the court. And the decree has gone out. And he sends a message into the palace to her. And he says, "Listen, Esther, don't think that you're going to escape from all of this because you'll be discovered sooner or later and you'll be in trouble as well, and remember, you're an orphan."

And Esther's initial reaction is, "What am I going to do? I've lost the king's favor. He hasn't called on me for thirty days." See, she wasn't a faith automaton either.

And then Mordecai sends the message back into the palace and he says, "Don't think you're off the hook, and maybe God has put you there for this particular reason." You remember the outcome? I'll give you the reference. We won't turn there. It's Esther 4, if you'd like to go back and read it.

When the message goes back into the palace from Mordecai, Esther says, "Okay. Okay. I'll get my maids together, and we'll all fast. We'll fast for three days and three nights. And we'll fast together." And she says, "I'll go into the king, even if I've lost his favor, and if I perish, I perish." She gathers her strength; she gathers her faith; she gathers her courage. It's a wonderful object lesson of someone else who is not a faith automaton, just like your not, and I'm not. It's not the unpardonable sin when we go through a circumstance in life where our faith is tested, where we feel this perplexity inside of us.

The big question, the big question for members of the church of God is NOT — do you ever have a moment where your faith wavers? That is not the question. The big question for you and for me is — where do we go, where do we go after we've entered that moment where our faith is tested, and we're troubled, and we've got the perplexity inside of us, and we sit on the knife edge between faith and doubt. Where do we go from there? I'd like you to turn with me to Psalm 73. Because Psalm 73 is a beautiful, beautiful Psalm, It's actually not David; it's Asaph, but it includes one little thought that we can read over rather easily. I want to read a big chunk of Psalm 73, the first seventeen verses. Don't read Verse 17 yet. You don't watch the end of the movie and ruin it, okay?

The big question is actually answered in Psalm 73 about what we do when we sit on the knife edge of faith and doubt. Here is Asaph, he was apparently one of the leading Levites in David's time. He was in charge of some of the responsibilities in the temple, perhaps some of the music, and he penned several of the Psalms. Also a servant of God, but also somebody who's faith was challenged.

Psalm:73:1Truly God is good to Israel, even to such as are of a clean heart. — Truly God is good to Israel, to such as are pure in heart. Great, fine, we all believe that. God rewards people, doesn't He? When they do the right thing.

Verse 2 — But as for me....says Asaph...my feet had almost stumbled; my steps had nearly slipped. Why? His faith was challenged as well.

Verse 3 — Here's the challenge to his faith. (For) I was envious of the boastful, when I saw the prosperity of the wicked. Bad guys getting away with it. Bad guys getting all the goodies, and good guys not getting the goodies. You ever seen that? Several of the Bible writers wrote about that, this problem. Philosophers have a term for it, by the way. They call it the problem of theodicy, you know. Why do the wicked prosper? And Asaph addresses the question of why the wicked prosper and here his faith is being challenged in a way somewhat different from Abraham and Sarah. Why are they getting away with it? And it really troubles him....I was envious of the boastful...

Verse 4 — (For) there are no pangs in their death, but their strength is firm.

Verse 5 — They are not in trouble as other men, nor are they plagued like other men.

Verse 6 — (Therefore) And pride serves as their necklace;...

When I read that verse it reminds me of the Feast of Tabernacles I had several years ago. I went to Columbia for the Feast and enjoyed it, by the way. It's a lovely country to keep the Feast of Tabernacles, but I was sitting in a restaurant with Pastores Hernandez, our Missionary Pastor there in Columbia, and we're looking around the restaurant. It was very interesting. Mr. Hernandez was quietly mentioning certain individuals. And he said to me, "You can pick out the people in this country who are involved in the drugs trade by the way they dress." I didn't want to look too closely, I carefully looked at this guy that he was talking about wearing this thick gold necklace, and the women very heavily dressed up and everything, and he was explaining to me that in Columbia what's happened is that the big drug traders have been wiped out and it's all kind of gotten smaller, but it's still there, and that the Columbian people can often tell who's involved in this illicit drug trade and of course, they're making a lot of money. ....pride serves as their necklace violence covers them like a garment. Again, I think of people who get away with things apparently, apparently.

Verse 7 — their eyes bulge with abundance;...I love that image. Here's the bad guy whose eyes are bulging out of his head, he's eaten so much food, stuffed himself so much, his eyes bulge out of his head. ...they have more than heart could wish.

Verse 8 — They scoff and speak wickedly concerning oppression; they speak loftily. Boy, if you ever read the news these days, you know, read about some of the things going on in the news, you're probably troubled by the same thought — bad guys getting away with it, right?

Verse 9 — They set their mouth against the heavens, and their tongue walks through the earth.

No God's going to get me, or so they think.

Verse 10 — Therefore his people return here, and waters of a full cup are drained by them.

Verse 11 — And they say, "How does God know? And is there knowledge in the Most High? He's not going to do anything against us. We're going to keep on getting away with it, with our drug trade and illicit trading and violence and murdering people. It troubled Asaph.

Verse 12 — Behold, these are the ungodly, who are always at ease; they increase in riches.

Verse 13 — Surely I have cleansed my heart in vain, and washed my hands in innocence. Perhaps in our lowest moments, we have that thought as well. Served God all these years — shouldn't I have had more of a payoff? Asaph had that same thought.

Verse 14 — For all day long I have been plagued, and chastened every morning.

Verse 15 — If I had said, thus, If I had said, "I will speak thus," behold, I would have been untrue to the generation of Your children.

Verse 16 — When I thought how to understand this, it was too painful for me — It hurt me. It hurt me because everything I've ever learned says, Asaph is, yes, there is a payoff when you serve God, but I look around me and it seems like it's not working that way. It seems as if the bad guys are getting away with it. And so my faith is troubled just like Abraham, just like Sarah, just like Asaph here, just like you. Now, Verse 17 tells us the solution.

Verse 17 — Until I went into the sanctuary of God; then I understood their end. You see, when you and I are troubled in our faith; when something comes along in our lives and we look at the physical circumstance, we say, it's impossible. I haven't been rewarded for being a bad guy. I look at what's going on and things ...it just isn't working out right. My faith is being troubled. Where do you go from there? Answer, you go into the sanctuary of God and then you understand the end of the story. This is the answer to your moment of perplexity. In that moment of perplexity, what you and I must do is draw closer to God, spend extra time maybe a day of fasting and prayer, extra time and then He gives us the answer. And then, AHHH, faith reasserts itself, and that difficult time when it's so battling itself out inside of us comes clean. It comes clear. How does it come out? We end up saying, "Okay I know it's impossible." But God specializes in the impossible.

Point number Four was — Faith knows moments of perplexity.

Point number Five — What happens after you've been through these experiences? I think many of us know what happens. After we go through all of this, then our faith emerges strengthened. Faith emerges strengthened.

Let's go back to Abraham and Sarah in Genesis 21. Genesis 21. It's a wonderful, wonderful story, and you know, we can read it and we can say well, it's just history. We wouldn't be here if God had not fulfilled these promises. We probably wouldn't have even come into existence. There would certainly not have been any physical Israel, and no spiritual Israel because ultimately, of course, Jesus Christ came from all of these events, didn't He, and He founded the church.

Genesis:21:1 And the LORD visited Sarah as he had said, and the LORD did unto Sarah as he had spoken. — (And the Lord) The Eternal visited Sarah as He had said, and the (Lord) Eternal did for Sarah as He had spoken. That word — visited — is an idiom in the Hebrew. It doesn't necessarily mean that God appeared to her. It simply means that at this juncture in history, God re-engaged; He got involved in her life in this very special way. He did what was to be done, what He promised.

Verse 2 — For Sarah conceived and bore Abraham a son in his old age, at the set time...at the moed, there's a wonderful Hebrew word here. It's the same Hebrew word that's used to describe the holy days of God — moed, at a fixed time. God fixes times. That's why we're looking forward to the Feast of Tabernacles because we know when the Feast of Trumpets and Day of Atonement and the Feast of Tabernacles are coming up, God fixes holy time, and so Sarah gives birth to the child at the time appointed that God has said. At the moed, at the specific time in his old age, at the set time (for) of which God had spoken to him.

Verse 3 — (And) Abraham called the name of his son who was born to him —whom Sarah bore to him — Isaac. Isaac means he is laughing. He is laughing. Now, isn't that wonderful? It's just tremendous. Both Abraham and Sarah laughed, and when they have a son, what's the son's name? Laughing boy. It's wonderful. Isaac.

Verse 4 — Then Abraham circumcised his son Isaac when he was eight days old, as God had commanded him.

Verse 5 — (Now)And Abraham was one hundred years old when his son Isaac was born to him.

Verse 6 — And Sarah said, "God has made me laugh,..." Isn't it wonderful? I think God likes making us laugh. There are times when God answers the prayers of his people, and I think God must enjoy getting a little giggle of laughter out of His people. We've all had the experience, I think, of asking God to answer a prayer and looking for where God is going to answer the prayer? You ever had this? I've had this happen. I've had this kind of experience in the area of employment. Our young people will have this experience if you haven't had this experience yet. You know, you cast your bread out on the water, so to speak, you think something is going to happen in one particular corner or one particular direction, and God causes the answer to come from a complete different direction. You ever had that experience? Bet you have. I have. And I think when those things happen, I think to myself, "Well, God must really enjoy having us giggle at the way in which He's fulfilled what He has promised.

"...God has made me laugh. and all who hear will laugh with me." Her laughter of perplexity, a moment of doubt has turned into a laughter of celebration. She's ninety years old, and she's had a child.

Verse 7 — She also said, "Who would have said to Abraham that Sarah would nurse children? For I have borne him a son in his old age."

Verse 8 — (So) And the child grew and was weaned. And Abraham made a great feast on the same day that Isaac was weaned. Laughing boy. God is laughing now, and He taught something to Abraham and Sarah, and He taught something to you and me as well, that when the trial is over, when faith is rewarded, faith emerges strengthened. *Hebrews:11:11Through faith also Sara herself received strength to conceive seed, and was delivered of a child when she was past age, because she judged him faithful who had promised.* and 12. I think if I get the chance, as we sit around the table at the wedding supper, I'd like to ask Jesus Christ how it feels to make people laugh when the prayers are answered.

Hebrews 11: 11 — Put that on your "to do" list. We'll all do that. By faith Sarah herself also received strength to conceive seed, and she bore a child when she was past the age, because she judged Him faithful who had promised.

Hebrews:11:12Therefore sprang there even of one, and him as good as dead, so many as the stars of the sky in multitude, and as the sand which is by the sea shore innumerable. — Therefore from one man, and him as good as dead, were born as many as the stars of the sky in multitude — innumberable as the sand which is by the seashore. Amazing event that took place when the trial was over and their faith emerged strengthened. Of course, that wasn't the end of the story for Abraham and Sarah. They had more to go through, and more experiences to go through. And you and I do as well, of course, but our faith should be strengthened as we go through this entire wonderful dynamic that takes place in our lives as people of faith.

Point Number Six - We are people of faith, and faith sees things through a spiritual lens. Faith sees things through a spiritual lens. I want to go back to an earlier event, back in Genesis 13. In a sense, it's not central to the birth of Isaac and the whole theme of the continuity of the promised line, but it's very indicative of something about the character of Abraham. In Genesis 13, this is the goings on between Abraham and Lot. Lot was his nephew. They are both very, very wealthy. And things begin to go bad. And Abraham reacts in a very unusual way.

Genesis:13:1And Abram went up out of Egypt, he, and his wife, and all that he had, and Lot with him, into the south. — (Then) Abram went up from Egypt, he and his wife and all that he had, and Lot with him, to the South...the Negeb, which is the Northeastern Sinai Peninsula. So they traveled together, a large extended family. Look at what goes on here.

Verse 2 — Abram was very rich in livestock, in silver, and in gold. He had a lot. He had a lot. God made him wealthy, and yet he wasn't the kind of person to grasp and hold on to it.

Verse 3 — (And) he went on his journey from the South as far as Bethel, to the place where his tent had been at the beginning, between Bethel and Ai. He'd been there before, and he built an altar.

Verse 4 — (to) the place of the altar which he had made there at first. And there Abram called on the name of the Lord. Remember there's no temple, so what we see in the lives of the patriarchs is this kind of spontaneous building of altars, and then they kind of call out to God as they build this kind of structure which is going to be a place of worship. But reading in Verse 5.

Verse 5 — Lot also, who went with Abram, had flocks and herds and tents. And as often happens, one of the strange quirks of human nature, have you ever noticed? People have a harder time getting along when they've got money. Poor people often get along better than rich people. And that's what we're about to read here.

Verse 6 — Well, the problem actually didn't stem from Abram and from Lot. It stemmed from the men who worked for them. (Now) the land was not able to support them, that they might dwell together, for their possessions were so great that they could not dwell together.

Verse 7 — And there was strife between the herdsmen of Abram's livestock and the herdsmen of Lot's livestock... This is a disagreement over range lands. They want their cattle to roam around and they've got a lot of cattle and a lot of flocks, and they're fighting it out over where the cattle and the flocks are going to be. ...The Canaanites and the Perizzites then dwelt in the land. You look at that and we say, "Why am I reading that? What does that have to do with the argument between Abram and Lot? Actually, what we're being told here is that there are these tribes of people there, and this is not the time when you want a family feud. You know, because if you've got a family feud, the Canaanites and the Perizzites might come down and kill the whole lot of you, and then what's going to become of your wealth and your cattle and your flocks, and so on, so it's a little cautionary note.

Verse 8 — (So) Abram said to Lot, "Please let there be no strife between you and me, and between my herdsmen and your herdsmen; for we are brethren.

Verse 9 — "Is not the whole land before you? Please separate from me....You go to the left, I'll go to the right. You go to the right, I'll go to the left. (If you take the left, then I will go to the right; or, if you go to the right, then I will go to the left.") Now Abram knows where he is geographically. And he knows that if you look from the north, and you look down toward that valley, some of the land is good land, and some of the land is bad land. And this is what I want to highlight here.

Verse 10 — Look at the way Lot reacts. Lot was not the same man of faith that Abram was. (And) Lot lifted his eyes and saw all the plain of Jordan...remember what we said in the beginning of the sermon, that to prosper in the ancient world, you had to be by the water. The Jordan valley was fertile. In order to prosper and to have flocks and cattle you had to be by the water and Lot takes what appears to be a good deal. He acts in a somewhat self interested way. ... (that) it was well watered everywhere (before the Lord destroyed Sodom and Gomorah)...a little hint of what's going to happen a few chapters hence.... like the garden of the Lord, It was so beautiful, this is like the garden of Eden. ... like the land of Egypt as you go toward Zoar.

Verse 11 — (Then) And Lot chose for himself all the plain of Jordan, and Lot journeyed east. And they separated from each other. Lot said, "I want that nice parcel of land. I want to go down by the river." Lot acted in the physical way and Abram agreed to it.

Verse 12 — (Abram) He dwelt in the land of Canaan, and Lot dwelt in the cities of the plain and pitched his tent even as far as

Sodom. Faith sees through a spiritual lens. What went through Abraham's mind? What went through Abram's mind? Probably he thought to himself, "Look, in the interest of settling this dispute, I'll let him take the good part. I'll take the bad part of land. I've already seen what God can do for me. I don't need to worry."

And perhaps we should think that way a little more frequently as well, and not worry about some of the physical things, not be so attached to some of the physical things and stop and think to ourselves, "I know what God can do for me. I don't need to worry."

II Corinthians 5:7 — This is a very famous verse. It tells us — (For) we walk by faith, not by sight. Abraham was the father of the faithful. He walked by faith. He said, "Okay, I'll take the dry scratchy part of land, and you, Lot, can take the nice part of land, and of course, a little bit later on, was when Lot got embroiled in the battle of the four against five. Sometimes things that look as if they're a good deal aren't such a good deal. When we make decisions through a spiritual lens, we tend to make good decisions.

We should, brethren, as members of God's church and people of faith, from time to time be willing to take an apparent loss. Be willing to take an apparent loss, and all too often people in the church today won't do that. But if we're people of faith, we should be willing to do that. We have too many disputes in the church, brethren. We really do. Too many disputes and sometimes the disputes that break out in the church would not be present if we thought the way Abram thinks. If we said, "Look, okay, I'm going to take a loss on this, maybe it isn't perfectly just right on the surface of things, but I know God can take good care of me, and so I'll let it go." And there are too many brethren in the church these days who won't do that.

I Corinthians 6:7 - Until recently, one of our church pastors said he did a full sermon on this. I just want mention it in passing. The apostle, Paul, corrected them, didn't he, back in Corinth? Also very wealthy, also too many disputes, too many squabbles. Now therefore,...says Paul... it is already an utter failure for you that you go to law against one another. Why do you not rather accept wrong? ...When was the last time you accepted wrong? When was the last time I accepted wrong? And said, "Okay, all right, it's a little injustice, but fine. In the interest of peace in the family of God, I'll just drop it." ...Why (do you not) don't you rather let yourselves be cheated?

I Corinthians 6:8 — No, you yourselves do wrong and cheat, and you do these things to your brethren! If we're people of faith, that should happen once in a while in our lives. We should let ourselves be cheated. Don't make a big deal out of it. Just let it slip. That doesn't apply to everything. There are times when you have to stand your ground. But too often as members of God's church, people will not take an apparent loss and want to fight over things that really don't merit being fought over. Talk to church pastors, and they'll tell you the stories. Faith sees through a spiritual lens.

And finally, point number Seven — Faith brings an ultimate reward. You know when God gave Abraham those promises, He actually gave him more than one promise. As is so often the case in the Bible, you get something on the surface, and then you get a layer of meaning below the surface. And of course there was a very important layer of meaning below the surface.

What was probably the first thing that went through Abram's mind when God said, "In you all the nations of the earth shall be blessed? The obvious meaning is — everybody else, Egypt and all of the city states, and all the little people in the neighborhood are going to come and trade with you, and you'll all make money, and that did happen. It was fulfilled, and maybe he thought, "Well, downstream, there will be other nations that will come from my family, and they'll trade and they'll make money and everybody will receive physical blessings. ...in you all the nations of the earth shall be blessed. And when they entered the promised land under Joshua, it was fulfilled.

God had said they would receive land; there would be prosperity; there would be good physical things. But I wonder to what extent

Abram understood the other level? Because you and I have in front of us a Bible, one third of which is New Testament, and we know what the New Testament says, and we know that what was promised through Abram was more than fertile land and trade and kings, and it went beyond kings. It went to the king of kings, and Abram must have had some idea about it. It's one of the wonderful things about the Bible. We can stop and sort of tease ourselves with the knowledge of the New Testament and say, well, how much did these folks in the Old Testament really understand? They had to have understood. Abram definitely understood but he probably didn't have the complete picture, that we have the complete picture.

Anyway, let's look at *Genesis:13:15For all the land which thou seest, to thee will I give it, and to thy seed for ever.* because there's something else here that in a sense is much greater than national prominence, and trade, and money and kings. *Genesis:13:15For all the land which thou seest, to thee will I give it, and to thy seed for ever..* Again, a reiterating of the same promise.

Genesis:13:15For all the land which thou seest, to thee will I give it, and to thy seed for ever. — "for all the land which you see I give to you and your seed as it says in the Hebrew...(descendant) forever. Permanence...Well, we're going to get land forever. No?. Well, yes, but that wasn't the whole story.

Genesis:24:7The LORD God of heaven, which took me from my father's house, and from the land of my kindred, and which spake unto me, and that sware unto me, saying, Unto thy seed will I give this land; he shall send his angel before thee, and thou shalt take a wife unto my son from thence. — This is the story of the bride for Isaac. We could spend a lot of time in that chapter. It's a wonderful chapter, but I just want to pick this one verse here, *Genesis:24:7The LORD God of heaven, which took me from my father's house, and from the land of my kindred, and which spake unto me, and that sware unto me, saying, Unto thy seed will I give this land; he shall send his angel before thee, and thou shalt take a wife unto my son from thence.* where it's got the same phrase. Here's Abram, Abraham, talking to Isaac's servant. The Lord God of heaven, who took me from my father's house and from the land of my family, and who spoke to me and swore to me, saying, "To your (descendants) seed I give this land," He (will) shall send His angel before you, and you shall take a wife for my son from there.

Seed. Okay. Who's the seed? Well, the seed is Isaac; the seed is Jacob; the seed is Joseph; the seed is Judah and the twelve tribes and so on. But the seed is someone much more than that. The apostle Paul interprets it for us in the New Testament in *Galatians:3:16Now to Abraham and his seed were the promises made. He saith not, And to seeds, as of many; but as of one, And to thy seed, which is Christ..* I'm going to have a conversation with the apostle Paul someday because he obviously had not gone to seminary. No good seminary student would every interpret that particular scripture the way the apostle Paul interpreted it, but he drew something out of it that was inspired of God. It was of course true, and you and I know who's the seed? The New King James translators obligating used an uppercase letter to make it clear just in case we couldn't figure it out, which we can.

Galatians:3:16Now to Abraham and his seed were the promises made. He saith not, And to seeds, as of many; but as of one, And to thy seed, which is Christ. — Now to Abraham and his Seed ...Capitol "S," no capital letters in the Greek, but they wanted to make it clear to us....were the promises made. HE does not say, "And to seeds,"...I don't know that anyone would have said that back in Hebrew, in the Hebrew language, but the apostle Paul is drawing out a very important point... as of many, but as of one, "And to your Seed."...Jesus Christ... (Who is Christ.) Who is to come ultimately from Abraham, Jesus Christ. You go down a few generations, of course, it's easy for us to do, through Isaac, through Jacob, down into Judah and several generations down from that, and we get to Jesus Christ the Savior of all humanity, and of course, the Feast of Tabernacles is approaching. We're making plans. We're going all over the world, and one of the things that we need to keep in mind when we go to the Feast of Tabernacles is that there was another level of promise. There was another layer, the Seed, Jesus Christ, through whom God will ultimately offer the chance of salvation in the very family of God to everybody. To everybody. So faith brings an ultimate reward, and of course in this wonderful way, from the offspring of Abraham, the Seed, Jesus Christ, Abraham, himself, will receive eternal life in that kingdom. He's awaking something. Hebrews 11:-8-10.

Hebrews:11:8By faith Abraham, when he was called to go out into a place which he should after receive for an inheritance, obeyed; and he went out, not knowing whither he went. —By faith Abraham obeyed when he was called to go out to the place which he would receive as an inheritance. And he went out, not knowing where he was going.

Verse 9 — By faith he dwelt in the land of promise as in a foreign country, dwelling in tents with Isaac and Jacob, the heirs with him of the same promise.

Verse 10 — for he (Abraham) waited for (the) a city which has foundations, whose builder and maker is God. Did Abraham see it, six thousand years ahead of time? Yes, he did. Four thousand years, excuse me. Did he see it way ahead? Yes, he did. Did he see it in as much detail as you and I can when we go to this years Feast of Tabernacles and listen to sermons that describe what the kingdom is going to be like? I would venture, he didn't. After all, he didn't have any scripture. He just had what God made known to him, but he knew it was out there. He knew it had to come, and he probably had in the back of his mind an inkling. Yeah, there's going to be a promise and there's a blessing, and the blessing must be more than just physical. There's got to be a spiritual level to it as well.

Faith ultimately brings a spiritual reward in God's kingdom. *Hebrews:11:39And these all, having obtained a good report through faith, received not the promise:* and 40. Abraham is awaiting the same destiny. Many of us, probably most of us here are descended from Abraham and yet isn't it wonderful the one who is our father physically, and our father, the father of the faithful, is waiting in the grave, and the same destiny is awaiting Abraham as awaits us.

Hebrews:11:39And these all, having obtained a good report through faith, received not the promise: — And all these,...including Abraham... having obtained (a) the good testimony through faith, did not receive the promise,

Verse 40 — God having provided something better for us, that they should not be made perfect apart from us.

Seven footprints of faith, from starting point to destination, and the payoff, when you walk through all the seven footprints, is a tremendous thing. God gives the ultimate reward that He promises to those who are the people of faith.

THE FOOTPRINTS OF FAITH

INTRODUCTION

BELIEVE, RESPOND, OBEY

When we are learning to do something, it is always helpful to have someone after whom to model our actions. Having a prototype will get us started, and from there we can adapt our role model's actions to our own pace. That's what we propose to do in this book.

In learning how to walk with God, let's take a close, long walk with a man who dominates the Old Testament. He is, in fact, mentioned seventy-three times in the New Testament, more than any other Old Testament figure. He's one of the central figures of the entire Scripture, related not only to those of the Old Covenant, but to those in the New as well. Without knowledge of him, I dare say that we do not completely know who we are. I'm referring to Abraham.

Abraham towers at the very beginning of the Scriptures as a man whom God sought out amidst the whole of the earth. He touched that man and entered into a covenant with him, a covenant that has so firmly bound the Lord God to His people that thereafter He was known as "the Lord, the God of Abraham".

An important statement was made in the book of Isaiah:

Listen to Me, you who follow after righteousness, you who seek the LORD:/ Look to the rock from which you were hewn/ And to the hole of he pit from which you were dug./ Look to Abraham your father. (Isa. 51:1,2)

Often in the book of Isaiah, it is as if the Lord God is really trying to get our attention. "Listen to Me, you stubborn-hearted,/Who are far from righteousness" (46:12). And, "Hear this, O house of Jacob,/Who are called by the name of Israel,/And have come forth from the wellsprings of Judah" (48:1). And again, "Listen to Me, O Jacob,/And Israel, My called:/I am He, I am the First/I am also the last" (48:12). Then, "Listen, O coastlands, to Me,/And take heed, you people from afar" (49:1)

Single Minded Service

It is easy to be distracted by all kinds of things, good things as well as bad. We may say, "Well, I do have a busy life", or I have to go to work in the morning", or "I have a family. I just don't have consistent times to concentrate on the Lord". Or you might even say to me, "If I had the time you've got, and was able to spend my full time in the service of the Lord, then I would be able to concentrate". That's not true. Jesus spoke of distraction in terms of Martha, who was distracted by what was going on around her. She served the Lord, but in her concentration on her service, she was distracted from His presence, and so was distracted from responding to Him. We, too, can be so busy serving the Lord that we do not listen to Him.

If we Christians, we must, to some extent, engaged in the pursuit of righteousness. The most distinguishing characteristic of our God is not His great power, or His infinite knowledge and wisdom; it's His absolute holiness. God dwells in light. There are no shadows in His life or in His character. In seeking Him, we must deal with righteousness. It is stinking that all the verses about listening have to do with righteousness. In all of them, He is calling us to focus on the fact that He is a holy God.

It is no accident that the Spirit of God is referred to as the Holy Spirit. One of the chief ministries of the Holy Spirit is to conform our lives to the will of God. This means it is His job to sanctify us, that our lives may become increasingly more holy and more in harmony with the purpose, the will, and the character of God. Our service to Him is to be single-minded.

From the perspective of the New Testament, we are able to say that we stand in the righteousness of Jesus Christ. It is perfectly clear in 2 Corinthians 5:21, "For He made Him who knew no sin [Jesus] to be sin for us, that we might become the righteousness of God in Him."

He took our sin, we took His righteousness. A fair exchange, you might say; that's what the whole gospel is about – the reconciliation of God and man. It was our sin that erected a wall of separation, but that's been overcome by the Lord Jesus Christ. That's why He is our Savior. That's why He is our Righteousness.

Look!

Again, it's all too possible to look at Isaiah 51:1 and read it with New Testament eyes and think, "Well, of course, the passage is talking about the Lord God." Many times in Scripture, particularly in the Psalms, the Lord God is spoken of as "our Rock" or "the Rock of our salvation." In the New Testament (see I Cor. 10). Jesus is expressly spoken of as "the rock". He is "the Rock of Ages," as the hymns describe Him. Yet, as you study the context of this challenge from the Lord God through the prophet Isaiah, He was not here speaking about Himself. He was not even speaking about Jesus. He was speaking about Abraham!

Now, you might wonder about that. After all, Abraham lived as far on the other side of Jesus as we live on this side. He lived almost two thousand years before Jesus, so you may well ask how anyone who lived four thousand years ago could have relevance in our life today. Abraham is an absolutely pivotal person in the whole of Scriptures. He dominates the Old Testament in a unique way, as you will see.

The first eleven chapters of the book of Genesis are a kind or prologue to the whole of the Bible: they tell us what we need to know in order to understand it. If we don't understand the foundation laid in Genesis 1 through 11, we will not understand anything else in Scripture. These chapters tell us that every thing that exists was created by the hand of God. They say that among the vast creation of God, we are a special creation, special because we were created in God's image. The Bible does not obscure the distinction between Creator and creature; we are not God, but are related to Him in a way that allows a relationship to develop between us. We're also told that God gave us a will, one that we can use to respond to Him and walk with Him – or to refuse to respond to Him and choose to walk in our own way.

Our ancient parents used their God-given will to resist the will of God. Rebellion is at the start of the Bible. Right off, rather than obeying the Lord, rather than choosing Him, people chose to "do their own thing" and chose to go their own ways. Adam and Eve succumbed to the blandishments of the evil one who said to them. "Well, if you take from that tree, you'll become as God". Of course, that was a lie; Satan is, after al, a liar and the father of all lies. Yet there was, like many lies, a bit of truth in it. They didn't become like God, they just acted like they were.

The word Adam in Hebrew (from which the name Adam is derived) simply means "man" in a generic sense. When we talk about the fall of Adam and Eve in the Garden of Eden, don't think of it as a quaint and curious tale. People, that's our story. It's about you! It's about me, it's about everyone ever born or who ever will be born. There is a time for us all when, for the very first time, we consciously choose to do something that is not right. That's your story, it's my story, and the story of the entire human race. "There is none righteous," the Scripture says in Romans 3:10, "no not one."

Discover Our Roots

In order for us to understand our God and ourselves and the tension that lies between us from the root of the bible, we have to know something about those early chapters. We find it them immediately that brother killed brother. Right off, our family album reeks of devastating of the social order. We find a description a few chapters later that says that "every intent of the thoughts of his heart was only evil continually" (Gen. 6:5) in the sight of God. We read about the first judgment that came upon the earth, one of water and destruction, but God did not destroy all. He saved one man and his wife, their three sons and their wives, and the whole story started over again.

The real story of the Bible begins in chapter 12. God created us to be His own, to walk with Him in obedience. He didn't just squash the whole of His creation when it didn't turn out very well, as we might have done. Instead, He decided to see if there were people who would choose to serve Him. He could have made robots, who would have had no choice, but he didn't do that – He wanted to be chosen, and so He made a choice.

God chose one man, a man by the name of Abram. It's to this man that we look, because he's related to us. In learning of him, we learn something of our roots, our heritage. We're going to discover something about the family of God, and about how we are to walk (and not to walk) with our Lord. There are some skeletons in the closet. There are shameful chapters, but there are glorious moments, too. As we look at the family album, there will be some pictures that will cause us to laugh – for instance, the birth of Isaac, whose name means "laughter", to a mother at ninety years of age. (Need you be reminded that age is a bit beyond the normal child-bearing years?). They named the child Isaac – "laughter" – not just because of the joy that he brought them, but because every time they looked at him, it struck them funny!

There are moments of high drama, too. After Isaac, the dearly beloved child of promise, grew older, Abraham was asked by the Lord God to sacrifice him on an altar. We'll sense something of Abraham's anguish as his world came crashing in on him. The soap operas of today have nothing to compare with this intense struggle between obedience to God and the affection of the heart in this terribly hard step of faith.

There will be moments of weeping, times when we wonder at a man with such firm faith in God. Abraham had faith that if he sacrificed his beloved son, God would be able to raise him from the dead. That was a new idea at the time; no one had ever thought that before (and one would have to be really sure he had heard the voice of God). Abraham risked it all; he had to be sure that no matter what, God would fulfill His promise.

Abraham's Children

All sorts of people call Abraham "father". To the Jews, Abraham, is the founder of the Jewish faith and the Jewish nation, descended through his beloved Isaac. To the Muslims, Abraham is the founder of the Islamic faith and the Arab race, descended through Ishmael, Abraham's son by his wife's maidservant Hagar. Seven hundred million Muslims read a Koran that begins with the story of Abraham, because that's where it started for them.

The origins of Christianity go back before Bethlehem, all the way to Abraham. Christians are children of Abraham. There are some people, however, who thought they were children of Abraham but weren't. Mere lineal descendancy from Abraham does not make a person his child, according to Jesus. One can be a descendant of Abraham after the flesh, and in the biblical sense not be a child of Abraham at all.

Jesus made it even more difficult, because He made it even clearer. He was talking to people who actually believed in Him – not just to the scribes and Pharisees, but to people who had heard Him speak and had begun to respond to Him. (One characteristic of Jesus – He seemed not to want to win disciples easily; He wanted them to know what they were getting themselves into!).

In John 8:31 we read: "Then Jesus said to those Jews who believed Him, 'If you abide in My word, you are My disciples indeed. And you shall know the truth and the truth shall make you free"

Listen to their response: "They answered him, "We are Abraham's descendants, and have never been in bondage to anyone. How can you say, "You will be made free?" (v. 33)

What kind of memory did they have? Why, even as they spoke, they were slaves of the Roman Empire; they had Roman taskmasters over their heads. They had a Roman governor; they had part of the Roman legion stationed among them to keep order. Had they forgotten that? What's more, before the Romans, they had been under the heel of Greece, and before Greece they were under the domination of the Persians, and before the Persians, under the rule of Babylonia; before the Babylonians, they were under the Assyrians, and before the Assyrians, they were oppressed by the Egyptians! They had never been free! Yet they asked, "How can you say, 'You will be made free?'"

Jesus replied,

"I know that you are Abraham's descendants, but you seek to kill Me, because My word has no place in you. I speak what I have seen with My Father, and you do what you have seen with you father". They answered and said to Him, "Abraham is our father". Jesus said to them, "If you were Abraham's children, you would do the works of Abraham. But now you seek to kill Me, a man who has told you the truth which I heard from God. Abraham did not do this. You do the deeds of your father". Then they said to Him, "We were not born of fornication; we have one Father – God". (vv 37-41).

Well, that's a step up. At first they claimed that Abraham was their father, but then they moved on to claim they were children of God. It was sort of a last Court of Appeals.

Jesus said to them, "If God were your Father, you would love Me, for I proceeded forth and came from God; not have I come of Myself, but He sent Me. Why do you not understand My speech? Because you are not able to listen to My word. You are of your father the devil". (vv 42-44).

Jesus would not allow people to presume to be children of Abraham simply because they were descended from him. What were His standards for being Abraham's child? Three short passages answer that. The first is Galatians 3:6: "Just as Abraham 'believed God and it was accounted to him for righteousness." Belief. Abraham heard the call of God, responded to it, and obeyed. Those who believe, respond, and obey, then, are Abraham's children.

The second passage is Romans 4:11: "…..that he might be the father of all those who believe, though they are uncircumcised." Circumcision was an outward sacramental sign of belonging to God. Parallel to that under the New Covenant would be baptism in the church. We are not accepted by God because we are baptized any more than Old Covenant men were accepted because of their circumcision! Faith save us – "those who believe". Those who believe, respond, obey.

The Greek word for church is ecclesia. It comes from two other Greek words, which together mean "to call out from." A church is an assembly of people who have heard the call of the Lord in some sense and have responded by gathering together in His name.

I suppose it's possible to hear the Lord and turn Him off, to close our ears, stop our minds, and go in an opposite direction. That's where obedience comes in. have you obeyed Him? If we've heard Him and believed, responded, and obeyed, then we are children of Abraham and a part of that ancient covenant.

There's one further passage, in Galatians 3:26: "For you are all sons of God through the faith in Christ Jesus." We are children of God by faith; by believing, by trusting, by accepting. "For as many of you as were baptized into Christ have put on Christ. There is neither Jew nor Greek, there is neither slave nor free, there is neither male nor female; for you are all one in Christ Jesus" (v. 28). Now here's the clincher: "And you are Christ's, then you are Abraham's seed, and heirs according to the promise" (v. 29).

When we belong to Christ, we are connected with ancient Abraham and the promise given to him centuries ago. We become heirs of those promises; that is part of our inheritance.

First Will And Testament

In the next few chapters, we will look at the first will and testament. We will examine the document, find out what God promised Abraham, and then see the whole promise is available to us today as we walk in Abraham's footsteps. I pray that God's word will be real, personal, significant, and transforming in our lives.

As we look through our family album at the travels of our forefather with God, why not begin to keep a traveler's journal of your own? I've prepared a few questions at the end of each chapter to help us recall where we've been, what we've seen, what we've done, and where we're going as we walk with God. You may find it helpful to record your thoughts in some sort of notebook so that you could look back from time to time at what God taught us as we were learning to walk with Him by emulating the actions of Abraham.

THE FOOTPRINTS OF FAITH

CHAPTER ONE

MOVING WITH GOD.

Listen to Me, you who follow after righteousness./ You who seek the LORD:/Look to the rock from which you were hewn,/And to the hole of the pit from which you were dug./Look to Abraham your father. (Isa. 51:1,2).

When we get to Isaiah 51 and read those words, we're already prepared to listen. This wasn't the first time the voice of the Lord attempted to arrest the attention of His people, crying through the lips of the prophet. (see 46:12, 48:1, 49:1).

It's as though the Lord God was making a special effort to get the attention of His people. I don't have to point out that He has to do that from time to time!. There are so many distractions that cloud our minds, dampen our enthusiasm, and make it hard for us to hear the Lord. We need to hear, and we must heed.

"Listen to Me….." Those words were addressed to those whose hearts are inclined toward God. That was true when they were first spoken eight centuries before Christ and has been true ever since. Those words are addressed generally to the whole of the people of God. There are those who will hear, and those who won't hear, it's always been that way.

Continual Consistency

The most distinguishing characteristic of the God of Abraham, Isaac and Jacob, the God and father of our Lord Jesus Christ is HIS HOLINESS His Holy character, with no dark spot, no shadows, rather light all the way through and through. His Holiness means a consistency of purpose that is never deflected and a constancy of devotion in continual and eternal covenant.

If we are going to be among those who seek the Lord, we must concern ourselves with His Holiness and concentrate on responding with a personal Holiness that conforms to the will and purpose of God.

Holiness is not a popular idea to day. There is a form of Christianity that is devoid of holiness, an eloquent testimony that it's god is not the God of Abraham nor is the father of our Lord Jesus Christ people fashion on their own terms, because their gods are the products of self- creation and limitations.

The only time we can deal with god and not be impressed with our needs is when we fashion a god after our own liking and worship that god. We can deal with that God and remain the same; but if we come into the presence of the living God, we are struck with our own need. If we are unwilling to deal with the things in our lives that re contrary to the purpose of God, then we are not dealing with the hold God. We're dealing with an idol of our own imaging.

Look To The Rock

"Look to the Rock from which you were hewn..." It's very easy to read those words with New Testament eyes and Imagine "The Rock "refers to the Lord God, or imagine (as in 1 Corinthians 10:4) that it refers to Jesus. But in this context it is neither. It says clearly look to Abraham your father "as we begin to pursue our roots, let's look at Gen. 12:1.

The Beginning of God's redemptive purpose started with His Sovereign choice of one man out of all the peoples of the earth. It doesn't tell us how God spoke to Abraham just that he (God) did speak to him. The scriptures tells us in Hebrews 1:1 that "God, who at various times and in various way, spoke in times past to the fathers by the prophets. God sometimes spoke through vision s, sometimes through dreams, sometimes through the circumstances or experiences; people began to hear the word of the Lord. It doesn't matter how the Lord arrested Abraham's attention, but it's virtually important that He did. Our faith is dependable upon the fact that God spoke to a man more than four thousand years ago, and that man, Abram responded. He is our father, apart from him. We would not be here.

What did the Lord say to him? Get out! The double motion of getting out of one state of affairs and going in the direction of another is directed by the Lord God. "Get out of your country.... your family.... your father's house. "God sought to create a people who would respond to him. He sought a people who would chose Him as their God, even as He had already chosen them as His people. Please understand the difference here. We know that all the people of the world are the creatures of God; God is our creator. The early chapters of Genesis tell us that God created us for a relationship with Him that we might have fellowship with Him. We are all created in the image of God. That does not mean that we resemble Him spiritually. We are created spiritual beings capable of a relationship with our creator. God made us capable of response, but interestingly enough, one of the aspects of His image that we possess is our WILL. We are able to respond and also able to refuse to respond. God gave us that ability!

Way back in the dim beginnings of the human race, our first parents exercised their free choice against the Lord. They refused Him and rebellion entered the heart of the human race. In every one of us, in the depths of our being, there is a rebelliousness against any who would presume over us, even God Himself. Yet it was He who gave us the ability to stamp our feet, spit in His face, and go off and do whatever we want to do.

After mankind's rebellion and the earth's destruction by flood, the new start, and the Tower of Babel (where humanity again wanted its own way) you'd have thought God would have given up. Had I been God, I would have squashed the whole enterprise, like one would swat a fly. I would have cast it aside and started over again without the nuisance of free will. But our most merciful, loving, gracious, patient God is changeless He did not give up; instead, He said to Himself, " I'm still going to call a people who will somehow heart, respond, and obey my leading o the pathway to divine destination.

Abram Of Ur

God began with one man, Abram from Ur of the Chaldees. On might ask, "why did the Lord tell Abram to leave his county? "God was fashioning a people unto Himself in the midst of this world, a people who would be separated and consecrated unto Him by following His perfect will.

We are given some insight into this concept in Joshua 24:1-3. After Moses, Joshua emerged as the new leader of the people of God, a position he held for about 50 years. He was the one who led them across the Jordan River into the Land of promise. He was the one who conquered the nations already situated in the land and divided the land among the 12 tribes. Chapter 24 records Joshua's last words to his people. He knew that his time with them was short, that he was soon going to lay aside the mantle of leadership. The phrase beyond the River is a significant one. It means "beyond the Euphrates", not the Jordan, and it speaks of the people who lived on the other side of that river. The passage says that they worshiped other gods.

God sought to bring about a people would be His people exclusively, and it was necessary to deal with the false gods, the idolatries, and the other things of honor, reverence, and importance in people's livers as they learned to walk with Him. That is still true.

The Idols In Our Lives

A functional definition of God (or your gods) is essentially whatever concerns us ultimately, whatever is the controlling dynamic of our life, is our god. For some people its family; for others, careers, or getting ahead and reaching the top. Whatever is dominating our life is our god; and if it is anything other than the Lord God Himself, that's idolatry. Before we can walk with Him, God has to deal with those things. He wants His people to allow

Him to be supreme,. And so He told Abram t leave his country, his people, and his father's house. He told him to throw away the gods of his forefathers so he could start afresh, so he could learn to serve Him in singular faithfulness. From Joshua 254:15, its obvious ultimately the choice to follow God's direction is entirely up to the individual.

It was against his pagan background of idol worshipers that God's word came to Abram to leave his country, his people, and his father's house. I wish I could say that Abraham's response was immediate and absolutely faithful to that call. Unfortunately, it was mot. He did leave, and we're told the route he took. He moved directly northward following the course of the Euphrates River- a green belt with a seemingly endless desert on both sides. Plenty of water and plenty of food were near the river the route was one of the major highways north. Abraham began in obedience to the Lord and pushed northward about seven hundred miles, until the came to a little town by the name Haran and then something happened; Genesis 11:31 says ... They settled there. (NIV) they weren't camping out anymore, they settled there. The place Haran where they settled not the promised land; that's not where they were told to go. I think it might have been because Abram did not leave his father's house; he took his father Terah with him. God knew the persuasive power of human relationships and family ties. Terah's heart was not turned unto the Lord, and yet he went along with Abram. The scripture says, "they set out... to go to Canaan". But when they came to Haran, they settled there. That explains why Chapter 12 began with the words., "Now the Lord has said to Abram (Emphasis's mine) indicating a previous time.

Stephen provides a little more information in Acts of Apostles 7:2-4. its strange! After the death of his father he obeyed God. I see something important in that story. Abraham was delayed because he disobeyed; he was told by God to leave his father's house. God knew that Terah's unbelief would corrupt him, and it did. A human relationship deafened his ear to the Lord God, and Abraham disobeyed.

Move Out!

I must ask you- have you started with God and come to your own Haran and settled in? When God calls us to move out, to commit our lives to Him, its easy to be seduced by the requests or demands of a loved one and be turned aside by those who are supposed to walk by our side. I believe that if like Joshua we are to obey the Lord, our families would be strengthened. Compromise rarely converts; faithfulness and obedience do.

I am not saying we should move out from our marriage relationships and leave our spouse. I'm pointing out the dangers of unpacking our bags in Haran when we haven't yet arrived at the promised land of settling down and settling for less than God's intended blessing, of burning out to the vision. Abram and his family stopped because they had come to the end of the green belt, the end of their visible supply of resources. Many people can't seem to move beyond that comfort zone in their lives. The stop when they get to the end of their own resources and say, "No further! This is the place where we'll settle down".

Our Lord says, "No, I want to take you beyond that level. I want to show you that I can provide for you. I can even set a table for you in the wilderness. I can rain manna from heaven; i can provide all your needs, I can command the raven to feed you. But you've got to learn that, and will never learned it if you settle in Haran. You'll only learn of my divine provision when you move beyond the range which your eyesight and experience can see "scary, isn't it? Its true!

Well, Terah finally died we don't know how long they lived there. The Acts passage says that after the death of his father, Abram began to follows the Lord. God is a God of mercy- He is a God of the second chance, when we come to Him-even though we've been walking in the wrong direction, even if we've stopped for a time and have not been moving along in the pathway of divine direction at all- if we recognize that we've been disobedient, and genuine conversion. We can start over again right away. God's forgiveness cleanses, and the grace of God again begins to flow toward us and in us for the race, then the joy of our salvation is restored (Psalms 51).

How do you hear God's instruction to you? Whose voices compete with God's for your attention? What pre-occupies most of your attention and orders direction? Where are you headed? Do you have a path or on whose path are you following? I do not know where you are but you do! It is possible to settle down before you get to where He would have you go. It is possible to listen even occasionally to the voice of idols. Some within your own family and deflected from a single-hearted devotion to the Lord god. If that is or has been your experience before you go on reading please, pause and acknowledge that before Him. Confess it, receive the forgiveness and the absolution of God, and be released to move on with Him, getting back on track, right on His pathway.

Traveller's Journal

Reflect

How do you hear Gods instructions to you?

Whose voices compete with God's for your attention?

What occupies most of your attention?

Where are you headed? Do you have a path that you are following?

Recommit

In your own words, deal with those things that keep you from obedience to God. Confess, repent, restart anew. Date this entry in your journal so you can record how things change for you in the coming days, weeks, months, and years as you walk by faith with God.

CHAPTER TWO

THE BLESSINGS OF GOD

I will make you a great nation; I will bless you And make your names great; And you shall be a blessing. I will bless those who bless you, And I will curse him who curses you; And in you all the families of the earth shall be blessed. (Genesis 12:2-3).

I want to focus attention on the first statement of the covenant God made with Abram. The seven promises, interestingly enough, are made without any strings attached. All of these are things that the Lord God said He would do. Later on there would be something for Abram and his descendants to do, but not here. Here the Lord declared His purpose on behalf of Abram and his descendants.

A Great Nation

First of all, God said He would make Abram and his descendants into a great nation. Understand that the Lord said this to Abram when he was a very old man and had no children at all. From a human point of view, he had no possibility of having a posterity after him, or descendants that would flow from his body. Yet, in that time when all human expectation could be dampened by the circumstances, the Lord made a promise to Abram: "And I will make your descendants as the dust of the earth, so that if a man could number the dust of the earth, then your descendants also could be numbered" (Gen. 13:16). "You shall be a father of many nations" (Gen. 17:4). Genesis 15:5 states another way: "Look now toward heaven, and count the stars if you are able to number them….. so shall your descendants be".

In other words, "If you can count the specks of dust or count the stars, Abraham, you'll have some small grasp of the number of people who will flow from your body and be your descendants – people who will be heirs to this covenant that I am making with you". That was the first promise of the Lord God to Abram: to make him a great nation.

The Blessing of God

The second promise was that God would bless him. Have you any idea what it means to live under the blessing of God? It means that God looks out for and moves on your behalf; that God concerns Himself with your life; that God desires always to bless you, never in any way to put you down. When this is later amplified in the book of Deuteronomy, the Lord said through Moses:

And the LORD will make you the head and not the tail; you shall be above only, and not be beneath, if you heed the commandments of the LORD your God, which I command you today, and are careful to observe them. (Deuteronomy 28:13).

God's intention is always to bless His people. We don't have to question that! His purpose is to advance them, to increase them, to make their lives more abundant, more rich, more full. God's purpose toward His people has never changed, and never will! And so if we know the Lord Jesus Christ and are Abram's descendants, this promise is to us, also. No wonder Jesus was able to say of his followers, "I have come that they may have life, and that they may have it more abundantly" (John 10:10).

To have life to the full, to live abundantly, under the blessing of God is to know that the hand of God rests upon us for blessing, not for evil, to understand that God's intention is to make us the head and not the tail, to realize that God wants to make our lives move only upwards, toward the top, and never downwards to the bottom of the heap. That is part of the covenant promise, and it has never changed over the long centuries since. God wants to bestow blessings on His people.

Great Name

The third promise was that God would make his name great. How strange is our God to take a man from Ur of the Chaldees. From there the Lord chose our obscure man (who ever heard of him? Nobody, at that time) and led him out of the land, away from his people, even from his father's house. God was beginning to call a people to Himself, and He selected one man and promised him his name would be made great.

The promise that Abram would be the father of many nations was fulfilled. A significant portion of the people of the earth today trace their origins back to Abram. That promise was renewed with Abram's son. Isaac and with Isaac's son Jacob, who became the father of twelve sons. Later in life, the Lord God changed Jacob's name to Israel, and his twelve sons became known as the Children of Israel. Those twelve children became the fathers of the twelve tribes, and all Jews trace their origins to Abram.

But there was a misstep between the promise and its fulfillment. God waited a long time after He made the promise to fulfill it, and Abram became nervous because he was getting older all the time. Not only that, but his wife was getting older, too, and in his anxiety he felt he had to help the Lord God out a bit. On one occasion he brought his servant Eliezer before the Lord and said, "Well, probably, what you meant Lord, was that you want me to take my faithful servant and adopt him as my legal heir." (That was something that could easily be done in those days, under the code of Hammurabi. Eliezer was a Syrian from Damascus). "Surely, this fine man is the one that you mean". The Lord said, "No, Abram, that's not the one I was talking about".

Sarai, Abram's wife, became worried about the whole thing, too. After all, she was getting well past the age of childbearing. "Now Sarai was barren; she had no child" (Genesis 11:30). So she suggested that Abram father a child by her servant, Hagar. (This was not an immoral arrangement, it was a part of the culture and understanding of the day, also from the code of Hammurabi). So Abram did as his wife suggested, and sure enough, he fathered a son and named him Ishmael. Abram brought that little boy before the Lord, and said, "Here he is, Lord. Surely this is the on." But the lord said, "No. Abram, strike two! Wrong again; that is not the child I've promised. Your wife Sarai shall conceive and bear a son, and through that son My promise shall be fulfilled".

God did not ignore Ishmael. He also became the father of twelve sons. God made a promise to him that he would also be a father of many nations. And today all Arab trace their origins back to Abram through Ishmael. Not only, then do Jews trace their origins back to Abram and regard him as the Great One, so do the Arabs.

Galatians 3:6-7. Contain a clear and important statement. "Abraham 'believed God, and it was accounted to him for righteousness". Therefore know that only those who are of faith are sons of Abraham". And again in verses 26 – 29.

For you are all sons of God through faith in Christ Jesus. For as many of you as were baptized into Christ have put on Christ. There is neither Jew nor Greek, there is neither slave nor free, there is neither male nor female, for you are all one in Christ Jesus. And if you are Christ's, then you are Abraham's seed, and heirs according to the promise.

All Christians trace their origins to Abraham also, and are part of the fulfillment of the promise. God kept His promise to Abram, and we are part of it. Through the heritage of Christians, Jews and Arabs, God has made Abram's name great.

To Be a Blessing

The fourth promise the Lord gave to Abram was that he would be a blessing. It's wonderful to receive and enjoy the blessing of God on our life, but it's equally wonderful to be a blessing to someone else. But God never blesses us so that we might simply bask in the blessing. It is rather His way to bless us so that we may bless others, so that we may be a blessing. That important principle is found all the way through the scriptures.

On a pilgrimage trip to Israel, I boarded a boat with fifty-one people and set off from Tiberias on the Sea of Galilee. We went out into the middle of the sea, stopped the engine, and I taught them a bit about their surroundings. I pointed out that in the land of Israel there were two bodies of water; the Sea of Galilee in the north, and the Dead Sea in the south. The Sea of Galilee is forty miles long and ten miles wide at its widest point. It's a jewel, gleaming in the sunshine. It's a wonderful place, teeming with fish, with rich vegetation all around it.

Seventy miles south of the Sea of Galilee is the Dead Sea, which occupies the lowest place on the face of the earth. It is 1,306 feet below sea level and has a mineral content of 24 to 26 percent, compared with 4 to 6 percent mineral and salt content for the oceans of the world. There are no fish, no life of any kind in the Dead Sea. Nothing can live in it, and until recent times, nothing could live around it. With the modern miracles of irrigation and cleansing of the earth itself, such as the washing of the sand, it is now somewhat possible to grow things on the edge of the Dead Sea, but the water itself still prohibits life.

Here is a possible reason for this: The Sea of Galilee is beautiful and fresh because all the water that flows into the north end from the Jordan River flows right through it and out through the southern end. It then tumbles down the Jordan River for seventy-five miles, but so winding is the course that it would be two hundred miles if you followed it. Then the water dumps into the Dead Sea. There is no exit from the Dead Sea; nothing moves through it, it just receives. It receives and gives nothing. It is dead and spreads death to all around it.

Do you understand the comparison? Abraham was blessed to be a blessing, and it's exactly the same with us. God wants to bless our lives, but not so that we are the end of the blessings. He does not want us only to receive; He wants us to pass on to others the blessing we have received. This is terribly important, and I'll use two brief sketches to illustrate this.

In 2 Timothy 2:2, Paul wrote to his young disciples: "And the things that you have heard from me among many witnesses, commit these to faithful men who will be able to teach others also".

Whatever we learn from and about God is not intended to stop with us. It is intended to pass through and far beyond us so that others may learn of God, too. For heaven's sake, we must not go to church just to learn for ourselves. We must learn all we can of God so that we may be able to share and teach others. It's important that we grow in our own understanding, but this lesson is part of it: if our understanding of God does not go beyond our heads, it is absolutely worthless – to us and to Him – and such learning will die and turn to ashes in our souls.

In 2 Corinthians 1:3-4 we find this wonderful passage:

Blessed be the God and father of our Lord Jesus Christ, the Father of mercies and God of all comfort, who comforts us in all our tribulation, that we may be able to comfort those who are in any trouble, with the comfort with which we ourselves are comforted by God.

That is a convoluted sentence, and you may have become tangled up in it, but its meaning is straight-forward: God ministers to us, so that we may be able to minister to others. If we receive any ministry, it is not to end with us. It is intended to move through us, so that we may touch and minister to others. Then we will understand the great promise of the Lord God: "I will bless you..... and you shall be a blessing".

Bless and Curse

The fifth and sixth promises the Lord gave to Abram were that God would bless those who bless him and curse those who curse him. The meaning of these two distinct promises is simple and clear: Abram was the man chosen to be an instrument of fulfilling God's purpose for the world. Those who align themselves with the purpose of God will come under His blessing. Anyone who goes against God's purpose will experience His judgment.

This is a universal principle. When we speak of the curse of God, we're not to imagine Him subject to fits of anger when He calls out various epithets and hurls thunderbolts about. That's not the kind of God we have. Judgment is the other side of mercy; God's curse is the other side of His blessing. Our choice is the same as Abram's, and his descendants. Go with God, know the blessing. Go against God, know the curse. We have His word on it. If we run contrary to the purpose of God, the only result is to know His judgment. And it is exactly the same today as it was then, that's part of having a changeless God.

The Lord gave the prophet Jeremiah an illustration that brings this point home.

Thus says the LORD: /"Cursed is the man who trusts in man/ And makes flesh his strength, /Whose heart departs from the LORD./ For he shall be like a shrub in the desert,/ And shall not see when good comes,/ But shall inhabit the parched places in the wilderness,/ In a salt land which is not inhabited,/ Blessed is the man who trusts in the LORD,/And whose hope is the LORD/ For he shall be like a tree planted by the waters,/ Which spreads out its roots by the river/And will not fear when heat comes;/But its leaf will be green/And will not be anxious in the year of drought,/Nor will cease from yielding fruit? (Jeremiah 17:5-8)

Clearly, the curse of God is not a capricious act, but a consequence of disobedience. God's promise to Abram was to bless those who blessed him, to bless those who followed Abram's example of obedience to the Lord. Those who went against God's purposes were going to find their way a tough, sometimes desolate route to take.

Blessings for All

The seventh promise, that all the families of the earth would be blessed through Abram, was the greatest of all. Although this covenant was made with Abram and his physical descendants called the Jewish people, the original statement of this covenant makes it clear that God's ultimate intention was to bless the whole earth through what he was prepared to do through Abram. The Lord was saying, "One day, I'm going to bring into the world someone who is a physical descendant of yours, Abram, and when He comes, He's going to bring blessings on the whole earth". Jesus is a son of Abraham. He is the fulfillment of the covenant promises; the one through whom the whole earth will find blessing. When we commit ourselves to Him, we find ourselves walking through life with the blessing of God. When we ignore him, we don't. it's as simple as that,

Our Prayer

Father in heaven, we stand before you as your people. We need your Holy Spirit to be our teacher, He who inspired the Word, we ask that You will do mighty things in and through us in fulfillment of Your promises. May they be the truth that becomes bread upon which we may feed; truth that becomes light upon our pathways, truth that may be a blessing through us to others. Let your voice be heard in us, we pray, in the name of Jesus Christ. Amen.

Traveller's Journal

REFLECT

What does it mean to receive unconditional promises?

How are you now experiencing the blessing of God in your life?

How are you a channel of His blessing to others? Is anything blocking the flow of God's blessing to, or through, you?

RECOMMIT

Unblock the channels of blessing in your life by recommitting yourself to obedience to God's purpose in your life as you know it. In your own words, flowing from the circumstances in the life He has given you, take the time to state how your walk with God will change.

CHAPTER THREE

FOLLOWING GOD'S WAY

Abram responded to the command and to the promise by faith. Faith taught Abram how to enter into the place of promise and the place of blessing. Remember, the Lord had promised him a land, and then made seven great promise in reference to His covenant:

I will bless you

I will make your name great

You will be a blessing

I will bless those who bless you

I will curse those who curse you.

I will make you a great nation all the people on earth will be blessed by you.

If Abram had remained in Ur or Haran, not heeding the word of the Lord, and not acting upon His promise, he would not have come into the place of blessing that God had appointed for him. God would not make Ur or Haran, the land of promise; God's plan called for Abraham to get on the route of God, get on the pathway to move toward the blessings; his receiving them was contingent upon his obedient response.

God deals the same way with us. He has plan for our lives. "for we are His workmanship", Apostle Paul stated, created in Christ Jesus for good works, which God prepared beforehand that we should walk in them (Ephesians 2:10) God's plan for our lives included good works that He has prepared ahead of time for us to do, but that does not mean that God foreordains or predestines those good works. The fact that God has a plan does not guarantee that we will either find or fulfill it on the platter of Gold. To be led toward the good works that he has prepared for us to do, requires of us the dame thing it required Abram: Absolute obedience without compromise to the Lord and belief in His promises.

If we don't totally obey, we will not leave our present circumstance and move towards fulfilling God's plan. There's a sense in which all of us are called to leave something in order to enter into the promise of God. That doesn't mean that we are all called to pack our bags and take off for a foreign continent, though it could mean that. It doesn't even necessarily mean that we are going from one place on earth to another. Most times that leave-taking we are called to do is emotional or psychological, because the things that hold us down and keep us back from fulfilling the purposes of God -are oftentimes things to which we have a firm emotional attachment. Sometimes the leave-taking is of a particular habit or lifestyle moving from one form of behavior to another. It may be moving from one career to another, whatever it is, unless we are prepared to move from those things in obedience to God's command, we never will enter into the place of His blessing and possess the promise land.

God has a place of blessing for all of us a place where we can find fulfillment and perfect His will, a place in which our personality, temperament, and talents flow together into the completion of the very reason for which we were given life and we can miss it entirely! Unless we are prepared to move out, we will never move in, unless we are prepared to let go, we will never take hold. Such is God's working in our lives.

The "Exodus mentally" we find laid down in the history of the people of Israel is one that recurs time and time again. God tool His people out go Egypt as led by Moses in order to take them into Canaan. On their own, they would have stopped midway and some did. A whole generation died in the wilderness and never came into the Promised Land. It is not guaranteed that we will automatically find God's will. Abraham did not leave Ur with a map in his land showing the way to Canaan or even a guide for all first led of the journey. It was absolutely a journey of faith. He left with a command ringing in one ear and a promise in the other. That's all he had. The command was to leave; it did not include a detailed description of where Abram was to go. The same principle occurs throughout the whole of scripture and is true for us today.

I think of the time when Jesus dealt with some men who had leprosy. They were social outcasts who wanted desperately to be healed: Read Luke 17:11-14. The Old Testament law required that people with leprosy had to go and show themselves to the priest, and they were submitted to certain tests to see whether they were cured or in a continual state or illness. "As they went, they were cleansed." Jesus did not heal them first and then say, "now go and shoe yourself to the priests. They first had to Act on their instructions, and then they received the blessing. At the wedding ceremony of Cana in Galilee, Mary admonished the servants to simply obey whatever instruction Jesus would utter. And in flowing his directions, the shame that was to disgrace the couple turned into a glorious provision and miraculous testimony (John 2:5-11).

When Peter who was an expert fisherman, toiled all night without success, Jesus stepped onto his boat and gave instruction for a great catch Peter almost missed the miracle because he was counting on his several years of experience and expertise but when he obeyed the lord's direction. The great catch was overwhelming. Read (Luke 5:4-7).

The same principle has been since the Old Testament, obey regardless of what you see in order to see the miraculous. In Exodus 15, God told Moses to stretch the Rod towards the Red See for it to part, no own had ever seen or heard such a thing before that occasion. When Moses obeyed, the Israelites saw the amazing wonder of God, which is unparallel. Joshua gave similar instruction as God had directed him before they could cross over River Jordan (Joshua 3:13) Also, at the great walls of Jericho in Joshua Chapter 6 following divine orders will consistently guaranty victorious celebration.

The poor widow of Zaraphath enjoyed surplus with her household in the time of famine, simply because of obedience to the instructions from prophet Elijah (1 Kings 17:15-16). Whereas, Naaman the Syrian army general who was a leper could have missed his miracle due to pride and premonition when prophet Elisha gave instruction on what to do to get healed and cleansed from leprosy, but thank God for his servants who persuaded him to activated the words of the prophet and be cured. (2 Kings 5:13-14). If Naaman had ignore the counsel then he would never receive his healing. When Achan disobey God's instruction as given by Joshua, a little town of Ai defeated Israel at was. (Joshua 7).

In this book, I want to persuade you to lay aside pride, prejudice and position in order to get what God would communicate to you, consistently, we're to Act on the Instruction of God for Him to fulfill His promises in our life and it was the same for Abram. Picture yourself in Abram's place. He was, I am sure a substantial citizen of Ur of the Chaldees. When he received his call from the Lord, he began to prepare to leave. When word got round that he was leaving, friends, naturally would have wanted to see him off. The conversation with his friends might have gone something like these lines:

Friends: Abram, where are you going?

Abram: Oh God! It's not easy to explain pal!

Friends: Well, in what actual direction are you headed?

Abram: Umm…..I'm not too sure about that.

Friends: Well, then, how far are you going to go?

Abram: Oh! I really don't know.

Friends: Abram, you're awfully indefinite for a man who is leaving town. If you don't know where you're going, well how will you know when you get there?

Abram: Well, I'm not sure, but I know I'll definitely know when I get there!

You see Abram didn't know, and neither do we! God just doesn't work that way. He lets us know that He's moving and incites us to go with Him, but its rare that He shows the end from the beginning. Usually, a promised is attached, just to get us started, most likely, we have to step out, then step out again, and yet again and again as the Lord directs, as the plan gradually unfolds in the process. One of the most important things we need to learn as Christians is that our earthly Christian life is a journey, not a destination. When we become christens, we have not arrived, we've only embarked. And so it was with Abram. Faith taught Abram how to come to the place of promise and blessing, and faith taught him how to live in the land when he finally got there. When Abram arrived with his entourage as we later find out that he had over three hundred people he had pocked up in Haran, he never unpacked his bags. "Abram passed through the land to the place of Shechem, as far as the Terebinth tree of Moreh (Genesis 12:6) that tree was a gathering place for the people. We know nothing whatever about the tree except the name Moreh, the Hebrew (Mowreh) for "teacher". That place was no doubt one in which God had revealed His purpose and instructed His people. (An interesting fact: Sixteen hundred years later, Jesus sat at that same place, near the same tree, and at the water well, He taught a woman about the depths of her need and His sufficiency to meet it. See (John 4) and it there Abram arrived. The Bible says " Then the Lord appeared to Abram and said, " to your descendants I will give this land." And there he built an altar to the Lord, who appeared to him (Genesis 12:7).

That's the first time Abram understood that he was going to be given the land. All he had known was that he would be shown the land, and he may have expected to fight for it. Now he knew that he had arrived and that the land was his. But notice that its not the end of the journey for Abram. "and he moved from there to the mountain east of Bethel, and he pitched his tent with Bethel on the west and Ai on the east; there he built an altar to the Lord and called on the name of the Lord (Genesis 12:8). He Pitched a tent!

Life for Abram was not destination, it was a journey. Even though he was in the place of God's will, he did not unpack because he knew that it was not the end. A great lesson for us to learn from Abram. There is always more to God's will than has been revealed to you. If you settle down in one area, you can stop your spiritual development. A pilgrim is a person who moves on. Let's read again, "By faith he dwelt in the land of promise as in a foreign country, dwelling in tents with Isaac and Jacob the heirs with him of the same promise. (Hebrew 11:9). He had arrived in the land of promise, but he did not settle down. He still regarded himself as a stranger in a foreign land. The image of a tent speaks of detachment. Abram knew that even though he was in the place of God's will for him, there was more to God's revelation and God's purpose for his life. He didn't just settle down; he lived in tents. He was ready to go on.

I love the great hymn of the church, "Lead On O King Eternal" which says, thy tents shall be our home. "This world is not our home. We are strangers here, pilgrims passing through. The great danger is t hat we will fall by the wayside on our faith walk with God towards divine direction when distracted by the scenery, perhaps and build ourselves a house and settle down. We will find in scripture and in life that the people of God exhibit tow lifestyles: one is of a pilgrim people; the other of settlers. Things happen to people when they move from the pilgrim posture to a settlements state. The truth, Christianity neither denies life, nor ignores the world. God puts us into this environment, and this is where we are to serve Him. We can't try to run from the world and think we will find our service to God somehow in solitude. We can't be snared into thinking that everything around us is permanent. It's not. Our lives are not, our health is not, our jobs our careers are not, our relationships, even our physical beings are not, our height, weight, color of hair, and number of teeth change. Nothing is permanent. Life is a progression, a journey on the pathway of God's direction.

We need to understand this truth applied to the church of Christ too. We as the church are called to be pilgrims on the pathway of divine direction, not settlers. What happens to a church when it loses its pilgrims posture? It begins to be more concerned about the building of the church than the life of the church, more concerned with the form of the service than the reality of the worship life of the people. When the church becomes more obsessed with its past than concerned with its future, the settlers state has begun to take hold. That is death, not life to the church. We must always realize we do not worship in a church building or cathedral, we are the church. And we've got to be pilgrims on the move, following God's pathway.

Something happens to people when they spiritually unpack their bags, when they reach a certain level of growth where they are comfortable and say, " I don't want to go any farther, I like it here. I'll settle down. I've had enough. This is fine. I've got it all down pat. I'm saved. I'll get into heaven anyway, do lets stop here. "That is spiritual death. Let's think about the man named Demas in the New Testament for a moment. He's not an all important prominent figure in the scriptures. In fact, he's hardly mentioned at all. In his letter to Philemon (v 25), Paul the apostle wrote that he sent greetings from Demas, a fellow laborer. Yet in the last letter Paul wrote, he said, "Be diligent to come to me quickly, for Demas has forsaken me having loved this present world, and has departed for Thessalonica (2 Timothy 4:9-10). In the first passage we find Demas a vigorous servant for the Lord, in the second we find Demas a Deserter, because he fell in love with the world. That is easy for all of us to do. The snares about us are so many and varied. It is easy to be a spiritual dropout on the pathway, and it happens all the time.

As Christians, however, our strength cannot be derived from the world. Our vision cannot be set by the world's standards. Our behavior cannot be governed according to the dictates of the world. We are to live in the world. We are to live in the world and be responsible citizens in it, but at the same time we are to know that we are stranger here and not live in a way that would deny our faith. Abram learned by faith that to lived in the land of promise is to live as a strange and a pilgrim. Faith taught Abram to keep his eyes always on the Lord, and so when he arrived, he checked n when he got to the site of the great tree at scheme, he built an alter to the Lord. It was there that Abram "called on the name of the Lord" Gen 12:8 is the first recorded verbal response coming from Abram to the Lord, and in fact the first time the expression appears in scripture. Not only does this signify that Abram knew that God was mysteriously calling him to Himself, but that Abram, in obedience, began to communicate with Him and built an altar.

Prayer

Our father in Heaven, we pray that you will speak to us now. as we come before you in quiet reflection, allow the searchlight of your truth to prevail upon our hearts and lives. This can be painful Lord, it's like a bright light shining in our eyes after we've been in the dark for a while. We may not like what we see, but we want to deal honestly with those things that scurry about to know what we've talking about when we come before you to humbly confess.

Give us specifics, Lord, show us those places where we've settle wrongly, where we've stopped short of your perfect will for us, where we've settled for only partial obedience to you. Lord, let our spirit bring to the surface those things that we've buried deeply within us, help us to deal with them squarely, not to reject or deny them. We are aware of the fact that we're unable to express worship that really arises from the heart in truth and spirit without the quickening of your Holy Spirit. Our ears are so filled with the sounds of all sorts that it's sometimes hard for us to hear your voice. O God help us to hear, Lord and to obey totally.

Precious father, we know ourselves to be citizens of two kingdoms at the same time. Sometimes the tension between the one and the other is not easy to live with. Like Demas, we are easily seduced by that which is around us, tempted to be spiritual dropouts. Oh Lord, as we've seen Abram your servant and learned from his experience, we understand that you have called us to press on to obey your commandments and to continually believe your promises. We understand something about how we're to live in this world. Sometimes we want to settle down; we just don't want to press on. Sometimes we did rather be comfortable that obedient, but Lord, please help us to retain our pilgrim heritage. Father, teach us to worship you daily erecting altars of praise and sacrifice, Altars of fellowship and prayer throughout the course of our days wherever we are; living lives that are holy and acceptable to you; that we may be a people who bring a great glory to you; people who furnish great hope and inspiration in this very dark world around us. Oh Lord, it's our desire to stand in your presence; to offer you the worship of our hearts, to beg your forgiveness, your mercy, your cleansing; to hear your words to us to be fed from your table of fellowship and to go forth as pilgrims on the pathway of your divine direction in this word.

Dear father, none of this can happen apart from your holy grace manifested in us and upon us and vital part of our live lord, as we pray in the most precious name of our Lord and Savior Jesus Christ, Amen.

Traveller's Journal

REFLECT

What has been the consequences of some of the choices you have made ?

Would you say that you have a pilgrim or shelter mentality?

Which of the promises of God that you are aware of do you have the most difficulty moving toward in faith ?

Would God be ashamed to be your God ?

RECOMMIT

In your own words, recommit your life to be one of a living sacrifice.

Say specifically what that would mean in your case-you are unique to God, and your life is not the same as anyone else's.

CHAPTER FOUR

EVEN SAINTS MAKE MISTAKES

The Bible makes no effort whatever to try to hide, obscure, or in anyway cover up the sins of the saints.

Noah was called a "preacher of righteousness" and yet, close to the end of his story, we find him in a drunken stupor.

Moses was a deliverer of God's people from bondage and a great lawgiver, and yet he himself was not able to bring the people into the Land of Promise because of his sin of impatience and his failure to sanctify the name of the Lord before the eyes of the people of Israel.

David was called "a man after God's own heart", and yet there are chapters in his life that we would not be called to emulate, for he was an adulterer, and to cover his adultery, be became a murderer.

Likewise, Abraham was called "the father of faithful", yet there were times in his life when he was not a man of faith. We can learn as much from the mistakes of the saints as we do from their great victories.

Faith had brought Abram into that Land of Promise. To be there was to be in the place of God's will. He had followed the Lord across trackless wastes; he had been led into the land; he knew he had come to the place where God wanted him. He pitched his sent, built an altar, and called on the Lord's name. A happy ending, one would think. But not so.

Problems in the Promised Land

A person can be in the will of God, the place of God's appointing, and still have to face problems.

I am not of the same mind-set of those who say if we commit our lives to the Lord, are filled with the Holy Spirit, and walk in obedience to Jesus, it's roses, lollipops, and smiles all the way. I do not find that true in my own life's experience or that of anyone I know, furthermore, I find that teaching does not square with the experience of God's people throughout history, nor with the written or living Word of God.

Jesus, the Son of God, said, "For I have come down from heaven, not to do My own will, but the will of Him who sent Me" (John 6:38). And, "For the works which the Father has given Me to finish – the very works that I do – bear witness of Me, that the Father has sent Me" (John 5:36).

Perfect obedience led Jesus to a torturous death on a cross! Throughout the three years of His ministry He was constantly in a place of peril, at the mercy of the wrath of those people who hated Him.

I reject the kind of teaching that lures people into Christianity with promises that say, "Commit your life to the Lord, walk in obedience to Him, and everything you do will prosper, you will become a healthy, wealthy, and wise person".

If people are prey to a faith such as this, it will not sustain them when the hard time come. Not only will they have to deal with the problems, but they will bear the added pain of having to deal with their thoughts that somehow they are not right with God or they wouldn't be in such a mess.

We'll look now at one of those times when Abram walked contrary and counter to the purpose of God.

Now there was a famine in the land, and Abram went down to Egypt to dwell there, for the famine was severe in the land. And it came to pass, when he was close to entering Egypt, that he said to Sarai his wife, "Indeed I know that you are a woman of beautiful countenance. Therefore it will happen, when the Egyptians see you, that they will say, "This is my wife': and they will kill me, but they will let you live. Please say you are my sister, that it may be well with me for your sake, and that I may live because of you." So it was, when Abram came into Egypt, that the Egyptians saw the woman, that she was very beautiful. The princes of Pharaoh also saw her and commended her to Pharaoh. And the woman was taken to Pharaoh's house. He treated Abram well for her sake. He had sheep, oxen, male donkeys, male and female servants, female donkeys, and camels. But the LORD plagued Pharaoh and his house with great plagues because of Sarai, Abram's wife. And Pharaoh called Abram and said, "What is this you have done to me? Why did you not tell me that she was your wife? Why did you say, "She is my sister?" I might have taken her as my wife. Now, therefore, here is your wife: take her and go your way" So Pharaoh commanded his men concerning him; and they sent him away with his wife and all that he had. (Genesis 12:10-20).

Abram exemplified being in the very center of the will of God, and yet he was being faced with a terrible problem: There was a great famine in the Land of Promise. Several options were open to him. He could easily have said to himself: *Well, God brought me this far, and He has given me many great and wonderful promises. He said He would take me into a land that He would show me, and He has. He said He would make a great nation, that I would have descendants like the sand of the sea and the stars of the sky. He said that He would bless those who bless me and curse those who curse me. He said that I will be a blessing. He said that there will come a day when someone of my lineage will bring blessing to the whole earth.*

He could have strengthened himself with the memory of the promises that God had given to him. After all, God gave those promises to Abram at a time when he had nothing whatever to look to in support of them, yet he believed. At that point, however, he forgot to put his faith in the God who had made (and had already begun to fulfill) those promises to him.

But Abram forgot who he was at this critical point. Abram was a man with a destiny, with a purpose to accomplish in life. And he forgot that the Lord God had given a pledge to be his God and that He would fulfill all that He had promised to him. So Abram was left to his own devices.

You may ask, "How could he forget?" yet think a moment. How often do we forget the many promises of the Lord God to us, and go off on our own? The promises from the very same God are available to us today. How often do we believe, appropriate, and follow? How much more often do we go on following our own intellect or judgment, and wind up living with consequences?

Abram, on his own, decided to go to Egypt. No place in Scripture specifically says he should not have gone there, but it is often that way in life. In the absence of specific prohibition, we are left to what, in the sports world, is known as a "judgment call". Abram was told to go to the Land of Promise, but he was not told not to go to Egypt. Yet as he approached Egypt, he became more and more frightened for his own welfare. When he was in the Promised Land, God had protected him and a great entourage – many menservants and maid-servants, much wealth in the form of cattle and sheep, and so forth. He probably felt that he could handle any opponent in the Land of Promise, for God had said that He would give the land to him and to his descendants. But now he was about to enter Egypt, and that was another matter altogether. Somehow he knew that God's protection did not extend to Egypt.

Egypt was an ancient land with a great civilization. The pyramids of Gaza were already a thousand years old when Abram got there. Egypt had a great and glorious history; it had long been governed by powerful pharaohs. Abram also understood the custom of the times. It was quite within the prerogative of an emperor, king, or pharaoh to take unto himself any woman that he desired. If a chosen woman was married, it would not have been unthinkable that the ruler would have ordered the death of the woman's husband so that he could have her all to himself. It was precisely this knowledge of the ways of the world that frightened Abram, because Sarai was a beautiful woman.

We know that Abram was seventy-five years old when he left Haran before he entered Canaan. We also know that Sarai was ten years younger than Abram, so she was least sixty-five years old.

We know that Abram was ninety-nine years old when his son Isaac was born, and his son Ishmael, by Hagar (one of the maidservants Abram took with him when he left Egypt) was then thirteen years old. So there is a space of about ten years time during which Abram's travel to Egypt took place.

Sarai was very likely at least seventy years old, but she was still a very beautiful, desirable woman. Abram determined to involve her in his deception, to protect himself. He asked her to say she was his sister so that the Egyptians would treat him well and spare his life.

The strange thing is, Abram and Sarai were, in fact, half-brother and half-sister, so what he told her to say was, in one sense, the truth. But the truth was told with the intent to deceive, and that made it a lie.

Genesis 20 records the same situation some years later. It was a different set of circumstances, and in a different land, but Abram's fear was the same, and he again asked his wife to say that she was his sister.

The Intention of the Heart

We can lie truthfully and tell the truth in a lying way. It's all a matter of our intentions. The intention of Abram's heart was to deceive, out of self-protection, and even though what was said was actually and technically true, it became a lie because its intent was only to deceive. When we talk about sin, we don't mean only what we do, but also the intention of the heart that is behind the action.

A good example of this is an incident that took place hundreds of years after Abram. A husband and wife named Ananias and Sapphira, two Christian believers, sold a piece of property that they owned. They gave part of the money to the apostles; no problem in that. They didn't have to give any of the money to the apostles. What was wrong was that they gave part, but created the impression that they were giving everything. That was a lie, that was deception, and God's immediate judgment came upon both of them. In those days of a fledging church, God wanted His people to know that if it was the intention of their hearts to deceive, their act was wrong. The deceiving husband and wife were struck dead on the spot in front of everyone. (See Acts 5). What a lesson!

The only way to live in the Promised Land (that is, in the will of God) is with integrity of heart. It would have been possible for Abram to have said to himself, *Well, I'm going down to Egypt to get food, but because God has promised these things to me and I believe Him, I will trust that He will protect me.* It would have been possible for him to live with integrity in the will of God in the face of problems. He didn't do it.

E-G-Y-P-T- Spells Trouble

Abram's travel to Egypt is the first mention of Egypt in the Bible. God's servant, Abram, the one who is going to be the founder of the whole people of God, was going to Egypt for help. As we look at subsequent Scripture, we will find again and again the temptation that came to the people of God to do this. In Genesis 26, Abram's son Isaac found himself in exactly the same situation. There was a famine, and this time a word came to Isaac from the Lord.

There was a famine in the land, besides the first famine that was in the days of Abraham. And Isaac went to Abimelech king of the Philistines, in Gerar. Then the LORD appeared to him and said: "Do not go down to Egypt; live in the land of which I shall tell you. Dwell in this land, and I will be with you and bless you; for to you and your descendants I give all these lands, and I will perform the oath which I swore to Abraham your father" (Genesis 26:1-3).

Isaac was definitely told not to go down to Egypt. In the Old Testament, Egypt is synonymous with the place of bondage. The descendants of Abraham all moved down to Egypt, and over a period of four hundred years, they were reduced to slavery. They found themselves in chains and shackles as bondservants in a foreign land. They weren't supposed to be in Egypt, they had been given the Land of Promise, but they wandered away from God. They moved out from the place of His will and into the place of bondage. You will continually find the prophets of the Lord warning the people of God about "going to Egypt" – not because of Egypt's location, but because of what it represented. "Going to Egypt" symbolized moving out of the will of God, leaning on one's own understanding, and following one's own will rather than following the Lord's will.

"Woe to the rebellious children," says the LORD,/"Who take counsel, but not of Me,/And who devise plans, but not of My Spirit,/That they may add sin to sin;/Who walk to go down to Egypt/And have not asked My advice,/To strengthen themselves in the strength of Pharaoh,/And to trust in the shadow of Egypt!/Therefore the strength of Pharaoh shall be your shame,/And the trust in the shadow of Egypt/Shall be your humiliation" (Isaiah 30:1-3).

What is wrong with people? In a time of trouble we fail to place our faith in the Lord, but rather lean on their own understanding. What was wrong with the Israelites? Why did they want to go down to Egypt for help? Why did they begin to make and carry out plans that were not of the Lord? Why did they begin to form an alliance that was not by the Spirit of the Lord? They wanted to add to their strength by calling on the might of Egypt!

The people of God went down to Egypt without consulting Him. They didn't turn to the Lord. That was Abram's problem; he wanted to form an alliance that was not of the Spirit. He apparently went down to Egypt without consulting the Lord.

In Isaiah 31 there is yet another: "Woe to those who go down to Egypt for help,/And rely on horses,/Who trust in chariots because they are many,/And in horsemen because they are very strong,/But who do not look to the Holy One of Israel,/Nor seek the LORD!" (Isaiah 31:1). Perhaps it would make a more contemporary comparison if I paraphrased it to read, "Woe to those who go down to the bank for help, who rely on their investments, who trust in the multitude of their possessions and the great prestige of their position, but do not look to the Holy one of Israel, or seek help from the Lord, "You and I know about that. We've all done it. We trust in the temporal rather than the eternal, in our prestige or insight, in our own scheming and plans. We invariably will get ourselves into difficulty, even as Abram did.

Now in whom do you trust, that you rebel against me? Look! You are trusting in the staff of this broken reed, Egypt, on which if a man leans, it will go into his hand and pierce it. So is Pharaoh king of Egypt to all who trust in him. (Isaiah 36:5,6)

"Going down to Egypt" when we meet problems in our walk of faith is turning away from God and trusting the arm of flesh. Trusting in our own intelligence, our own resources, always brings problems".

Affliction or Consequences?

Abram's decision resulted in an increase of problems for everybody – including Pharaoh and Abram himself. You may wonder why the Lord would afflict the Pharaoh when the sin was Abram's. after all, Pharaoh was innocent; he didn't know that he was being deceived. But no sooner had Sarai come into his household than problems began to arise.

We know that the practice in those times was that a sovereign king, emperor, or pharaoh could take a woman into his harem, but there was a waiting period of one full year before he could touch her. (This is also illustrated in the story of Esther, who was brought into the court of King Ahasuerus). It was during that year, that time of waiting, that all kinds of calamities fell on Pharaoh and his household.

Scripture doesn't tell us how Pharaoh drew the connection between the troubles that occurred and the presence of Abram's wife. Perhaps Sarai himself told him; there might have come a point when she would have confessed that the story of her relationship to Abram was not quite true. Yes, she was Abram's sister, but she was also his wife. Pharaoh, when he discovered that, had every reason to be incensed against Abram. He confronted him and said, "What is this you have done to me? Why did you not tell me that she was your wife? Why did you say, 'She is my sister?" (Genesis 12:18-19).

Think of the implications of that. How tragic it is when some of the children of the world enter into judgment because of the sins of believing people. Our sin always affects others. How tragic, when a worldly has cause to point to a child of God and say, "What you did was wrong!" How tragic it is to find a higher degree of morality in the world that within the household of God.

What kind of testimony could Abram have among Egyptians unbelievers? He was a man under orders from the Almighty God, but he couldn't talk about it! He couldn't influence anyone for God because he was a liar and a deceiver in a foreign land. I wonder if he felt guilty when he received all those gifts from Pharaoh when their bestowal was based on a lie.

If we lie, we are out of the purpose of God! For example, it's not necessary to cheat on income tax or follow everybody-does-it business practices in order to have a few more dollars. Or if a husband lies to his wife, no matter how he rationalizes, it is wrong. Likewise, if a wife lies to her husband, or children to their parents, it is wrong. When we rationalize our behavior, it is wrong. "Rationalizing" is no more than another way of describing "lying to self".

Look at the problems Abram created for himself when he deceived Pharaoh. And yet, in Genesis 20 we find that he did the same thing all over again. Why didn't he learn? Well, isn't it easier to sin a second time and a third or a fourth if it works the first? Once done, a pattern of disobedience is established and this pattern becomes more and more entrenched the longer it is allowed to go on. Abram created the pattern, and his son Isaac did the same thing some years later. Have you noticed how often children reproduce the sins of their parents because of the example they've had?

Well, fortunately for Abram (and for us), it's not the end of the story. In a rather disgraceful way, Abram was kicked out of Egypt by a man more righteous than he was at the moment, and he went back to the Land of Promise.

> *Then Abram went up from Egypt, he and his wife and all that he had, and Lot with him, to the South. Abram was very rich in livestock, in silver and in gold. And he went on his journey from the South as far as Bethel, to the place where his tent had been at the beginning, between Bethel and Ai, to the place of the altar which he had made there at first. And there Abram called on the name of the LORD. (Genesis 13:1-4).*

Abram had been wandering in Egypt and was kicked out. He had been going on his own and the consequences caught up with him. No credit to him, he had to go back until he came to Bethel. Bethel was the last place that Abram had a hold on God. That's the place where he built his altar to the Lord and first began to call upon His name. He had wandered away off the path with God and he had to go back to that place where he began.

The same principle was present in the story of the lost son, popularly known as the "prodigal son". He had left his father's house with great promise and squandered his money in wild living, ending up envying what the pigs had to eat. Whatever was a good Jewish boy doing with pigs? You can be sure that was never a part of God's plan for his life! That wasn't the boy's intention, either, but that was the consequence of his actions. Then there's that wonderful part of the story.

But when he came to himself, he said, "How many of my father's hired servants have bread enough and to spare, and I perish with hunger! I will arise and go to my father, and will say to him, 'Father, I have sinned against heaven and before you, and I am no longer worthy to be called your son. Make me like one of your hired servants". And he arose and came to his father. But when he was still a great way off, his father saw him and had compassion, and ran and fell on his neck and kissed him. (Luke 15:17-20).

Why is it only in times of desperation that we realize we are out there somewhere far from God – even alienated from ourselves – and the only way to wholeness again is to go back?

When we are separated from God, we are headstrong in our intention to do what we want to do and to accomplish our own will. We silence the inner voice that tells us, "No", "Danger ahead!" "Don't go in that direction".

When the prodigal came to his senses, he said, "I will set out and go back to my father". He knew there wasn't any other way! If he had kept on going, even if he had acknowledged that he was in the wrong, that would not have been repentance. He had to make the decision to go back to the place where he and his father were last in fellowship. It was exactly the same with Abram. He had to go back to Bethel because that was the place where God and he had last spoken to each other. He wanted to start all over again.

There are actually two "prodigals" in Jesus' story: the son, who was wasteful and extravagant, and the father, who was profuse in giving, lavish in forgiving, and accepting of the wasteful son's return. This is a message from the Word of God that we all need to hear. Remember, there will be problems in the Promise Land, but we can be in the place of God's will and face them! The question is not whether we have the problems, but how we respond to them. Thank God, we have a prodigal Father who lavishes forgiveness and welcome upon us. There are times of restoration to those who repent and turn around and go back again.

When God stops our headlong plunge into destruction, it is His mercy, not His judgment. When He convicts us and we feel a sense of shame and guilt, that's the blessing of God seeking to draw us back from that which would entangle and ultimately destroy us.

I don't know if there is a problem that you are facing at this moment, but I do know that life has problems even for those who try to fulfill the will of God. We make wrong choices at times and find ourselves in Egypt. Take a moment to allow the Holy Spirit to cast the light of the His truth upon your life, to open any dark places, to reveal or expose anything that is contrary to His will. This is always painful, but it's the kind of pain that one experiences with surgery. The cut enables healing. If something comes to your mind, deal with it right now.

The following prayers will be helpful. As you read through them slowly and deliberately, allow the Lord to refresh you with His forgiveness.

Most merciful God,

We confess that we have sinned against you

In thought, word and deed,

By what we have done,

And by what we have left undone,

We have not loved you with our whole heart.

We have not loved our neighbors as ourselves;

We are truly sorry and we humbly repent.

For the sake of your Son, Jesus Christ,

Have mercy on us, and forgive us,

That we may delight in your will.

And walk in your ways,

To the glory of your Name. Amen.

Almighty God have mercy on you, forgive you all your sins through our Lord Jesus Christ, strengthen you in all goodness, and by the power of the Holy Spirit keep you in eternal life.

Traveller's Journal

REFLECT

Where have you come to a fork in the road and taken the turn that led away from God?

What things in your life represent Egypt?

How often is the phrase "I can do it myself" in your vocabulary?

RECOMMIT

In your own words, describe your duty to God and your duty to neighbors. Tell what the Ten Commandments are and why we have them. Explain the concepts of sin, penitence, and grace.

CHAPTER FIVE

CHOOSING GOD.

Life is made up of a series of choices and decisions. Some of the choices are of little consequences. For instance, we may have faced the choice of corn flakes or oatmeal this morning for breakfast – and I suspect that nothing of eternal significance will result from our decisions. Some choices we make, however, at the very least affect the rest of our lives. The choice of a college, for instance. If we choose to go to a particular school, it is clear that we will make different friendships and have a different education than had we chosen another.

The choice of a lifetime is another decision with lasting consequences. Years ago I read a poem by Robert Frost that touched me greatly, "The Road Not Taken" is a poem about choices. Frost pictured one walking in the woods and coming to a fork in the path, and he described the decision to take the less traveled road in preference to the other, and the knowledge that he would never return to that same point again.

The Road Not Taken

Two roads diverged in a yellow wood,

And sorry I could not travel both

And be one traveler, long I stood

And looked down one as far as I could

To where it bent in the undergrowth;

Then took the other, as just as fair,

And having perhaps the better claim,

Because it was grassy and wanted wear;

Though as for that the passing here

Had won them really about the same.

And both that morning equally lay
In leaves no step had trodden black
Oh, I kept the first for another day!
Yet knowing how way leads on to way,
I doubted if I should ever come back.

I shall be telling this with a sigh
Somewhere ages and ages hence;
Two roads diverged in a wood, and I –
I took the one less traveled by,
And that has made all the difference.

We will see in this chapter how choices make the difference. Not for us alone, but for many; not for the present only, but for the future.

Problems of Prosperity

As we move into Genesis 13, the focus shifts a bit from the central character of Abram to his nephew, Lot:

Lot also, who went with Abram, had flocks and herds and tents. Now the land was not able to support them, that they might dwell together, for their possessions were so great that they could not dwell together. And there was strife between the herdsmen of Abram's livestock and the herdsmen of Lot's livestock. The Canaanites and the Perizzites then dwelt in the land. (Gen. 13:5-7).

Abram acquired wealth while he was Egypt, as did his nephew, Lot. Their prosperity brought problems. In that part of the world, there is a shortage of rain and a resultant shortage of grassy lands. It was not possible for the large herds and flocks of Abram and the flocks and herds of Lot to be sustained on the same land – along with those of the Canaanites and Perizzites. Abram made the first move to resolve the problem.

So Abram said to Lot, "Please let there be no strife between you and me, and between my herdsmen and your herdsmen; for we are brethren. Is not the whole land before you? Please separate from me. If you take the left, then I will go to the right; or if you go to the right, then I will go to the left." (Gen. 13:8,9).

Abram was the patriarch – no one would have expected him to give Lot the first choice. Very graciously and generously, however, Abram gave up the rights and said to his nephew, "You take first choice. Anywhere you decide will be quite all right; I'll take what's left over". Then came the moment of decision:

And lot lifted his eyes and saw all the plain of Jordan, that it was well watered everywhere (before the LORD destroyed Sodom and Gomorrah) like the garden of the LORD, like the land of Egypt as you go toward Zoar. Then Lot chose for himself all the plain of Jordan, and Lot journeyed east. And they separated from each other. Abram dwelt in the land of Canaan, and Lot dwelt in the cities of the plain and pitched his tent even as far as Sodom. (Gen. 13:10-12).

Territorial Terrain

Bethel is on a high, hilly, mountainous territory, and from there Abram and Lot could survey the whole of the Jordan Valley at their feet. The Jordan Valley is part of one of the most remarkable physical features on the face of the earth. If we were to see that portion of the world from outer space, we would see a huge scar that cuts across a lot of it, touching the two continents. This Jordan Valley actually begins in the north of Israel at Mount Hermon, a great mountain over 9,000 feet high. It is often snow-covered, and more often encompassed by clouds so that we cannot see the top of the mountain except on very rare occasion at certain times of the year.

The Jordan River begins to flow down the valley that starts at that place. When it comes to the Sea of Galilee, it is already 600feet below sea level. It then plunges out the southern end of the Sea of Galilee and goes farther down the Jordan Valley until it empties into the Dead Sea. The Dead Sea is 1,306 feet below sea level, making it the deepest place on the face of the earth. But even that is not the end of the valley. The valley continues beyond the Dead Sea into Africa, and ends as part of the Rift Valley, which is a part of Eastern Africa in what is known today as Kenya.

The portion of land that Abram and Lot saw as they looked out from Bethel was the Jordan Valley, the part that begins with the Sea of Galilee in the north and ends seventy-five miles further south at the entrance to the Dead Sea. Because the valley was watered by the Jordan River, it was a fertile land – and perhaps the most fertile portion of that country in ancient times. It's not surprising that Lot, having been given the first choice, looked to that valley and perhaps said to himself: *Well, that's certainly the best place to graze herds and flocks.* Looking to the mountains around Bethel, he saw that the vegetation was scraggly, the grass sparse. He chose the very best for himself. He chose to graze his flocks at the Jordan Valley, but he moved his dwelling place further south and pitched his tents near Sodom.

Note that it is seventy-five miles from the Sea of Galilee to the Dead Sea, and the Dead Sea itself is seventy-five miles long. Sodom was one of the cities way down at the southern end of the Dead Sea, in the Valley of the Salt Sea. (No longer was it called the Jordan Valley, because the Jordan River ended when it entered into the Dead Sea). Lot chose to dwell seventy-five miles from where the herds and flocks were grazing. Lot was a gentleman farmer; he didn't tend the flocks himself. He had many, many servants to take care of things.

Selecting Sodom

Lot pitched his tents near Sodom, and the Bible gives a one sentence description of the city of Sodom: "But the men of Sodom were exceedingly wicked and sinful against the LORD" (Gen. 13:13). Sodom was already a city with a bad reputation, a city known for its paganism. Yet Lot chose to leave the Land of Promise and settle near it.

That's the end of Act I. We already see the beginning of a tragedy in this drama. It gets worse as it goes along, because of the escalating force of a decision – a decision innocently made, I suppose, when first determined, and yet a decision that had consequences that lasted for generations after.

Act II opens in Genesis 14. There was a war in the Valley of the Salt Sea, and four kings were engaged in war against five other kings. The word kings in this chapter does not refer to rulers of nations, but to tribal chieftains, like Abram and Lot. Those tribes could involve thousands and thousands of people. They were settled tribes, nor nomadic tribes, and they built cities. The cities were in that lower plain called the Valley of the Salt Sea, and one of them was Sodom.

This little dogfight in the Valley of the Salt Sea would never have been included in Scripture, were it not for the fact that it touched upon the story of Abram in a striking way. ***"Then he took all the goods of Sodom and Gomorrah, and all their provisions, and went their way. They also took Lot, Abram's brother's son who dwelt in Sodom, and his goods, and departed" (Genesis 14:11-12).***

Did you notice the progression? In Act I, Lot moved near Sodom. In Act II, we find that he lived in Sodom. When Sodom was attacked by the four kings from the north, the city was defeated. Among the people and treasure carried away into captivity were

Lot, his family, and possessions. News of this reached his Uncle, Abram.

One who had escaped came and reported this to Abram the Hebrew. Now Abram was living near the great tress of Mamre the Amorte, a brother of Eshcol and Aner, all of whom were allied with Abram. When Abram heard his relative had been taken captive, he called out the 318 trained men born in his household and went in pursuit as far as Dan. During the night Abram divided his men to attack them and he routed them, pursuing them as far as Hobah, north of Damascus. He recovered all the goods and brought back his relative Lot and his possessions, together with the women and the other people. (Genesis 14:13-16).

When Abram heard that Sodom had been conquered and that Lot and his family had been taken into captivity, he assembled his militia. It's interesting that the Bible says that they were three hundred and eighteen trained men who were born in Abram's household. Where did all those people come from? When Abram was on the way from Ur of the Chaldees to the Land of Promise, he had settled for a time in Haran. Part of his entourage had come into the Land of Promise from Haran, and the other part had come out of Egypt.

These were people born in his tribe and in his family, and they were trained men. He dispatched them in hot pursuit after the kings of the north to rescue his nephew Lot, and Abram's men pursued them as far as Dan, located on the northern border. (In the Bible, the borders of the Promised Land are often described as "from Dan to Beersheba." The ruins of the ancient city of Tell Dan are still there). They were able to liberate Lot and his family and take them back home again. Act II finds Lot living in Sodom, taken from the city, recovered and rescued by his uncle, and returned home.

Abraham and Lot

Having intervened in Lot's life, Abram no doubt wondered how; and why; Lot was living in the land near Sodom. In the theater these are, at times, asides – scenes that take place with other characters that have bearing on the main plot of the story. We have one with Lot's drama, also. Between the time that Abram returned Lot to Sodom and the conclusion of the story, Abram touched on Lot's life in a way that we can see, but we have no idea if Lot ever knew.

And the LORD said, "Shall I hide from Abraham what I am doing, since Abraham shall surely become a great and mighty nation, and all the nations of the earth shall be blessed in him? For I have known him, in order that he may command his children and his household after him, that they keep the way of the LORD, to do righteousness and justices, that the LORD may bring to Abraham what He has spoken to him" (Gen. 18:17-19).

The Lord was about to take Abraham into confidence concerning a decision He had made that would affect the lives of his relatives. But what God had to say was hard for Abraham to here:

> *And the Lord said, 'Because the outcry against Sodom and Gomorrah is great, and because their sin is very grace, I will go down now and see whether they have done altogether according to the outcry against it that has come to Me; and if not, I will know"*
> *(Genesis 18:20,21)*

God knew all the gory details, but because of His righteousness, He decided to send messengers to seek any redeeming qualities in the life of the city. In legal procedure, investigation precedes inflictions. Thought the guilt of Sodom was great, God would not let loose His vengeance until it should seem perfectly just. 'Then the men turned away from there and went toward Sodom, but Abraham still stood before the LORD" (Gen. 18:22). Abraham wanted to respond to God. Imagine his heavy heart.

And Abraham came near and said, "Would you also destroy the righteous with the wicked? Suppose there were fifty righteous within the city, would you also destroy the place and not spare it for fifty righteous that were in it? Far be it from You to do such a thing as this, to slay the righteous with the wicked, so that the righteous should be as the wicked; far be it from You! Shall not the Judge of all the earth do right?" So the LORD said, "If I find in Sodom fifty righteous within the city, then I will spare all the place for their sakes" (Gen. 18:23-26).

An amazing exchange! God agreed to spare the city if there were fifty people found to be righteous. Abraham was learning that God is open to entreaty, unwilling to destroy.

Then Abraham, answered and said, "Indeed now, I who am but dust and ashes have taken it upon myself to speak to the Lord; suppose there were five less than fifty righteous; would You destroy all of the city for lack of five?" (Genesis 18:27-28).

Abraham pointed out that if the difference were only five, it would be a tragedy to destroy so many for such a small number, and God agreed. Abraham then posed increasingly smaller numbers of righteous people to be found in Sodom: What if forty? Thirty? Twenty? Ten? "For the sake of ten", God promised He would not destroy Sodom. (See vv. 29-32).

Abraham exhibited holy boldness – unrestrained, almost audacious prayer on the behalf of his nephew and those he lived among. Abraham was humble at the same time, acknowledging repeatedly his personal unworthiness to be heard. But he kept on, logically and steadily, until he got what he asked of the Lord – a promise to spare the city if ten righteous people could be found there. Obviously, he had second thoughts about the righteousness of Lot's entourage if he dropped from fifty to ten, but surely, in a huge tribe such as Lot's there would remain ten people! In any case, Abraham felt he had reached the limits of his intercession, and he went home to await news of what was about to happen.

The scene fades out, and Act III of Lot's drama begins in chapter 19: "Now the two angels came to Sodom in the evening, and Lot was sitting in the gate of Sodom" (v.1). The gateway of the city in those days was a public place where courts were held and decisions given; it was the place from which those governed ruled, the place where the elders of the community assembled. If Lot was seated in the gate of the city, he was not only living in Sodom, he had become a major citizen, an important person, one of the rulers. (This is also illustrated in Ruth 4:1:2, which describes Boaz inviting the kinsman-redeemer and ten elders of the town to sit with him at the town gate).

The town gate was the place where the elders of the city met, where important decisions were rendered, where justice was meted out. See the progression: first Lot decided to settle near Sodom, a city described as "one of the great wickedness in the sight of the Lord"; then he lived in Sodom; finally he became a substantial citizen. And this town ruler was about to be visited:

When Lot saw them [the angels], he arose to meet them, and he bowed himself with his face toward the ground. And he said, "Here now, my lords, please turn in to your servant's house and spend the night, and wash your feet; then you may rise early and go on your way" (Genesis 19:1,2).

Two strangers arrived in town, and Lot, sitting at the gate, welcomed them to his house. His concern was born also out of knowledge of the danger to which strangers were exposed.

And they said, "No, but we will spend the night in the open square". But he insisted strongly; so they turned in to him and entered his house. Then he made them a feast, and baked unleavened bread, and they ate. Now before they lay down, the men of the city, the men of Sodom, both old and young, all the people from every quarter, surrounded the house. And they called to Lot and said to him, "Where are the men who came to you tonight? Bring them out to use that we may know them carnally."
(Genesis 19:2-5).

Some of you have heard the word *sodomy,* which refers to homosexual relationships. The term comes from the city of Sodom, that was judged wicked and evil in the sight of God. At the giving of the law to Moses, this sin was punishable by death. What happened? Lot welcomed two visitors – described as "angelic visitors" – into his home, and we can presume them to be exceedingly attractive. Before they retired that night, all of the men of the city, young and old, surrounded Lot's house and demanded that Lot bring the two visitors out so that they could have sex with them. This was a town utterly given over to the practice of homosexual relationships.

Lot's response to the citizens is significant:

So Lot went out to them through the doorway, shut the door behind him, and said, "Please, my brethren [Brethren! What kind of friends did her have?], do not do so wickedly! See now, I have two daughters who have not known a man; please, let me bring them out to you, and you may do to them as you wish; only do nothing to these men, since this is the reason they have come under the shadow of my rood." (Genesis 19:6-8).

You may think that a strange exchange, but so circumspect was the pledge of protection by a man toward the guests of his household, that he would rather have his daughters violated than the honor of his house. Still, that was a horrifying thing to have happen, and Lot was clearly distressed.

And they said, "Stand back!" then they said, "This one came in to stay here, and he keeps acting as a judge, now we will deal worse with you than with them." So they pressed hard against the man Lot, and came near to break down the door. But the men reached out their hands and pulled Lot into the house with them, and shut the door. And they struck the men who were at the doorway of the house with blindness, both small and great, so that they became weary trying to find the door. (Genesis 19:9-11).

The angels then told Lot about the Lord's coming destruction of Sodom and asked him who else lived with him in order that they would all escape safely. But Lot's sons-in-law thought he was joking. When the morning dawned, the angels took the lingering Lot by the hand, along with his wife and two daughters, and warned.

"Escape for your life! Do not look behind you nor stay anywhere in the plain. Escape to the mountains, lest you be destroyed." Then Lot said to them, "Please, no, my lords! Indeed now, your servant has found favor in your sight, and you have increased your mercy which you have shown me by saying my life; but I cannot escape to the mountains, lest some evil overtake me and I die. See now, this city is near enough to flee to, and it is a little one; please let me escape there (is it not a little one?)_and my soul shall live." (Gen. 19:17-20).

Do you see what happened to Lot? He was a man who made a decision – an innocent decision, or so it seemed – to live outside the big city. But then he was drawn into the vortex of its life. He moved into the city and became so involved in its affairs that he ended up one of the rulers, one of the elders sitting at the gate. He had such a stake in the city, and had invested so much in it that he couldn't bear to leave. Even though judgment sounded in his ears, he couldn't bear to leave. His home and family were there; his friends were there; his business was there. He has invested a lot in Sodom. He had developed the mentality of a settler and had lost his pilgrim spirit; Sodom had entered into his heart. Even when he was pulled out and told to escape to the mountains, he answered with a counter offer to escape to a close city. And the two angels agreed. (See vv 21-22). You can just imagine Lot saying to himself, *Well, after the heat is off of Sodom, I'll go back.* He believed, but only partially. He had lost some of the sense of the holiness of God, and it really hadn't sunk in that the city of Sodom, and Gomorrah, too, would be ashes.

As we read on in Genesis 19, we find out that as they were fleeing the city, Lot's wife turned back. Perhaps she said to herself, *I wonder what's happening to our home? To our beautiful garden? And what about our business?* She couldn't make the break. She had settled, and Sodom had crept into her heart. She became a pillar of salt, never to move again. (see v. 26).

Since life is a series of small decisions, one following another, lot didn't realize that he was getting in deeper and deeper and deeper. The nature of sin is that, little by little, through a series of wrong choices, people gradually get to the place where they lose their freedom to choose. There is a time when an alcoholic can take it or leave it; when a drug addict can decide, "I don't need it anymore", when sexual perversion is not an established habit. The trouble is, there is always something so alluring about sin – and addiction to it – that the person caught up in it loves it and hates it at the same time. That's what happened with Lot.

Contemporary Commentary

A devastating, and current, commentary on the lure of sin is described in 2 Peter 2:

But there were also false prophets among the people, even as there will be false teachers among you, who will secretly bring in destructive heresies, even denying the Lord who bought them, and bring on themselves swift destruction. And many will follow their destructive ways, because of whom the way of truth will be blasphemed. By covetousness they will exploit you with deceptive words; for a long time their judgment has not been idle, and their destruction does not slumber (2 Pet. 2:1-3).

How does a society become corrupt? It starts with leaders who convince others that truth is in error and then substitute their error as truth. The people of Sodom were not born perverts; they allowed the patterns of error to take hold, and they gave in to them. The majority accepted ways that were alien to God's purposes in creation, and judgment followed.

THE FOOTPRINTS OF FAITH

[For if God turned] the cities of Sodom and Gomorrah into ashes, condemned them to destruction, making them an example to those who afterward would live ungodly; and delivered righteous Lot, who was oppressed by the filthy conduct of the wicked....then the Lord knows how to deliver the godly out of the temptations and to reserve the unjust under punishment for the day of judgment t, and especially those who walk according to the flesh in the lust of uncleanness and despise authority. (2 Peter 2:6-10).

We read that Lot was a righteous man and that the wickedness of the people around him troubled him. I've some questions for you. Did he try to stop it? Did he protest it? Obviously not, since he called the townsmen *brethren* and was one of their leaders. Lot had learned to coexist with evil. He hated it, yet he loved it at the same time. That is the deceitfulness of sin.

I'm not only talking about Lot. How do you and I react to that which we know is wrong? When we choose consciously to look away and to walk away from the Lord, we are in danger. We don't realize the tremendously seductive power of evil. We don't realize that we can become slaves of sin, of passion, alcohol, drugs, money, or whatever. Sin just takes over a while, and we can reach a place where we can't do much about it.

A most interesting test was once conducted in an experimental laboratory. A frog was placed in a container of water, and the water was heated at 0.036 of a degree per second. The frog did not notice this slight increase in the temperature of the water each second. When the temperature reached 140 degrees, the frog died. He could have jumped out at any time in the process, and his life would have been saved. But the frog did not notice the danger he was in because the change was so gradual. He was dying by degrees! That is a good illustration of the spiritual death that occurs when we are not alert to the subtle ways of the sin in our lives.

An example of the subtleties of sin is sex – one of the most vital areas of life where many wrong choices are made. We can't afford to be fooled by what we see on television. We are being led to believe that out biological urges are the most important aspect of our lives and that we must satisfy that area. That is a lie. Indeed, sex is important. It is a part of our God-given nature, and He can indeed bless it. The problem is that sex in itself, without God, is a terrible tyrant. It can take over and dominate people's lives.

The "liberation" of the world is bondage of the spirit, and those so liberated are enslaved as if in shackles. "They are presumptuous, self-willed. They are not afraid to speak evil of dignitaries, whereas angels, who are greater in power and might, do not bring a reviling accusation against them before the Lord" (2 Peter 2:10-11).

Judgment and accusation are reserved for the Lord, no matter what. The destruction of Sodom and Gomorrah were at his command. The angels, who were there on a fact-finding mission, found utter depravity.

Today, homosexual relationships are glamorized and widely accepted as simply another variety of sexual expression. It's weird, single sex marriages and gay bishops and naked wedding, Don't you believe it! Homosexuality is an offense against God, and those who choose it will find themselves enslaved. "But these, like natural brute beasts made to be caught and destroyed, speak evil of the things they do not understand, and will utterly perish in their own corruption" (2 Peter 2:12). It is blasphemy to go against the created order of God, to declare that which God has said is wrong to be right. Judgment will follow, at the sovereign decisions of God.

Not a very attractive drama, this play about a man who made a decision on a mountaintop and chose a fertile valley. Once there, he saw the bright lights of the city and moved near it. He didn't intend to go any closer, because he knew the reputation of the city. But then, going in and out of the city so much, he probably thought to himself, *why not settle in the city itself?* He moved in, made friends with the people, rose in popularity, put down deep roots built a business and a home, raised a family, became a leading citizen – and destroyed his life. He destroyed his life by gradually dulling his sense of holiness, compromising God's ways, and accepting as right those things which God said were wrong. He betrothed his daughters to men of Sodom, and allied his family with the sin of the city. He did not present a heritage of righteousness, though some remained in his heart.

The angel told Lot to flee quickly. When Lot reached Zoar, "the LORD rained brimstone and fire on Sodom and Gomorrah" (vs. 24). The cities were destroyed – imagine the horror! "Then Lot went up out of Zoar and dwelt in the mountains [where he was told to go in the first place!], and his two daughters were with him; for he was afraid to dwell in Zoar" (vs. 30). Do you wonder that he would be afraid? And out of fear, he obeyed. How common is that scene!

The rest of chapter 19 tells how they lived in a cave in the mountains (from riches to rags!) and how the daughters tricked their father into impregnating them. The immorality of Sodom had been passed to the next generation, and Lot's grandsons were born of incest. Out of that sin came two separate peoples, the Moabites and the Ammorites, and these people constantly tormented the people of God for many generations. Long after Lot was dead, the effects of his decision were still being felt by hundred of thousands of people.

"[Abraham] looked toward Sodom and Gomorrah, and toward all the land of the plain" (v. 27). Abraham had learned much about the God he served. Have we?

I shall be telling this with a sigh

Somewhere ages and ages hence:

Two roads diverged in a wood, and I –

I took the one less traveled by,

And that has made all the difference.

Father, give us the ability to hear, and heed, Your holy word in the precious name of our Lord Jesus Christ . Amen.

Traveller's Journal

REFLECT

How have others in your life determined your thoughts and actions?

What choices have you made in life that have made a difference?

What choices do you regret making?

Can you see the consequences clearly?

RECOMMIT

In the world today, the straight paths of God are often "the road not taken". In your own words, express those things that have obliterated the guidance for you, and express your desire to walk with God on the road that makes all the difference.

CHAPTER SIX

ONE PRIEST – ONE SACRIFICE

Then Melchizedek king of Salem brought out bread and wine; he was the priest of God Most High. And he blessed him and said:

> *"Blessed be Abram of God Most High,*
>
> *Possessor of heaven and earth;*
>
> *And blessed be God Most High,*
>
> *Who has delivered your enemies into your hand"*
>
> *And he gave him a tithe of all. (Gen. 14:18-20).*

Of all the incidences recorded in Abraham's life, this is the strangest. This event is dropped down in the center of the story, seemingly without preface or follow-up. It simply appears; a text without a context. It is as though the write of Genesis began to say one thing, moved quickly to another, and then returned to his original thought.

The story is hardly self-explanatory, and I cannot imagine that it would have been included in Holy Scripture were it not for the fact that much, much later on, very important truths were built on this very short story. A thousand years later, David, in one of the psalms, made reference to this obscure character by the name of Melchizedek. A thousand years after that, the writer of the epistle to the Hebrews made an extensive commentary on this obscure passage. How do we explain the appearance of this man who came without announcement, disappeared from the stage of history as mysteriously as he came, and yet had such a profound impact on our father Abraham?

The name *Melchizedek* is a Hebrew compound: *melek* means "king"; *tsedeq* means "righteousness". So *Melchizedek* means "King of Righteousness". We are told that he is the king of Salem, the most ancient name for Jerusalem. Salem is the Hebre *shalem*, anglicized to *Shalom*, which means "Peace". Melchizedek is, then, the king of Righteousness, the king of Peace.

Melchizedek brought bread and wine; he was the priest of the Most High God. Where did he come from? He appeared more than six hundred years before any sort of priesthood would be established in Israel- and when that priesthood was established and began to offer sacrifices, bread and wine were not a part.

This is the very beginning of the redemptive story. Yet, as Abram returned from the battle of the kings, he met this strange man, who was not only a king, but a priest. Where did he get his priesthood? Who ordained him?

We don't know, but it's clear that Abraham recognized his priesthood. We know nothing about him, where he was born, where or how he died.

We know that he was likely a Gentile, certainly not a Jew. He was not related to Abraham or the covenant people. Yet he was a God-worshipping priest from whom Abraham received a blessing. "Blessed by Abram of God Most High/possessor of heaven and earth".

Where did Melchizedek gain that insight? That kind of understanding was ahead of its time – people didn't yet have the notion of creation. How did he get that revelation? By whom did that word come to him? He not only blessed Abram, but he blessed the Lord! Abram responded to his priesthood by giving him a tithe, or 10 percent of all he possessed.

The Order of Melchizedek

Yet hundred of years later, Melchidezek is mentioned again, in a psalm attributed to King David. Psalm 110 is significant; it is the one most quoted in the New Testament. Jesus referred to it a number of times, as did the apostles Peter and Paul. "The LORD said to my Lord, /Sit at my right hand, / Till I make Your enemies Your footstool" (Psalm 110:1).

"The LORD" translates to the term used to refer to the Lord God. Who is the "my Lord" that David referred to? David was king; he didn't have anyone over him. Further on, David said, "The LORD has sworn /And will not relent,/'You are a priest forever/ According to the order of Melchidezek" (Ps. 110:4).

Great mystery surrounds this psalm. For what occasion was it written? Was it written for the coronation of some great king? Could it have been written, for instance, for David's son, Solomon? It doesn't make sense if addressed to any human king. Who is the one so great to provoke the Lord God to swear? There is none higher than God by whom He can swear. Certainly a man can take an oath in the name of God when called to bear witness, but how can God take an oath? Yet God made an oath.

In the epistle to the Hebrews, Melchidezek is mentioned several times. We might even say that the epistle serves as a commentary on him. "For this Melchidezek, king of Salem, priest of the Most High God, who met Abraham returning from the slaughter of the kings and blessed him, to whom also Abraham gave a tenth part of all" (Heb. 7:1,2). This is simply all of the information we have! The author of the epistle got that information form the book of Genesis, the same place that we did. He summarized in those opening two verses every blessed thing Scripture says about him! His sermon on the subject is better than mine:

First being translated "king of righteousness," and then also king of Salem, meaning "king of peace," without father, without mother, without genealogy, having neither beginning of days nor end of life, but made like the Son of God, remains a priest continually. (Hebrews 7:2,3).

Normally, if a New Testament writer was going to make a comparison between someone and an Old Testament character, he started with the person at hand. He would say "this one is like that one back then". Not here! He described Melchidezek as "like the Son of God". Why? The Son of God came into the world (to be sure, He was announced) and made His entrance among us; He blessed us while He was present with us; and He remains a priest forever. This passage is talking about none other than the Lord Jesus Christ, priest, and king.

The priesthood of the Old Covenant contrasts with the New. More than six hundred years after Abraham, the Lord sovereignty chose Moses' brother to be the first high priest of the Old Covenant, and his male descendants were to be priests in Israel. This means that priests under the Old Covenant were direct lineal descendants of Aaron. Aaron and Moses came from the tribe of Levi. All priests were Levites, but not all Levites were priests, only those who were descended from Aaron. Under the Old Covenant, men were born into the priesthood.

The New Covenant changed the priesthood as well as the covenant, and the high priest of the new covenant is the Lord Jesus Christ: "Therefore, holy brethren, partakers of the heavenly calling, consider the Apostle and High Priest of our confession, Christ Jesus" (Hebrews 3:1).

Jesus was neither a descendant of Aaron nor a Levite. He descended from David, of the tribe of Judah. Nobody from the tribe of Judah had ever been a priest in Israel. Just as there was a new beginning, so there was a New Covenant. Just as God sealed the Old Covenant and appointed a priesthood to administer it, so God sealed the New Covenant and appointed Jesus the high priest.

Jesus is the one mysteriously referred to by David. Peter explained:

Men and brethren, let me speak freely to you of the patriarch David, that he is both dead and buried, and his tomb is with us to this day. Therefore, being a prophet, and knowing that God had sworn with an oath to him that of the fruit of his body, according to the flesh, He would raise up the Christ to sit on his throne, he, foreseeing this, spoke concerning the resurrection of the Christ, that His soul was not left in Hades, nor did His flesh see corruption. This Jesus God has raised up, of which we are all witnesses. Therefore being exalted to the right hand of God, and having received from the Father the promise of the Holy Spirit, He poured out this which you now see and hear. For David did not ascend into the heavens, but he says himself:

> *"The LORD said to my Lord,*
>
> *'sit at My right hand,*
>
> *Till I make your enemies your footstool."*
>
> *Therefore, let all the house of Israel know assuredly that God has made this Jesus, whom you crucified, both Lord and Christ. (Acts. 2:29-36).*

The function of the high priesthood of Jesus is most relevant to our lives. First Timothy 2:5,6 says: "For there is one God and one mediator between God and men, the Man Christ Jesus, who gave Himself a ransom for all, to be testified in due time".

If you and I had lived in the days of the Old Covenant, once a year we would be required to bring our sacrifice to offer it to the Lord, but we could not offer it ourselves. We would have to bring it to the priest. He would prepare the sacrifice according to the ritual law and then would make the presentation, offering it to God. God would not receive the sacrifice from you or me, under the Old Covenant, because He was training His people to understand the infinite chasm between our absolutely holy God and His very unholy people.

It's quite impossible for men to build a bridge across that chasm, but the Lord God built a bridge for the people of the Old Covenant. He instituted a mediatorial priesthood to stand between God and man, and if any person wanted to come to God, he would have to go through a priest. The mediation of someone whom God had specifically instructed was necessary.

Only One Mediator

In Israel there were as many mediators as there were priests, but now there is only one Mediator between God and man – the Man Jesus Christ. Think of it! Our only approach to the Father is through Jesus Christ. Is it any wonder we end our prayers by saying, "through Jesus Christ our Lord?" Jesus makes our prayers acceptable to the Father.

The epistle of the Hebrews says that we are welcomed into the presence of the Father through Jesus Christ our Lord. That is one of the reasons why some of us never refer to the Table of the Lord as an altar. Get the picture? We don't come to the table of the Lord as if it were an altar where sacrifices are made – other than our personal, living sacrifice of self. We are, rather, invited to a table of fellowship: "Behold, I stand at the door and knock, if anyone hears My voice and opens the door, I will come in to him and dine with him, and he with Me" (Rev. 3:20).

Picture it – restored fellowship between an errant humanity and a Holy God.

For indeed He does not give aid to angels, but He does give aid to the seed of Abraham. Therefore, in all things He had to be made like His brethren, that He might be a merciful and faithful High Priest in things pertaining to God, to make propitiation for the sins of the people. For in that He Himself has suffered, being tempted, He is able to aid those who are tempted. (Heb. 2:16-18).

Seeing then that we have a great High Priest who has passed through the heavens, Jesus the Son of God, let us hold fast our confession. For we do not have a High Priest who cannot sympathize with out weaknesses, but was in all points tempted as we are, yet without sin. Let us therefore come boldly to the throne of grace, that we may obtain mercy and find grace to help in time of need. (Hebrews 4:14-16).

Jesus became a human being and walked among us so that He might share our life and experience. He is completely able to understand us! There isn't a single temptation we have had that He didn't experience. He knows what it means to live in this world. He conquered death that we might not fear it. He is able to be a merciful and faithful high priest in the service of God.

Indeed, Jesus is the Son of God, our great high priest, the King of Kings and Lord of Lords. But Jesus also tasted human experience. He knew physical weariness and exhaustion. He was hungry and thirsty, tired and discouraged. He experienced many disappointments in his relationships with people and many times of discouragement in his life's work.

I can think of a few temptations I can hardly imagine Jesus as having had – maybe you can, temptations that are unique to our culture and day. What Scripture says is that he tasted and overcame everything that can be a temptation to man, and I believe that He did. Most temptations fall into the broad categories of what used to be known as "The Seven Deadly Sins" – pride, envy, malice, gluttony, avarice, lust and sloth. We don't hear very much about them these days, which makes them even more deadly!.

We can face no trial – remember that temptation means trial and difficulty – that he hasn't already faced. We are not strangers to Him, nor He to us, when we come to Him in need.

Did you notice the most gracious of invitations to approach "the throne of grace with confidence"? can you imagine being hauled before the throne of a holy and infinite God? Can you imagine His withering gaze, the fire of truly righteous indignation from His eyes? We might well fearfully approach. But not so! Our Mediator stands at His right hand and speaks on our behalf, and we are invited to come boldly to the throne of grace.

Come!

It's a strange thing about human beings. Often when we are the most needy, we are the least likely to come before the throne of God. When we are most aware of our need, we turn away. That's part of our sin nature, that rebellion we inherited from our parents at the dawn of the earth. In days post-Christ, it's less understandable, yet persistent. Why? Perhaps fear comes into our hearts.

When Adam and Eve became aware of their sin, what did they do? Rush to the Lord and throw themselves on His mercy? No, they went and hid themselves; they didn't want to see His face. They didn't know the grace of the Mediator. Hiding from God if not only unnecessary, its impossible!

Also there were many priests, because they were prevented by death from continuing. But He, because He continues forever, has an unchangeable priesthood. Therefore He is also able to save to the uttermost those who come to God through Him, since He always live to make intercession for them. (Hebrews 7:23-25).

He is able to save completely anybody who comes to God through Him. He is the Mediator, the door of the sheepfold, the way into the presence of God.

Jesus Christ is our great High Priest. He is the one who has paid the sacrifice. Is He going to condemn us when we come seeking to avail ourselves of that Which He Himself has provided? Of course not! He welcomes us. He bids us to come before the throne of grace to be saved to the uttermost – regardless of what our special need might be.

A Kingdom of Priests

Another wonderful thing about the high priesthood of Jesus is this: Although Jesus is the only high priest of the New Covenant, He has chosen to share that priesthood with us!

The church is just beginning to understand this concept, the priesthood of all believers. Most of the churches function on the Old Testament concept of the priesthood, and the people in the pews expect that. "He's the priest (or the minister) and we're the people; he's the one upfront." The mind-set is that the ministers minister, the congregation congregate, and that's it. This model bears no resemblance to New Testament Christianity, and it doesn't have a shred of apostolic truth about it!

The word *priest* underwent a change of meaning at the institution of the New Covenant. From the night that Jesus took the chalice in His hands and said, "This cup is the New Covenants in My blood. This do as often as you drink it, in remembrance of Me" (I Cor. 11:25), the word priest was never supposed to be applied to what we call a minister, a paid professional. It was to be used in ways from that moment on. First, *priest* would be used to apply to Jesus Christ, and second, to all believers in Him. In the New Testament sense of the word, you are a priest of God Most High. Not the High Priest, for there is only one – Jesus. But as His follower, under His instructions, a priest. Until you know that, until all of us know that, and are bale to exercise that priesthood, the church can never be what God intended it to be. We who believe are priests of the most High God and are made priests by the High Priest Himself, Jesus Christ.

Another image that the Lord would have us understand is found in 1 Peter 2:4,5.

Coming to Him as a living stone, rejected indeed by men, but chosen by God and precious, you also, as living stones, are being built up a spiritual house, a holy priesthood, to offer up spiritual sacrifices acceptable to God through Jesus Christ.

These symbols terms says that all who come to Jesus are priests and are built into the holy temple [our church] as living stones. We don't go to church, we are the church! All who stand on His name – all who are a part of the people of God – are priests of the Most High God, not after the order of Aaron (we weren't born to the priesthood), but after the order of Melchizedek, who appeared without preparation on the stage of history.

But you are a chosen generation, a royal priesthood, a holy nation, His own special people, that you may proclaim the praises of Him who called you out of darkness into His marvelous light; who once were not a people but are now the people of God, who had not obtained mercy but now have obtained mercy. (I Pet. 2:9,10).

We are chosen people, royal priests, parts of a holy nation, special people belonging to God. These words were not addressed to the sons of Aaron, or even to the sons of Abraham. They were addressed to all who come to the Lord Jesus Christ. If we belong to Jesus Christ today, we qualify for a royal priesthood. Why royal? Because Melchizedek was not only a priest, he was also a king; Jesus is not only our High Priest, he is the King of kings and Lord of lords. We share also His kingship and His rule.

Think of it! Now we are the people of God, that we may declare the praises of Christ Jesus our Lord – the functional description of our priesthood.

In Revelation we find a most extraordinary passage: "To Him who loved us and washed us from our sins in His own blood, and has made us kings and priests to His God and Father, to Him be glory and dominion forever and ever. Amen" (Rev. 1:5,6). Jesus made all who were redeemed by His blood priests.

Great favorite Scripture verses of mine are Revelation 5:9-10:

And they sang a new song, saying:

"You are worthy to take the scroll,

And to open its seals;

For you were slain,

And have redeemed us to God by Your blood

Out of every tribe and tongue and people and nation,

And have made us kings and priests to our God."

Who made us priests to serve God? The one who was worthy to open the scroll and to open the seals, the One who was slain, with whose blood we have been purchased for God, Jesus Christ.

Ponder these truths. They will feed your soul and direct your path. They will open a door to who you can be by God's grace. They will lift your spirits, energize your faith, strengthen you for service, widen your perspective, and deepen your faith.

Father, we thank You for Your Word. It's almost more than we can grasp; it's hard for us to take it all in. it's hard to understand who we really are – we have such limited perspective on our lives.

Grant us your Grace so that we may see ourselves as You see us, in the light of the Lord Jesus, our great High Priest. Help us to understand Your truth, and let it be for us a converting and renewing word, by the fullness of your Spirit, that we may approach your throne of grace with confidence, for we are a needy people and we need the mercy and grace that You offer us. As we pray, let us be aware that in repentance and faith we will be heard, and let us be confident in You; and strengthened and blessed so that we may be a blessing to others. Grant all of this in Jesus' name, we pray. Amen.

Traveller's Journal

REFLECT

What do you think it meant to Abram to meet Melchizedek? We have the perspective of Jesus, Abram didn't!

What do the titles *king of Righteousness and King of Peace* mean to you?

What does it mean to you to know that, because Jesus Himself suffered when He was tempted in His walk with God, He is able to help those who are tempted in their walk?

What does it mean to you to be "completely saved"?

RECOMMIT

Describe the way you would like to use your royal priesthood to serve the holy nation of the people of God. Be specific, plan and dream, using time goals and people you'd like to contact.

CHAPTER SEVEN

PROMISES MADE – PROMISES KEPT

God does not tell us exactly what to do in every situation and circumstance of our lives. What we find in the Scriptures are general principles that would apply to various situations, but we must make the application ourselves. One of these principles is clearly and expressly stated in Jeremiah:

The instant I speak concerning a nation and concerning a kingdom, to pluck up, to pull down, and to destroy it, if that nation against whom I have spoken turns from its evil, I will relent of the disaster that I thought to bring upon it. And the instant I speak concerning a nation and concerning a kingdom, to build and to plant it, if it does evil in My sight so that it does not obey My voice, then I will relent concerning the good with which I said I would benefit it. (Jer. 18:7-10).

I want to focus on the promise of God to Abraham concerning the land. You might ask what possible relevance that promise, made almost four thousand years ago, could have for us today. Understanding that promise will illuminate to some degree the situation in the Middle East. More than that, it will illustrate a basic biblical point. The message of this promise bears on our very existence.

As discussed in an earlier chapter, the promise that God made to Abraham concerning the land appears for the first time in the first verse in which the call of Abraham is recorded. (Gen. 12:1). The writer of Hebrews, commenting on this passage, said that Abraham obeyed. He went out not knowing where he was to go, but believing the promise of God. His ears rang with the command of the Lord to leave. The command and the promise together led Abram out of the place where he was. It was up to God to bring Abram to or show him a land somewhere.

The second statement in reference to the land is found in Genesis 12:7 "Then the LORD appeared to Abram and said, 'To your descendants I will give this land'"

The third reference is found in Genesis 13:14-17.

And the LORD said to Abram, after Lot had separated from him: "Lift your eyes now and look from the place where you are – northward, southward, eastward and westward; for all the land which you see I give to you and your descendants forever. And I will make your descendants as the dust of the earth; so that if a man could number the dust of the earth, then your descendants also could be numbered. Arise, walk in the land through his length and its width, for I give it to you".

Two promises are found together all the way through the story of the land: the promise of a land and the promise of a posterity. Notice the word *forever* - "to you and your descendants forever". The fourth and last mention of the land in reference to Abram is found in Genesis 17:7,8.

And I will establish My covenant between Me and you and your descendants after you in their generations, for an everlasting covenant, to be God to you and your descendants after you. Also I give to you and your descendants after you the land in which you are a stranger, all the land of Canaan, as an everlasting possession; and I will be their God.

God took Abram and his descendants as His people and made an everlasting covenant to give them the whole land of Canaan.

The Promise Renewed

This promise of the land and of posterity was given again to Abram's son, Isaac, after Abraham's death:

Then the LORD appeared to him (Isaac) and said: "Do not go down to Egypt; live in the land of which I shall tell you. Dwell in this land, and I will be with you and bless you; for to you and your descendants I give all these lands, and I will perform the oath which I swore to Abraham your father. And I will make your descendants multiply as the stars of heaven; I will give to your descendants all these lands; and in your seed all the nations of the earth shall be blessed." (Gen. 26:2-4).

Here we have a second image in reference to the progeny of Abraham – they will be as vast as the stars of the sky. The promise is again made to the descendants as well as to the principal, because the covenant is established with them. The Lord confirmed the oath he swore to Isaac's father, Abraham, "because Abraham obeyed My voice and kept My charge, My commandments, My statues, and My laws" (v.5).

The covenant is renewed a third time with Isaac's son, Jacob:

Then God appeared to Jacob again, when he came from Padan Aram, and blessed him. And God said to him, "Your name is Jacob; your name shall not be called Jacob anymore, but Israel shall be your name". So He called his name Israel. (Gen. 35:9,10).

When the Lord God entered into covenant with Abram, He changed his name from Abram to Abraham. (See Gen. 17). When the covenant was renewed with Abraham's grandson, He changed his name from Jacob to Israel. Jacob was the father of twelve sons. After his name had been changed, these twelve sons became known as the children of Israel. "Also God said to him [Jacob]: 'I am God Almighty. Be fruitful and multiply; a nation and a community of nations shall proceed from you, and kings shall come from your body" (Gen. 35:11).

After the Lord appeared to Abraham, He was known as "the God of Abraham". After the Lord revealed Himself to Isaac, he was known as "the God of Abraham and Isaac". After the Lord appeared to Jacob, the Lord God was known as "the God of Abraham, Isaac, and Jacob". God was picking up family as He went along. That's the whole point of the covenant. God was taking to Himself a people who would be His people, and He would be their God.

More than four hundred years after Jacob, the covenant was again renewed, this time with Moses, the leader of Abraham's descendants. "See, I have set the land before you; go in and possess the land which the LORD swore to your fathers – to Abraham, Isaac and Jacob – to give them and their descendants after them" (Deut. 1:8). All of this comes together in a very direct way:

> *He is the LORD our God;/His judgments are in all the earth./He remembers His covenant forever,/The word which He commanded, for a thousand generations,/The covenant which He made with Abraham /And His oath to Isaac,/And confirmed it to Jacob for a statue,/To Israel as an everlasting covenant,/Saying, "To you I will give the land of Canaan / As the allotment of your inheritance."*
> *(Psalm 105:7-11).*

As we survey those promises which were spread out over hundreds and hundreds of years of God's revelation of Himself to His people, Israel, we begin to understand that God meant it when He said he was going to give Abraham a vast number of descendants.

God's Land

Nowhere else does God identify Himself with a certain piece of land. We can find many places in Scripture where the Lord said, "This is My land" or to the Jews, "Why are you desecrating My land?" or "The day will come when I will bring all of the nations of the world together and they will fight on My land." No wonder it is called the Holy Land! The Holy God chose it.

Another passage about the land is found in Deuteronomy 11:8-12.

Therefore you shall keep every commandment which I command you today, that you may be strong, and go in and possess the land which you cross over to possess.... [It] is a land of hills and valleys, which drinks water from the rain of heaven, a land for which the LORD your God cares; the eyes of the LORD your God are always on it, from the beginning of the year to the very end of the year.

Who are the descendants of Abraham, Isaac, and Jacob? Because Abram's first son, Ishmael, was born to him by Hagar the Egyptian handmaid and is the father of those people we call Arabs, does that mean that the Arabs also have a claim to that land on the basis of the original promise?

Scripture answers that question directly. Abram spoke to the Lord about his son Ishmael, "Oh, that Ishmael might live before you (Gen. 17:18). The Lord answered, "And as for Ishmael, I have heard you.... But My covenant I will establish with Isaac, whom Sarah shall bear to you at this set time next year" (vv. 20-21).

Ishmael and his lineage are true descendants of Abraham, but they are clearly not the heirs of the covenant.

Sarah in her old age finally had a child and named him Isaac. Isaac and his older half-brother Ishmael didn't get along very well (a foretaste of the continuing rivalry between Jews and Arabs). Sarah was disturbed about this and told Abraham to get rid of that slave woman and her son. The master distressed Abraham greatly because Ishmael was his son also.

For God said to Abraham, "Do not let it be displeasing in your sight because of the lad or because of your bondwoman. Whatever Sarah has said to you, listen to her voice, for in Isaac your seed shall be called" (Gen. 21:12).

Biblically, (not politically speaking), the Arab people have no claim to the land of Israel. When Menachem Begin was Prime Minister of Israel, the believed in and referred to those promises every so often in his speeches. That was not and is not a common feature of Jewish political life. One of the reasons Begin was prepared to let the Sinai go was because the Sinai was at no time a part of the covenant. It was not given to the Jews by God. Similarly, one of the reasons Begin absolutely refused to give back the West Bank and the Gaza strip to the Palestinians is that they were part of the land intended by God for the Jewish people. On biblical grounds, he was absolutely correct.

Taking and Leaving the Land

Hundreds of years after the promise was given, Abraham's descendants actually came into the land. Moses led them to the very edge of the land, but he was not allowed to bring them in. Joshua finally led them in, but Moses was concerned about the rebellious people he had taken from slavery in Egypt and brought to the edge of the land. The entire book of Deuteronomy comprises four long speeches purportedly given by Moses to the children of Israel before his death. In those speeches he recorded the history of God's dealings with His people. Let's focus on two significant passages.

When you beget children and grandchildren and have grown old in the land, and act corruptly and make a carved image in the form of anything, and do evil in the sight of the LORD your God to provoke Him to anger, I call heaven and earth to witness against you this day, that you will soon utterly perish from the land which you cross the Jordan to possess; you will not prolong y our days in it, but will be utterly destroyed. And the LORD will scatter you among the people, and you will be left few in number among the nations where the LORD will drive you. (Deut. 4:25-27).

Moses was concerned. In effect he was saying, "Let me tell you something. After you get settled in the land and have a heritage, if you forsake the covenant of your God and turn back on His holy ways and serve other gods, you will lose that land. Not only that, but you will be scattered by the Lord Himself among the nations of the world, and only a few of you will be left". But he made an even stronger statement:

If you do not carefully observe all the words of this law that are written in this book, that you may fear this glorious and awesome name, THE LORD YOUR GOD.... The LORD will rejoice over you to destroy you and bring you to nothing; and you shall be plucked from off the land.... Then the LORD will scatter you among all peoples, from one end of the earth to the other, and there you shall serve other gods, which neither you nor your fathers have known – wood and stone.... Your life will hand in doubt before you; you shall fear day and night, and have no assurance of life. In the morning you shall say, "Oh, that it were evening!" because of the fear which terrifies your heart, and because of the sight which your eyes will see. (Deuteronomy 28:58-67).

The people of God did not obey the covenant when they got in the land. They did turn their backs on the Lord; they did serve other gods; and in God's time, He did exactly what He said He would do. He took His people out of the land, and scattered them among all the nations of the world. No other people have come close to the continual suffering the Jewish people have known. Over centuries of time, they have been persecuted by virtually everyone everywhere they went. Why? They were chosen by God, instructed by God, and pledged to God. And they were unfaithful. Read again the warning they were given before they ever entered the Land of Promise for the first time. I cannot imagine a more accurate description of what in fact has happened to them.

Under normal conditions, a conquered people would be absorbed by their surrounding cultures. One might have expected that to have happened, and it did – partially. The first great wave of extradition came in the year 722 B.C. when the Assyrians conquered and captured ten of the northern tribes, settling them around their empire. Gradually the people were culturally and ethnically absorbed, and they disappeared from sight. They are called "the ten lost tribes of Israel." From time to time a certain sect will claim to be descended from them, but it has never been possible to prove heritage.

Over a hundred years after the first dispersion, the Babylonians destroyed the temple and the city of Jerusalem, and scattered the rest of the Jews around the Babylonia empire. This time, however, the Jews had learned to preserve their heritage, and so they were not absorbed. During this Babylonia exile, they developed synagogues. The word *synagogue* never appears, not even once, in the whole of the Old Testament. Synagogues grew up when the people of Israel were in dispersion, scattered around the world. The people agreed that whenever ten heads of families could be found, they would establish a synagogue. A synagogue (unlike a church, which is a place of worship) is a place where the law is read and explained to the people and where a common heritage is shared. In this way, Jews have been able to hold on to their identity down through the centuries.

The third great wave came in A.D. 70. In A.D. 66 the Romans were into what was then called Palestine because there was a rebellion. So fiercely did the Jews fight to defend their land that it took the Roman four years to subdue them – and even then they could not subdue them completely. In March of A.D. 70, the general of the Roman Army, Vespasian, was made emperor by a decision of the Roman Senate. He left the battle for Rome. His son Titus succeeded him as general, and it was Titus who successfully conquered the city of Jerusalem. He destroyed the temple that was standing in those days and again slaughtered hundreds of thousands. Flavius Josephus said that 600,000 Jews were killed in a single day and that all of Palestine was left in desolation. Moses' words were literally fulfilled.

The Hand of God in the Affairs of Men

An extraordinary passage is found in Jeremiah 16: "Therefore behold, the days are coming,' says the LORD, 'that it shall no more be said, "the LORD lives who brought up the children of Israel from the land of Egypt" (v.14). in other words, they would not talk about the Exodus and how God delivered the children of God from the bondage of Egypt by His mighty hand. "But, the LORD lives who brought up the children of Israel from the land of the north and from all the lands where He had driven them'. For I will bring them back into their land which I gave to their fathers" (v.15).

The day will come when the Jews will not talk about the Exodus from Egypt, but the new Exodus when the Lord God Himself brings the people back into that land from all of the nations where He had driven them.

Some of you may have read the novel *Exodus* or seen the movie. Some of you know that we have seen the fulfillment of this prophecy to an extraordinary degree. Just before the turn of our century, a tiny little trickle of Jewish people began to go back to that land. But it wasn't until 1948, after World War II, that something was done about the "great Jewish problem," as it was then known. The United Nations – by a single act, in a single day – created the nation of Israel, and a great wave of immigration was begun. From all over the world, Jews returned to that land. They had not had a single inch of real estate that they could call their own for almost twenty-five hundred years!

The interval between the time the Jews lost their land and the time they regained it was very long, and they regained it during the lifetime of many who are reading this. No other generation of Christians in two thousand years of history has been able to say that they saw come to pass what the Lord had predicted. Other Christians have had to "SEE" it by faith. We've actually seen it happen.

What happened when the nation of Israel was established? Jews flocked to it from all over the world. Russian Jews came, German Jews, American Jews, Spanish Jews, Arabic Jews, African Jews, all speaking their native languages. They had to decide quickly what language they would speak. The nation of Israel then did something without parallel in the history of the world. They decided to revive a dead language, and to speak Hebrew! Nobody in the world spoke Hebrew. It has been dead since the days of Jesus. Even Jesus didn't speak it; He spoke Aramaic. Hebrew was maintained as a language of worship and law, but it was not spoken, not even by scholars. Hebrew, to the Jews of Jesus' time, was rather like Latin to the Roman Catholics of our own generation. It was the language of the service, but not the language of its people. Israel chose to revive the language in which God had spoken to His people thousands of years before. Israel chose to teach speak it to people who didn't know a word of it.

Ezekiel 37 contains a remarkable passage of scripture. Although it is familiar, often people don't realize the contemporary application of the story:

> The hand of the LORD came upon me and brought me out in the Spirit of the LORD, and set me down in the midst of the valley; and it was full of bones.... He said to me, "Prophesy to these bones,".... So I prophesied as I was commanded; and as I prophesied, there was a noise, and suddenly a rattling; and the bones came together, bone to bone. Indeed, as I looked, the sinews and the flesh came upon them, and the skin covered them over; but there was no breath in them (Ezekiel 37:1-8).

The prophet of the Lord was standing in the midst of a valley filled with all kinds of disconnected bones and the Lord asked, "Can these bones live?" Ezekiel replied, "O Lord God, You know". And the Lord told Ezekiel to speak His word to them and tell them that He would put flesh and sinew on them and breath in them and they would live.

Ezekiel spoke as he was told. He heard rattling sounds and saw bones move. Bones joined themselves. Muscles, sinew, and flesh came upon them. Finally there were complete bodies, but there was no life in them. Bones to skeletons to corpses, without life. God was doing something, but the lifeless bodies weren't aware of it.

One of the great movements that resulted in thousands of Jews coming to Israel was a movement known as *Zionism*. It was an utterly secular movement; not even in its roots was it remotely religious. It was a movement solely to find a homeland for the Jewish people. That was exactly what the Ezekiel passage referred to: a gathering taking place in unbelief. As yet, most of Israel is unaware that their existence is the work of the Lord. The population of Israel is composed of many factions of Jews. Although the majority are not observes of the ancient traditions, the government is strongly influenced by the powerful Orthodox Jews who have forced the majority to conform at least in part of the old law. Most Jews haven't the slightest idea what the Ezekiel passage means, or what the promise of the land means, anymore than most Christians do. We haven't yet seen the final fulfillment of the passage. We have only seen the re-gathering, of bone to muscle to flesh; we have yet to see life instilled. There is no life Israel as a nation – life as interpreted by the Scripture, that of following the Lord's commands.

Also He said to me, "Prophesy to the breath".… So I prophesied as He commanded me, and breath came into them, and they lived, and stood upon their feet, an exceedingly great army.… "I will open your graves and cause you to come up from your graves, and bring you into the land of Israel. Then you shall know that I am the LORD, which I have opened your graves, O My people, and brought you up from your graves. I will put My Spirit in you, and you shall live, and I will place you in your own land….. "David My servant shall be king over [the children of Israel]".(Ezekiel 37:11-14,24).

When those words were first spoken and written, David had been dead for more than five hundred years. This passage does not refer to David, son of Jesse, second king of Israel, but to David's greater son, Jesus. Even believing Jews today (that is, Jews believing in a Messiah to come) recognize that Messiah as coming from David's line.

David My servant shall be king over them, and they shall all have one shepherd; they shall also walk in My judgment and observe My statues, and do them. Then they shall dwell in the land that I have given to Jacob My servant, where your fathers dwelt, and they shall dwell there, they their children, and their children's children, forever, and My Servant David shall be their prince forever. Moreover I will make a covenant of peace with them, and it shall be an everlasting covenant. (Ezekiel 37:24-25).

The Scriptures illuminate for us the hand of God in the affairs of men. We are able to see that, played out against the background of world history, there is one people whom the Lord has ordained to be an object lesson of His way of working with the world.

The New Testament tells us that everything in the Old Testament was written for our sake so that we might learn from what happened. Ours is a God who will fulfill His promise. Ours is a God who will accomplish His purpose. He has told us over and over again: "If you want to live in My blessing, you have to obey. You have to keep My covenant and walk in My ways. If you don't, I will not fulfill the promises of blessing that I've given you".

When we fail to walk in His ways, we need to know that the Lord is constantly, personally seeking our restoration, that we might be brought back onto the paths of promise. If we walk in willfulness away from the Lord, we walk out from under His hand of blessing.

Do you wonder sometimes why the promises in the Bible don't seem to be true for you? God's promises are true – but only when we walk in absolute obedience. God is faithful to His word when His people are faithful in their response to his word when His people are faithful in their response to His word. We can't have the promises without the commands. We also can't be obedient to the commands and miss the blessings He promises! That is the word of the Lord.

Father, this is almost too much for us to take in. We do see Your hand in the sweep of history and we pray for Your ancient people, Israel. We believe that although they broke Your covenant, and You established a New Covenant through Jesus Christ, Your purpose for them is still not worked out; there is still more. Lord, we are a people who have heard bones ratting and coming together.

We are a generation that has lived to see the remarkable beginning of the fulfillment of Your promise.

We have seen flesh and sinew cover the bones, but there is as yet no life in them. We pray for that day, whom the breath of Your Spirit will blow over them that they might live; that all Your people may be united under our Shepherd, one Lord, so that the world will know that You are God and faithful to your promise.

Father, burn Your promises into our minds and then work within us that degree of obedience that will allows us to walk under Your hand of blessing. Allow us to profit from the experience of others, as well as from our own experience. We ask it in Jesus' name, and for His sake. Amen.

Traveller's Journal

REFLECT

Paraphrase Jeremiah 18:7-10, using your own name and a promise of God that you would like to see fulfilled in your life.

How do you react to the knowledge that God has fulfilled an ancient promise in our lifetime? What does that tell you about our God?

What does the passage from Ezekiel 37, beginning with verse 21 mean to you personally?

RECOMMIT

In your own words, as the Lord leads you, look toward the Promised Land under the eternal kingship of David's greater Son.

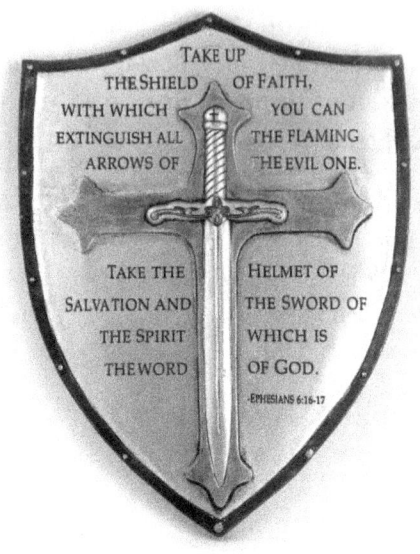

CHAPTER EIGHT

RECEIVE THE GIFT

"After these things, the word of the LORD came to Abram in a vision, saying, "Do not be afraid, Abram I am your shield, your exceedingly great reward" (Genesis 15:1).

After His rescue of Abram's nephew, Lot, the Lord God came to Abram in a vision and reassured him with those marvelous words. Remember, Abram was in the land with two promises: a promise that he would be given a posterity like the sands of the seashore and the stars of the sky, and a land that would also be given to his descendants forever, throughout all generations. Yet after about twenty five years had passed, and Abram had no children. What was even more difficult, his wife, Sarai, was getting older. By then they were well beyond normal child-bearing days. Although God had made the promise and Abram had responded to it, Abram could not see how it would work out.

Unquestionable, Abram was wondering why God had made him a promise that was not yet fulfilled. He was now in the land of promise, yet his heritage was yet to be established in it. So he said, "Lord God, what will you give me, seeing I go childless, and the heir of my house is Eliezer of Damascus?" (Genesis 15:2). Under the code of Hammurabi, if Abram had remained childless, all that he had could have passed by his will and decree to a servant whom he had appointed his heir. What Abram was really trying to do was to figure out a way for God to keep His promise and "save face". (Have you ever tried to do the same thing? Have you tried to figure out how God could do something and tried to advise Him, as if He hadn't figured it out for Himself?)

But the Lord told Abram, no, that's not what He wanted him to do, "This one shall not be your heir, but one who will come from your own body shall be your heir". (Gen. 15:4).

Genesis 15:6 is absolutely central to understanding Abram, and indeed, to understanding all of the New Testament, as well: "And he believed the LORD and He (the Lord) accounted it to him [Abram] as righteous.

It is at this point that we come to the very heart of the Christian Gospel. Before we continue, however, think back to the beginning of the book of Genesis, where Adam and Eve were created in the image of God. They were given a limited sovereignty over creation and were told to subdue it and bring it under their control. They were to be vice-regents under the authority of the Lord God. But God put them in the Garden of Eden with a prohibition – they could eat of all the trees in the garden but one. They disobeyed that prohibition and partook of that particular tree. The result of their disobedience was judgment upon them and the whole of creation.

Did you ever think about the effect of that sin on Adam and Eve? Early in their story, they walked freely and talked openly with the Lord. They were in intimate communion with God. After they disobeyed, two things happened.

First, they felt a new emotion in their hearts, an emotion called fear, They had no known fear before because they were secure in the place that God had put them.

Second, their eyes were opened and they perceived that they were naked. That's a powerful metaphor. Having sinned, Adam and Eve saw themselves before God, not as capable of open and free fellowship, but as exposed. They were completely unveiled. So what did they do? They hid themselves.

The day after the sin took place, the Lord took His morning walk and called, "Adam, where are you?" The Lord knew perfectly well where Adam was, but Adam and Eve came creeping out from behind the bushed where they were hiding, and do you know what they had done? They had taken fig leaves and sewn them together to provide a covering for their nakedness.

I believe that act to be the very first recorded religious act. The sewing of fig leaves together was religious in the true definition of religion – man's attempt to make himself acceptable in the sight of the god or gods. All religions in the world recognize to some degree that something is wrong with man, and they all call him to a higher existence. Judaism and Christianity differ from other religions at this point.

Adam and Eve tried to make themselves look right in God's sight. God, of course, did not accept it at all. He tore the fig leaves away and provided for them coverings made of the skin of animals. Two points are important here:

(1) God provided the covering for their nakedness, not Adam or Eve. They tried, but God did not accept it.

(2) The animal skins God provided required the shedding of blood. One doesn't get skins without taking lives.

All religious recognize to some degree that sin, or whatever it may be called, has to be overcome and dealt with. Muslims, for instance, must perform several acts. They must say prayers five times a day facing Mecca. They must give alms to the poor. They must keep the fast of Ramadan for an entire month once a year. Once in their lifetimes they must make a pilgrimage to Mecca. These acts will them access to Islamic heaven. If they don't do it all, they won't get there! The Koran recognizes that something is wrong between God or Allah and man, and the way Muslims overcome it is by doing certain things – man trying to provide the covering.

Buddhists (Buddhism is actually an atheistic religion – it doesn't have a god), also know that something is wrong with man. In order to achieve Nirvana or whatever Buddhist heaven they would like, Buddhists must climb the eightfold path. Ultimately, they are "saved", (if we can use the Christian terminology) by their own efforts. They are repeatedly seeking to advance themselves.

With Hindus it's the same story, only they have many gods and have to escape constant reincarnation. If they don't behave themselves this time around, then the next time they might become bedbugs – and try to work themselves out of that one! Gradually, after endless tries, they might emerge, if they do the right things.

But the Christian faith says that what has to be done has been done – and it's been done by God. You cant do it, and neither can I. the basic question is whether mortal man can be righteous before his God. That question is explicitly asked in the book of Job. God knows we're not righteous, and we know it, too. But can we stand before our Holy God? Can we be welcome, or even received, by a Holy God?

I believe that Jesus was the world's greatest enemy of religion. I think He hated it with a passion – and still does. Most of modern "Christianity", however, is still "religion". Religion is man's effort to make himself look right in the sight of God. Many people carry the concept of Christianity as a religion whereby if you do this or that you will be more acceptable to God.

Martin Luther was a priest, and a great biblical scholar. He translated the Bible into the German language, and his translation remains the standard, even today. His translation is to the German language as the King James Version is to the English language. Luther had an acute and sensitive conscience, and he was tormented because he knew that he wasn't righteous. He knew that there was nothing holy about him, and he said to himself, "How in the world can I stand before a congregation of people at the altar of the Lord?" (This question has plagued many clergy, before and after him). So he talked to his spiritual counselors, who gave him various suggestions. They told him to pray a set number of prayers so many times, and he did. They recommended that he go away on a spiritual retreat, get away from the demands of ministry for a while, and he tried that. He tried all kinds of dutiful acts. He even went to the city of Rome and climbed the steps of the Schola Septorum on his knees. But when he got to top, all he had was sore knees! He had no sense of spiritual relief whatever.

Luther did everything a man could do. He did everything he was told, yet was not released. Then one day, while translating the epistle to the Romans, he found his release. Keep in mind Genesis 15:6 ("[Abram] believed the LORD and He accounted it to him as righteousness") as you read the Scripture Luther found:

Now, we know that whatever the law says, it says to those who are under the law, that every mouth may be stopped, and all the world may become guilty before God. Therefore by the deeds of the law no flesh will be justified in His sight, for by the law is the knowledge of sin. But now the righteousness of God apart from the law is revealed, being witnessed by the Law and the Prophets, even the righteousness of God, through faith in Jesus Christ, to all and on all who believe. For there is no difference; for all have sinned and fall short of the glory of God, being justified freely by His grace through the redemption that is in Christ Jesus. (Rom. 3:19-24).

Abram wasn't any more righteous than you or I. righteousness is not something that we can attribute to ourselves. Righteousness comes through faith to all who believe.

Many people don't really believe that's true. We human beings have a way of comparing ourselves with one another. If we look hard enough or long enough, we will find someone who is actually worse than we are, someone who is more flagrant in his sin, more open in his rebellion. If we were to bring that person next to us, we might swell with pride and joy that we were so much better than he.

The trouble is, the comparison has two sides – there will always be others who are better than we are, who live lives more sacrificially, more openly, and more in harmony with the Word of God. That's a bit distressing, yet that's what happens when we measure ourselves against other people (and we do that ll of the time). We rather congratulate ourselves when we come off fairly well, and justify ourselves when we come off poorly. Have you ever noticed that it's always someone else's fault if we don't come up smelling like a rose?

What about this standard: Jesus said, "Be ye therefore perfect, even as your Father which is in heaven is perfect" (Matthew 5:48). How do you measure up on that? I don't measure up very well at all.

Or what do you do when you are confronted with these words of the prophet Isaiah: "But we are all like an unclean thing,/And all our righteousness are like filthy rags;/We all fade as a leaf,/And our iniquities, like the wind,/Have taken us away" (Isaiah 64:6).

The Hebrew root word used for "filthy" rags ed, means "menstrual" cloths. All of our righteous acts (can imagine what our sins look like?), all the good thins for which we are praised by one another, are seen by God as if they were filthy rags.

Jesus said, "When you have done your very best, still consider yourself to be an unprofitable servant" (see Luke 17:10). Man at his best is still judged as an unprofitable servant from God's point of view. There is simply, absolutely, no possibility that we can bring a recital of our righteous acts before God and gain a hearing!

I love the prayer, in the Book of Common Prayer, that begins "We do not presume to come to this thy Table, O merciful Lord, trusting in our own righteousness". The prayer acknowledges that there is a righteousness that we can possess, a righteousness that comes from God. That righteousness was accounted to Abram by God, because he believed. Abram was spiritually bankrupt, and so are we. We are absolutely bankrupt before God in the righteousness account. We will never have a chance to recite our virtues before the throne of the Almighty. We won't even have a chance to read our obituaries – that list of all the things we did while our earthly lives lasted. We will see as we are seen by god, and we will understand that we have no worthiness in ourselves to claim.

When we understand our spiritual bankruptcy, we begin to understand why we call Jesus "Savior." We begin to understand the reason for Christmas. Jesus came because we desperately needed Him! When we understand that we have no claim on the grace of God at all (understand not only intellectually, but existentially, right in the depth of our souls), then we're in the position to begin to understand the good news of the gospel. Because we believe in the Lord Jesus Christ, it is accounted to us as righteousness.

When a man works for something, his wages are not credited to him as a gift, but as an obligation. How would you feel if, at the end of this week or this month, you went for your paycheck and your boss said to you, "This is my gift to you". You might not say anything out loud, but you'd think, *Gift? What gift? I earned every penny of it. And what's more, I deserve more than I get!* A wage is not a gift. Salvation and a right relationship with God is not a wage; it cannot be earned. It is a gift, and we have to receive it.

Suppose someone comes to you with a beautifully wrapped package in his lands, and it has your name on the tag. Suppose he even walks up to you and shows it to you. You might admire it, look at it, thing it's interesting and attractive. But if you do not reach out and take it, really isn't yours, even if the gift has your name on it. So it is with salvation. We can sit in a church all our lives and never be saved. We have to appropriate the salvation from God, take it to ourselves. Nobody else can do that for us. Only we can reach out in faith and lay hold of what God has given us. He's given us a new life, a chance to start over. He's given us the forgiveness of sins and the gift of the Holy Spirit, and all of that becomes real in our lives when we believe in Him and receive His gifts by faith.

Have you received the gift? Perhaps you have gone to church all your life, yet you are not really sure how you stand in reference to Jesus Christ. If you are a man, woman, or young person who has no time in your life consciously said to the Lord, "I believe, help my unbelief," or "Yes, Lord, I believe that you are the Christ, the Son of God who has come into the world," or simply "I do receive you", do it now! There is no formula attached, just a reaching out and response form your heart to the Lord God.

There are times when the Lord, in His graciousness, brings us face-to-face with what He asks of us. If you are reading this book and have a sense of inner confusion or doubt where you stand with the Lord, don't miss the change to do eternal business with God.

PRAYER

Lord, I believe there are those who want to respond to the good news today. I believe that there arte those who want to reach out and take the great gift You offer them. They want to become members of your family. Lord; their faith is in Jesus alone, not in their own efforts to please You. They cast themselves wholly on Your mercy, that they may receive all you have for them.

Thank You, Lord, for revealing inwardly that truth which is bread to us, for those who have said that they want to feed on that truth. I thank You, Lord, that I am able to assure them that all who come to You, You will not cast away. I believe that there are those who are making decisions on earth that You are recoding in heaven, and that years from now they will remember this time and place as significant and life changing.

I reach out in Your love, Lord, to those who join us in the thousand of faith. We are all sinners saved by Your grace, and we rejoice in that. We thank you for Jesus, our Savior. We place our whole faith and confidence in Him. Never again will we depend on our own righteousness, but on the righteousness You given us through redemption in the name of Jesus Christ. Amen.

Traveller's Journal

REFLECT

Insert your name in the verse that begins with Genesis 15.

What does it mean to you to have God as your shield, your great reward?

What things have you "helped God" with? What were the results?

Is there any fear in the relationship between you and God?

RECOMMIT

Restate John 3:16, insert your name, and express what it means in your own words. How will it change your walk with God?

CHAPTER NINE

OUTER AND INNER SIGNS OF FAITH

The Lord God has primarily related Himself to the human race on the basis of covenant. The first covenant was made with Noah after the flood:

"Never again shall all flesh be cut off by the waters of the flood; never again shall there be a flood to destroy the earth". And God Said: "This is the sign of the covenant which I make between Me and you, and every living creature that is with you, for perpetual generations: I set My rainbow in the cloud, and it shall be for the sign of the covenant between Me and the earth" (Gen. 9:11-13).

This covenant was a promise from God the Creator, and it was secured with a sign, the rainbow as a symbol of God's promise to all people. But when the time came to call out from among all people a separated people, another covenant was made, the major covenant of the Old Testament.

The promise to Abram from God (see. Gen. 12:1-3) are known as the first statement of the Abrahamic Covenant. Remember that it was the Lord God who initiated the covenant. He is the one who chose Abram, revealed Himself to him, and called him into a covenant relationship. That covenant is the basis of the whole of the Old Testament!

As we read through the Old Testament writing, we find that the promises of the covenant were scarcely appropriated by God's chosen people, and the law was given to Moses so that the people could be more specifically guided in their obedience to the Lord and not miss His blessings. The law was an extension of the Abrahamic covenant.

God made the third covenant with Jesus Christ, and it extended to the whole of the peoples on the earth, but not as a general promise as in Noah's time. This is the covenant that is celebrated in the communication service and appropriated through faith in Jesus. When we say, "This is the cup of the New Covenant", we are recognizing that Jesus instituted a new covenant foretold in the Old Testament.

> *Behold, the days are coming, says the LORD, when I will make a new covenant with the house of Israel and with the house of Judah.... I will put My law in their minds, and write it on their hearts, and I will be their God, and they shall be My people...... for I will forgive their iniquity, and their sin I will remember no more (Jeremiah 31:31-34).*

David, King of Israel, through whom the physical line of Jesus descended, said in his last recorded words: "Although my house is not so with God, yet He has made with me an everlasting covenant, ordered in all things and secure. For this is all my salvation and all my desire; Will He not make it increase?" (2 Samuel 22:5).

What David knew and longed for, what Jeremiah proclaimed, is ours by faith in Jesus Christ. God is still dealing with us on the basis of a covenantal relationship. The New Covenant that Jesus instituted did not replace but completed the former ones. God in His great love for His people kept extending Himself through covenants, a greater one each time.

The first statement of God's promise to Abram occurs in Genesis 12. Notice the "I wills," because they prefaced what God was prepared to do. "I will make you a great nation; I will bless you/And make your name great." Then he added, "I will bless those who bless you,/And I will curse him who curses you."

Lest you think that is an empty oath, I want you to understand that the curses of God are the inevitable consequences of disobedience.

A curse is a choice against life. Now, if I were to go to the World Trade Center in New York City and decide to jump off, and then I did it, I would go splat! On the sidewalk – not because God had plummeted my body in a fitful rage to the sidewalk, but because I put into motion a chain of events with inevitable results. The curse of God is not an arbitrary malediction or anything of the sort. The curse of God is the inevitable result of walking contrary to the purpose of God. Oftentimes, however, we don't believe that we're under the curse of God because we do not see the consequences of our choices immediately.

If we want the blessing of God in our lives, we must choose life! We have to find the purpose of God and fulfill it. The blessings of God is connected to His purpose. It is true that the Lord says He wants to bless us, but He doesn't bless our will and our efforts unless they correspond to His will and His purpose.

Covenantal Requirements

Let's go to Genesis 17 for a fuller statement of the Abrahamic covenant: "When Abram was ninety-nine years old, the LORD appeared to Abram and said to him, 'I am Almighty God; walk before Me and be blameless. And I will make My covenant between Me and you, and will multiply you exceedingly" (vv1,2). This was not a case of Abram sidling up to the Almighty and saying, "How's about You8 and me getting together." The initiative was wholly from God's side. He introduced Himself – "I am Almighty God" – and instructed Abram to "walk before Me and be blameless". He gave him a promise, "I will confirm my covenant between me and you".

Then Abram fell on his face, and God talked with him, saying: "As for me, behold, My covenant is with you, and you shall be a father of many nations. No longer shall your name be called Abram, but your name shall be Abraham." (Gen. 12:3-5).

Abram's name was changed at the institution of the covenant. (That fact will become important later on). "And I will establish My covenant between Me and you and your descendants after you in their generations, for an everlasting covenant, to be God to you and your descendants after you" (v7).

The Bible is the story of how God calls to Himself a people to be His own. He calls all of us, but the fact that He calls does not mean that we respond. To come into covenant is to respond to the Lord.

"This is My covenant which you shall keep, between Me and you and your descendants after you: Every male child among you shall be circumcised" (Gen. 17:10). This is the first hint that there would be anything for anyone but God to do. Up to this point the Lord had said, "I will do this, I will do that." Then came the fine print of the contract. Abraham and every male among his tribe was to be circumcised. God equated this procedure with the covenant as a sign that Abraham had been chosen by God to be His own, that the relationship had been established.

He who is eight days old among you shall be circumcised, every male child in your generations, he who is born in your house or bought with money from any foreigner who is not your descendant. He who is born in your house and he who is bought with your money must be circumcised, and My covenant shall be in your flesh for an everlasting covenant. And the uncircumcised male child, who is not circumcised in the flesh of the foreskin, that person shall be cut off from his people; he has broken My covenant. (Genesis 17:12-14).

It's very important to understand that:

1. God intended the covenant
2. The purpose of the covenant was to establish a relationship.
3. Abram's name was changed to Abraham at the institution of the covenant.
4. The sign of the covenant was the rite of circumcision given to a male child. It was a sign that God has chosen the child. The child, of course, would have nothing to do with that choice; it was a choice of God for the child.

The responsibility for obedience to this command obviously could not fall upon the shoulders of the child since he was to be circumcised at the age of eight days. The baby would not know anything about it (other than that he wouldn't like it – when he grew up he would not remember it at all).

Responsibility for obedience to the covenant fell on the parent. It was the responsibility of the parent to bring the child to the rabbi, priest, or whoever was authorized to circumcise. Circumcision was not optional. Not to be circumcised was not to be numbered among God's people. It was the sacramental sign, the outward and visible sign of the covenant.

Under the Old Covenant, women did not receive an outward sign of the covenant, but they were included in the covenant: first, by their relationship to their fathers, and second, by their relationship to their husbands. This will become important later on.

Would you agree that a tiny child could be circumcised at the age of eight days and from that moment be able to be called "a child of God"? Would it possible for that child to grow up and have nothing to do with the Lord? Would it be possible for him not to be interested in the service of the Lord or for him not to be obedient to the Lord? Would it be possible for a child circumcised as a sign of his covenant inheritance to grow up and have no concern for the Lord whatsoever? Of course it would. What, then, did God really desire from His people in the covenantal relationship?

Deuteronomy 10:12-13 is a very clear statement of what God wanted:

And now, Israel, what does the LORD your God require of you, but to fear the LORD your God, to walk in all His ways and to love Him, to serve the LORD your God with all your heart and with all your soul, and to keep the commandments of the LORD and His statues which I command you today for your good?

God wanted His people (1) to love Him, (2) to serve Him, and (3) to obey Him. God wanted them to do those three things out of respect and honor for Him. (Respecting and honoring God is what fearing God means. Fearing God doesn't mean being afraid of Him, but desiring His company and approval so that we guard what we do. Our changeless God still desires this from His people!

The word *circumcise* in Deuteronomy 10:16 ("Therefore circumcise the foreskin of your heart, and be stiff-necked no longer") is not used in a literal sense, but in a figurative, or spiritual sense. To circumcise your heart means to dedicate or to set apart your heart to God. We are now talking about two kinds of circumcision: the circumcision of the flesh, as an outward sign of the covenant, and the circumcision of the heart as an inner sign of our commitment.

A question was raised in Jeremiah 9:25, "Behold the days are coming.....that I will punish all who are circumcised with the uncircumcised." How could that be? "And all the house of Israel are uncircumcised in the heart" (v. 26). A person could have the external sign of belonging to God, but not have the inner reality.

Being a child of the covenant in the full sense under the Old Covenant involved two parts: first, having the external sign, the sign of that child's being chosen; second, responding to the Lord God, the sign of that child's growing up and choosing to love, serve, and obey the Lord. That is the circumcision of the heart.

Saint Paul instructed us on this matter. In Romans 2:25, he spoke about circumcision and its significance: "For circumcision is indeed profitable if you keep the law; but if you are a breaker of the law, your circumcision has become uncircumcision".

What does it mean to keep the law? Jesus summarized the law as loving God with all your heart, soul, and mind, and loving your neighbor as yourself. He said the whole of the law and the prophets is fulfilled in those two commands. (See Matt. 22:37-40). So, if in fact you love the Lord and serve Him and obey Him, your circumcision is established. If you don't, your physical circumcision becomes as though it had not occurred.

External Sign, Inner Reality

A sacrament must have the accompanying grace of God to make it effective. There were two sacraments for the Jews – the sacrament of Passover, which directly corresponds to our Communion, and sacrament of initiation (circumcision), which directly parallels out baptism.

In our Church, we present the child to the minister. The parents and godparents are asked specific questions, and they agree before God and the congregation to see that the child is brought up in the Christian faith and life, by their prayers and witness. They renounce Satan, sin, and evil and put their whole trust in the grace and love of Jesus Christ, promising to follow and obey Him as Lord. The congregation agrees to support those who have taken the vows, with God's help, and starts immediately to pray for the child.

The parents present the child for the inheritance of faith, and they and the godparents pledge to make the child aware of that inheritance. The congregation welcome and accept the child into the household of faith, and the officiate bestows the external sign upon the child as the promise of God to that child. The child has yet to know all of what has occurred, has yet to choose to walk with God herself. The name given at baptism becomes that child's Christian name. (with Abram becoming Abraham, and ever since, in Jewish tradition, the child's name's given at circumcision).

Paul said in Romans 2:26, "Therefore, if an uncircumcised man keeps the righteous requirements of the law, will not his uncircumcision be counted as circumcision?" This verse speaks of the priority of the inner over the outer. When we look in the New Testament as the history of the early church, we find that children were always regarded as members of the New Covenant.

The first Christians were Jews who understood that the Old Covenant was established with Abraham and his children and descendants after him, and that the children were brought at infants. So also, under the New Covenant, they brought their children to be baptized, as a sign of their inclusion in the New Covenant. Everywhere in the Christian church, in the earliest centuries, children of believing parents were baptized.

Baptism was not instituted as a saving ordinance; it was instituted as a sacramental sign of a person's incorporation into the company of God's people. It is within that fellowship that we are intended to receive the instruction that brings us to believe in and accept the Lordship of Jesus Christ.

In the sixteenth century, a group of people within church circles said, "Look around. Everybody in Europe has been baptized, yet they are all pagans." They were right! Those observant people were called Anabaptists because they said, "There's a lot more to being a Christian than being baptized; maybe the thing to do would be to wait until people accept Christ and then baptize them."

In churches that came out of the Anabaptist movement (not only Baptist churches but others), infant baptism versus adult baptism is not taught. Rather, believer's baptism is taught. Anabaptists and their followers understand correctly that being a Christian in the full New Testament sense involves not only an outer relationship but an inner one, an inner working of regeneration.

This notion of covenant was very important to my mother and father. They were biblically grounded people; they understood perfectly well the spiritual responsibility of parents for their children. I grew up knowing that I was a child of the covenant. Prayer was an important part of household life, and we learned about the Lord as children.

It's important to understand the relationship of baptism to faith. If a child is brought before the Lord, the child is put in a particular relationship with God and is chosen to receive the inheritance of the covenant. But this inheritance is not like a trust fund that is dispensed at a certain age automatically. The inheritance cannot be received until that child chooses to become a believer in Jesus.

Individual Faith

John the Baptist said to the crowds coming out to be baptized by him, "Therefore bear fruits worthy of repentance, and do not begin to say to yourselves, "We have Abraham as our father". For I say to you that God is able to raise up children to Abraham from these stones" (Luke 3:8-9).

All sorts of people have been led to believe that because they've been baptized they are in the kingdom of God. Dear people, there is much more to being a Christian than being baptized. To be a Christian in the full sense of the New Testament is to come into the company of God's people by way of baptism. That's the way in, as circumcision was for the Jews. As with circumcision, if we have been baptized, we must still come to faith. If we have never been baptized, we still have to come to faith.

I would imagine that most of you who are reading this have been baptized. Has there also been a circumcision of the heart? Is there also the inner working of God's Holy Spirit whereby you have spiritually regenerated, given the gift of new life? Was your baptism merely an external ceremony and ritual with you? Or has its promise been fulfilled?

In Romans 2:28-9, Paul talked about who is a real Jew:

For he is not a Jew who is outwardly, nor is circumcision that which is outward in the flesh; but he is a Jew who is one inwardly; and circumcision is that of the heart, in the Spirit, not in the letter, whose praise is not from men but from God.

If the word Jew were changed to Christian. And the word circumcision to baptism, we would understand the New Covenant exactly right! A real Christian is not one who is merely an outward Christian, whose baptism is simply external and physical. A real Christian is one who is an inward Christian, whose baptism is by the Spirit. A real Christian is brought into a new life inwardly in response to faith, not according to the written code of the liturgy of churches.

Where do you stand? Are you a believer in the Lord Jesus, yet have never been baptized? If so, you should be! I have a friend who's a believing, living, witnessing Christian, but he's never been baptized. I've talked to him about it many times, I ask, "Why not?"

and he replies, "Well, I believe that faith is the important thing". I've assured him that's true, but told him that Jesus said we were to be baptized. I can think of only two reasons why a person might not be baptized. One would be ignorance, the other, disobedience.

If you have never been baptized but have come to faith in Jesus Christ, then you should be baptized. If you were baptized years ago and have never come to faith, never committed your life to the Lord, never accepted Him, never allowed the work of the Spirit to bring you new life in response to faith, then that is your need today.

I am concerned that you be children of God, heirs of the covenant, fully – in every way – and I pray to that end.

Father, I thank You that every person is an individual to You; You know their histories and everything about them. You know exactly when they are with You today. We understand, Lord, that You have called into being a people, for whom You will be their God, and they will be Your people, a relationship has been established, and You call people into it.

Lord, I pray for those who have been baptized years ago, and cannot remember it, yet they belong to You, were promised to You, and You to them through baptism. They are indeed part of the covenant, but Lord, we understand that inheritance of the covenant depends not really upon baptism, but upon faith; a responding to Jesus Christ as our Saviour and Lord, a baptism, of the heart, a spiritual regeneration, that quickening by Your Spirit, that new birth.

Lord, let there be none who read these words who will be content to trust in external relationship alone, failing to move on to that inward-heart relationship with You. If, Lord, there are those who walk in faith and know You and love You, but for some reason have never sealed this outwardly, we pray that You will put them on their hearts as well, that they may be a people who have been signed with Your sign, sealed with Your blessed Holy Spirit, moving in the new life of the Spirit, and living to the praise of Your glory. We ask that in the name of Jesus Christ our Lord. Amen.

Traveller's Journal

REFLECT

Are you a child of the new covenant?

What does the term "everlasting covenant" mean to you

How will understanding your responsibility toward God change your actions?

How will you pass on to your children their spiritual inheritance? If you don't have children in the physical sense, are there spiritual children?

RECOMMIT

What vows were taken on your behalf at baptism? What vows have you yourself made? Read through the service used when you were a child or an adult and recommit yourself to those vows. In your journal, in your own words, personalize these vows between you and God.

THE FOOTPRINTS OF FAITH

CHAPTER TEN

JOINED TO GOD

The time when Abram became Abraham is a small detail that could be overlooked. But we will be unable to understand his story completely (remember, his story is ours, too) if we fail to understand the significance of his change.

When Abram was ninety-nine years old, the LORD appeared to Abram and said to him, "I am Almighty God; walk before Me and be blameless. And I will make My covenant between me and you, and will multiply you exceedingly". Then Abram fell on his face, and God talked with him, saying: "As for me, behold My covenant is with you, and you shall be a father of many nations. No longer shall your name be called Abram, but your name shall be Abraham; for I have made you a father of many nations". (Gen. 17:1-5).

Abraham's name was changed in connection with the giving of the covenant. Two concepts are absolutely central to biblical revelation; they tie together the whole concept of the Bible from Genesis through the Revelation. The first is the concept of God's kingdom and the second is the concept of covenant.

An Intimate God

In the Bible the relationship between God and His people is described under various metaphors: God is our Father, we are His children, God is the shepherd, we are the sheep; He is the vine, we are the branches; He is the potter, we are the clay. These metaphors teach us something significant about the Lord and also about ourselves. But the most intimate and expressive of all the pictures the Lord gave us is the image of the marriage relationship.

In Ezekiel's prophecy, God took a people to be His own, and the descriptive figure is that of marriage: "Yes, I swore an oath to you and entered into a covenant with you, and you became Mine" (Ezek. 16:8). Even in the days of the Old Covenant, there was a clear prophetic word that the day would come when God would make a new covenant with his people.

Behold, the days are coming, says the LORD, when I will make a new covenant with the house of Israel and with the house of Judah – not according to the covenant that I made with their fathers in the day that I took them by the hand to lead them out of the land of Egypt, My covenant which they broke, though I was a husband to them, says the LORD. (Jer. 31:31,32)

Or, we could read in Isaiah 54:5, "For your Maker is your husband,/The LORD of hosts is His name".

God is the Creator of all the earth and all the people. The covenantal relationship, however, exists only among those who have responded to the gracious invitation of the Lord to come into a covenantal relationship with Him.

God is the initiator of the covenant, which is an intimate relationship, like that of a marriage. One of the features of marriage that still exists today, although it has been lessening somewhat in our country, is that the bride takes the name of her husband. The significance of that is much greater than most people realize. The husband gives his name to his wife, replacing the name of her father, thereby signifying his protection of her and his responsibility for the household they will build together. The same significance is attached to the changing of Abram to Abraham.

The name of the Lord God in Hebrew Scripture is unpronounceable. His name was considered so holy that the people would not read it aloud; they substituted the word Adonai, which means "Lord". In most English translations, Lord is used for the name of God. Sometimes it will be in capital letters (LORD) to signify the sacred nature of the name, but Lord isn't the true name. scholars are not able to prove conclusively how it should be printed, or how it should be given vowels, or how it should be pronounced. But the closet we can come to it in English are the letters JHWH. You cant pronounce that in English or Hebrew!

Today there are those who call God's name Yahweh. It is interesting that the *h* letter in English and its equivalent in Hebrew is an aspirated sound – like *hah* – that resembles breathing life into someone, and in a sense it is. When the Lord God changed Abram's name, He placed His own name, His own life, in the middle of his! His name was no longer Abram; he was to be called Abraham. God bound Himself to His man, and not only to him, but to Abraham's descendants throughout all generations.

Not only was there an inclusion of God's name, but there was an exchange of names, similar to that of brides today who take their husband's name and hyphenate it with theirs, giving one last name for both. From the moment that Abram's name was changed, the Lord God added the name of Abraham to His own. He is "the Lord, God of Abraham". Imagine, allowing Himself to take on the name of a mere mortal! A wedding had taken place, a marriage, a union. God gave Himself to Abraham, even as He gives Himself to us. God extended the covenant of Abram's wife:

Then God said to Abraham, "As for Sarai your wife, you shall not call her name Sarai, but Sarah shall be her name. And I will bless her and also give you a son by her; then I will bless her, and she shall be a mother of nations; kings of peoples shall be from her" (Gen. 17:15-16).

"Sarah shall be her name." Sarah – let's put in an *h* here, too. Again, the significance of God giving Himself to His people. God bound Himself to them saying, in effect, "I am yours, you are mine".

The Lord God named Isaac before he was born, so Isaac's name did not need to be changed. But Jacob's name was changed to Israel. El (*El*) is another one of the names of God – IsraEL. Jacob's new name indicated a connection, a link, a union, a marriage between God and those to whom He had bound Himself in eternal covenant.

The Sign of the Covenant

Along with the name change at the giving of the covenant, God gave instructions that there was to be a physical, external sign: circumcision – a simple operation, but one that required the shedding of blood. (There is always blood connected with the covenant).

This practice of giving the name and the covenantal sign, a Jewish tradition yet today, was a practice in Jesus' time. We find two examples, John the Baptizer:

So it was, on the eighth day, that they came to circumcise the child; and they would have called him by the name of his father, Zacharias. His mother answered and said, "No: he shall be called John" (Mark. 1:59,60).

And Jesus;

And when eight days were completed for the circumcision of the child, His name was called JESUS, the name given by the angel before He was conceived in the womb. (Luke 2:21).

We celebrate the birth of Jesus on December 25. Eight days later on the old church calendar we observe the Feast of the Circumcision (January 1), which celebrates the fact that Jesus Himself, who had come to institute the New Covenant, was circumcised and received the sign of the Old Covenant. (The name of this feast days is now called the Feast of the Holy Name – I rather like the name better myself, because it was on the eight day of His earthly existence that Jesus received His name, that Name above all Names).

Martin Luther said that when he was discouraged, he thought of his baptism, because that reminded him that God chose him before he chose God. Didn't Jesus say that to his disciples? "You did not choose Me, but I chose you" (John 15:16). In a sense they did choose Him – but they didn't have to follow Him. They responded to Him. That's the whole point! Life is a response to God.

The Name Above All Names

I want to look a bit at the name of Jesus. Let's look at four important passages of Scripture. The first is Matthew 1:21. The angel of the Lord spoke to Joseph about Mary and told him, "And she will bring forth a son, and you shall call His name JESUS, for He will save His people from their sins."

This is forgiveness in the name of Jesus. We so often take it lightly when saying the Apostles' Creed, but belief that God is over and over again, "I believe in the forgiveness of sins." Do we? Think about that. Where would we be if there were no forgiveness of sins? This is the very heart of the gospel: we have forgiveness of sins and we can come to the Lord Jesus in repentance and faith. It is no light consideration.

The church today wants to magnify the fact that God is a forgiving God, and indeed, He is. Sometimes, though, forgiveness is presented as if it were an automatic act of God. It is nothing of the sort! God is prepared to forgive any sin, and any sinner, but His forgiveness is not automatic. Forgiveness requires confession, repentance, and faith. If a sin is unconfessed and unrepented, it is unforgiven. It's as simple as that.

We must consciously deal with the fact that when we violate God's will it wounds Him, and we need to respond in godly sorrow. The word confession means "to say along together with," and that's what we do. We agree with God that what we have done in wrong, and we are prompted to confess our sins – to Him, and if the Holy Spirit prompts us to do so, to another whom we have wounded as well.

Repentance is altogether different. Repentance means we cast our sins aside and turn away from them. It does not do us any good to confess unless we repent. When God says, "That is a sin, that is a violation of MY will," it will not do for us to try to blame somebody else. You're no doubt familiar with that approach – it's known as self-justification:

"Poor toilet training, Lord; you understand...."

"My environment was (unloving/smothering/hard/easy)"

"My parents, Lord, (never/always) did...."

"My (spouse/kids/boss).... You see, Lord....."

"Everybody was doing it, Lord, and I couldn't resist...."

"_____" (You fill in the blank with your favorite!)

All these are simply excuses for why we did this or failed to do that, and we will much better off realizing that these excuses will never work with God.

The Lord said, "Their sins I will remember no more" (Jer. 31:34), and I think He wants us to do the same thing. Accepting and receiving His forgiveness are part of His healing.

This is healing in the name of Jesus. In Acts 3, Peter and John went to the temple at the usual hours of prayer, and found there are a man who had been crippled since birth. This man was taken every day and placed at the gate of the temple. Everyone knew him; he was a part of the whole temple scene. As people approached, he would beg assistance and alms from them.

On this particular occasion, as Peter and John approached the temple, this poor man turned to them, begging. Peter responded, "Silver and gold I do no have, but what I do have I give you: In the name of Jesus Christ of Nazareth, rise up and walk" (Acts 3:6). The man rose up, and walked – not only walked, but ran about jumped, screamed, and delighted in the Lord. A great crowd gathered, as you well might imagine. Peter seized the occasion to preach in the name of Jesus. Next to the temple courtyard the Roman Guard was stationed, and when the disturbance arose, soldiers arrested Peter and John and put them in jail overnight.

The next morning, Peter spoke to the Jewish ruling council with much power:

Rulers of the people and elders of Israel: if we this day are judged for a good deed done to a helpless man, by what means he has been made well, let it be known to you all, and to all the people of Israel, that by the name of Jesus Christ of Nazareth, whom you crucified, whom God raised from the dead, by Him this man stands here before you whole. (Acts. 4:8-10).

Not only that, but Peter went on to assert that salvation is found in no one else, for there is no other name under heaven given to men by which we must be saved.

Unfortunately, the word *salvation* has become a word of offense. We live in a day where folks like to make a "do-it-yourself," egalitarian religion – a little from this, a little from that, a bit from poetry, a sample from other writers or preachers – and make themselves a comfortable belief system. The popular view espoused in some high circles is that all religions basically are much the same. Don't believe it! That's a lie!

It is not true that all religions are alike and that all religions worship the same God. Many times God's people, thinking they were worshipping God under some other form, were rebuked by the prophets because they were worshiping idols, gods created in their own minds or manufactured by their own hands. The same thing happens today. Often the gods we worship are ourselves, our own desires.

Jesus said, "I am the way, the truth and the life. No one comes to the Father except through Me" (John 14:6). Some consider the exclusiveness of that statement offensive. Thinking people are bound to ask, "But, what about the millions of people who live and die and have no knowledge of other word religions? Are they totally bereft of hope?" the Scripture says that God has not left himself without witness in the whole of the earth. (See I John 5:7-9). There are basic truth about God, His eternal power, and His glory that are revealed in nature, so that the whole human race is left without excuse before Him (see Romans 1 and 2).

Some Christians have said those people are hopelessly damned because they have not heard the name of Jesus. In fact, that belief has been part of the impetus for missions. But Scripture does not say that anywhere. I want to tell you two true stories that may give a little glimpse into what I believe. The first has to do with Socrates, a Greek philosopher who lived four hundred and fifty years before Christ. There is absolutely no evidence that he ever, at any time in his life, came in contact with the Hebrew tradition, yet he was charged with atheism, among other things, and put to death. He said to the religious leaders of his day, in effect, "What you have done is to people the heavens and Mount Olympus with gods created in your own image. They are but men and women writ large". (if you know anything about Greek mythology, you will know that the Greek gods had all of the foibles of human beings and then some!) He declared, "I don't believe in the gods of the Greek peoples. What I believe is that there is one God, that's all; and he is a holy God, a righteous God. I'm not righteous; I'm not holy; if I am ever to get to God, he will have to provide a way".

That sounded like atheism to the Greeks, with their panoply of gods in their own image. It was Christian's faith more than four centuries before the coming of Jesus Christ! Socrates didn't trust in his own righteousness; he knew he wasn't worthy. He cast himself on the mercy of a God he but dimly apprehended, and I expect to see him in the kingdom, through Jesus Christ, of course.

The second story came out of China, before it was closed to Christian missions. A missionary in a remote area entered a village where the gospel had never been preached, and he began to tell the story of Jesus; how God had sent His own son into the world and that those who believed in Him would not perish but have everlasting life. As he talked, a woman smiled and her face lit up. When the missionary finished the story, she came up to him with great excitement and said, "I have always believed in Him. Today, you told me His name!"

Some people in the world have responded to a small glimmer of light, as inadequate as it may be, who have never heard the name Jesus. They will be in heaven, not because of their righteousness, but because of Jesus Christ. There is no other way, even if they have never heard of Him. I believed that there are probably people in this world who are right with God because they trust in a God they do not understand. They do no know the revelation of His mercy in Jesus Christ, but in some strange way they cast themselves on the mercy of this God, as Socrates did.

I need to say, however, that I don't believe it is possible to have the fullness of life apart from an explicit knowledge of Him and a relationship with Him. We have been commissioned to carry the message of Jesus to the whole of the earth, that as many people and possible can know that fullness. It is a tremendous opportunity and obligation. As far as the matter of eternal judgment, God has reserved that matter for His concern. We can but rest on His promise that if we seek Him with all our heart, we shall find Him. As the Lord said to Abraham, "Shall not the judge of all the earth do right?" (Genesis 18:25).

Whenever we came upon a situation for which we had no suitable answers. We read Deuteronomy 29:29, "The secret things belong to the LORD our god, but those things which are revealed belong to us and to our children forever, that we may do all the words of this law". Jesus is revealed to us, and we have our marching orders. We must trust God to do His job.

There is salvation in the name of Jesus. We have access to the Father through Jesus Christ; He is our only mediator. It is no accident that we end our prayers by saying "through Jesus Christ our Lord." He is the one who makes our prayers accessible to the Father, and we are taught to consecrate everything we do to the Lord through Jesus Christ.

THE FOOTPRINTS OF FAITH

The Christian faith knows nothing of the distinction between the secular and the sacred. Separation of the two is a pagan idea. The Scripture knows the distinction between the sacred and the sinful, but not the sacred and the secular. It is almost a blasphemous notion to think that a part of our life is unimportant to God, that somehow He is concerned with us only when we are at prayer and worship. It is just as important for us to be Christians in our work as it is to have a consistent Christian witness in our church – perhaps even more so. God is likewise concerned with what we do with our leisure time. He is concerned with how we use the talents that we have been given. God is concerned with our whole life – not simply the part we define as "religious"

Colossians 3:17 ("And whatever you do in word or deed, do all in the name of the Lord Jesus, giving thanks to God the Father through Him") tells us something important. It tells us to take everything – our whole life, all of it, not just our church experience, Bible studies, and prayer groups – and offer it to God through the Lord Jesus Christ. If we can't do that, then there is probably something wrong with what we are doing. We then need to examine our heart and conscience. Obviously, we are not to offer our sins to God and expect Him to sanctify them; we are to confess our sins and forsake them.

We also are not to offer Him plans that we've made on our own and expect Him to bless them; we are to seek His kingdom first and make our plans accordingly. We are to offer Him everything present in our life for His blessing. Our past and our future belong exclusively to Him, but our present is our time to share with Him. If we can't do that, we are trying to please someone other than the Lord God.

There is worship at the name of Jesus. Did you know that Saint Paul told the Christmas story? You have heard the passage many times, but perhaps you did not realize that it was the Christmas story. It bears none of the familiar accoutrements of Christmas; the shepherds, or the Magi. It is as though Saint Paul stripped all those familiar scenes away to let us stare at the bare truth of what happened nearly two thousand years ago.

[Jesus] being in the form of God, did not consider it robbery to be equal with God, but made Himself of no reputation, taking the form of a bondservant, and coming in the likeness of men. And being found in appearance as a man. He humbled Himself and became obedient to the point of death, even the death of the cross. (Phil. 2:6-8).

At Christmas we celebrate the eternal Son of God, one with the Father, equal to Him, sharing His glory, who laid aside not His deity but His glory, and came among us. Not only did Jesus become a man (which would have been humbling enough), but He came as a servant of men and was "obedient even to death".

Therefore God also has highly exalted Him and given Him the name which is above every name, that at the name of Jesus every knee should bow, of those in heaven, and of those on earth, and of those under the earth, and that every tongue should confess that Jesus Christ is Lord, to the glory of God the Father. (Phil. 2:9-11).

How terrible it is to profane that which is sacred and holy. Jesus is that name that the Father has decreed to be worshiped. To take His name and to throw it in the gutter and drag it through rubbish is an unspeakable insult.

It would take another book and it would be possible to show in both the Old and the New Testaments that God will raise from the dead ever person who has ever lived on the face of the earth. Scripture declares that the whole earth assembled will stand before Him on that day, and God will vindicate the holiness of His name, before all peoples.

God has decreed that every knee shall bow before Him and every tongue will confess Him as Lord. Hitler will be among those who bow, and so will Idi Amin and the Ayatolalh Khomeini. You will be there and so will I. we will bow willingly; for some it will be an awful moment of revelation and judgment – a dreadful scene – and yet they will bow just the same. The Father has decreed it. History is moving inexorably toward that moment. Jesus is the name that should evoke in us the worship not only of our lips, but of our lives.

Almighty God, Father of all mercies,

 We your unworthy servants give you humble thanks

For all your goodness and loving-kindness

To us and to all whom you have made.

We bless you for our creation, preservation,

And all the blessings of this life;

But above all for your immeasurable love

In the redemption of the world by our Lord Jesus Christ;

For the means of grace, and for the hope of glory

And, we pray, give us such an awareness of your mercies,

That with truly thankful hearts we may show forth your praise,

Not only with our lips, but in our lives,

By giving up our selves to your service,

And by walking before you

In holiness and righteousness all our days;

Through Jesus Christ our Lord,

To whom, with you and the Holy Spirit,

Be honor and glory throughout all ages. Amen.

Traveller's Journal

REFLECT

Do you know that God has joined His name to yours?

An intimate God – one who makes a commitment to His people similar to that which we know in a marriage relationship. What aspects of this relationship with God would you like to strengthen?

Does self-justification occur often in your speaking of your life?

How is your worship of Jesus expressed? How often?

RECOMMIT

To confessing more often, in more areas of your life, that Jesus Christ is Lord.

In Jesus' name. Amen

CHAPTER ELEVEN

RUNNING AWAY FORM GOD

Let's focus now on Genesis 16. The first verse brings us immediately into the midst of a problem: **"Now Sarai, Abram's wife, had borne him no children."**

Even if looked at from a purely human point of view, Sarai's barrenness could have been a tragedy. A woman's inability to bear children was regarded as a judgment from god. In this passage and many others, women who faced this problem spoke as if the Lord had "closed" their womb. I'm sure that Sarai's infertility was a disappointment fro Abram as well. Bearing a child was even more important to him and to most men, because in the back of his mind was the promise the Lord had given him. Abram had staked everything he had on the promise, and as yet he had no offspring- and he wasn't getting any younger.

Giving God a Hand

Even with the very best of our intention, God really does not need our assistance. He makes the promises; it's His job to fulfill them. Our difficulty is with His timing. He is an eternal God who exists outside of time; HE has all eternity in perspective, while we temporal beings are locked into a time frame. Learning to move in God's timing is one of the most difficult aspects of the Christian life. It's very difficult, perhaps close to impossible, due to our willful nature, to fully grasp that the intelligence and cleverness of man Is as foolishness before God. We tend to take the fact that we are made in His image a little too far. Forgetting that the might of men does not glorify Him.

Seemingly, faced with the situation of heir-less-ness, Abram came up with the first suggestion to "help God out," the Eliezer should be appointed in heir. The Lord said not. The heir was to be a blood descendant. Sarai offend the second suggestion to "give God a hand," that she give her servant to her husband, and the child born of that union he counted as if he was her own, a fairly common practice. (We see that in the cases of Rachel, Leah, and others in the Old Testament.) Sarai was Abram's wife. Hagar was "married" to Abram but was in reality a concubine. The difference between a concubine and a wife in that culture is that there was only one wife in the full sense of the term, though there were often many concubines. The wife was the woman who symbolized the joining of households, and the union between husband and wife was usually arranged by the parents. The wife's word was law over others in the household. The concubine had a certain status, but it was never equal to that of a wife. If a man had a child by a concubine and then wanted to get rid of her, he was unable to do so. She was a permanent part of his household from the moment of childbirth on.

You may be wondering where Sarai and Abram got an Egyptian slave. Remember when Abram to Pharaoh that Sarai was his sister? Scripture records that the Pharaoh was good to him for Sarai's sake, and Abram acquired sheep and cattle, male and female donkeys, menservants and maidservant and camels. Hagar was part of that package, and she went back to the Promised Land with Abram and Sarai. Hagar was acquired at a time when Abram was out of the will of God. With that beginning, what would the consequences be?

Abram agreed with Sarai that "marrying" Hagar might be the solution. Hagar conceived. She knew that she was bearing the long-desired son of her master. Scripture says that as the child began to grow in her womb, she began to despise Sarai, and apparently was not discreety about revealing that fact. She may have expressed disdain of the barrenness of her mistress, which created a great tension in the home.

Note Sarai's response to Abram, "May wrong be upon you! I gave my maid into your embrace; and when she had conceived, I became despised in her eyes. The LORD judge between you and me" (Gen. 16:5). Had Sarai forgotten that the whole originated with he? In fact, yes!

It is so very characteristic of our human nature to look around and find somebody on which to place the blame if things don't go right. There is a small sign on the door of our office: SOMEONE WHO CAN SMILE WHEN THINGS GO WRONG HAS FOUND SOMEBODY TO BLAME IT ON. We are masters at avoiding responsibility. If we take a step or make a decision that backfires, we shuffle a bit to the side, se we can avoid the flak. If our argument isn't logical, we simply protest all the louder. Sarai did just that.

Abram answered Sarai, "Indeed your maid is in your hand; do to her as you please" (Gen. 16:6). Sarai's response was to mistreat Hagar, and Hagar fled. The Hebrew word for *harshly*)'anab, "to depress") paints a picture of piling weight upon something. Perhaps in mistreating Hagar, Sarai overworked her, perhaps constantly nagged at her. But however she did it, Sarai made Hagar's life absolutely miserable.

Discord, pain, heartache, even torture when were found in the home of Abram-essentially because in it were trying to fulfill God's according to their understanding.

Hagar and the Angel of the Lord.

Having fled Sarai's presence, Hagar started running toward her homeland, Egypt:

Now the Angel of the LORD found her by a spring of water in the wilderness, by the spring on the way to SHur, And He said, "hagar Sarai's maid, hwre have you come from, and where are you going?" (Gen. 16:7,8)

Shur is the Hebrew word for "wall", and the village called Shur was located on the border between Egypt and points east. Records dating from as early as two thousand years before Christ tell of strong fortifications built by the Egyptians along an entire well separating Egypt and the area east of Egypt. Apparently, Hagar had made it all the way to the gate of the wall. She sat down beside a well to refresh herself when the angel of the Lord appeared to her.

Genesis 16:7 is the first occurrence of the phrase "the Angel of the Lord" in the Old Testament. Since it appears a number of times, we must distinguish between to the Angel of the Lord and the many references to other angels in Scripture. The phrase seems to indicate someone a bit different than the " usual" angel, if we can use such a term. The word *angel* means "messenger" both in Hebrew and in Greek, but this phrase is used, the implication is that the angel of the Lord actually takes the place of the Lord. Some biblical scholars have said that the angel of the Lord is actually a pre-incarnational appearance of Jesus-the Word that later became flesh. However we decide to think of it, we must that the term, and the person to whom it applies, is special. This angel received worship; no other angel would ever receive worship. The angel of the Lord spoke as though God were speaking, and was addressed as though the angel of the Lord were in fact God. It was the angel of the Lord who spoke to Moses in a bush that burned but was not consumed. It was the angel of the Lord that wrestled with Jacob (who ended up with limp) and said, "I will not let You go unless You bless me!"

When the angel of the Lord spoke to Hagar, he addressed her by name. he knew her! Then he asked where she was coming from and where she was going.

Hagar's answer was clear and direct. "I am fleeing from the presence of my mistress Sarai." Then the angel of the Lord told her to go back to Sarai and submit to her. That was the last thing in the world that Hagar wanted to hear.

If when a rocket takes off its trajectory is the slightest bit of course, that minute mistake winds up being a very big error. A small difference continued for a great distance results in a mighty gap. We could miss the moon, all because we were just a tiny bit off at the start and failed to change our direction. Life is like that, too. Sometimes, the only way forward is to go back, to start over, particularly if we are running away from God. If we are running contrary to His will and we know it, we need to go back! If He puts someone in our path who is kind and gracious enough to try to stop us and point out the error in our ways, we shouldn't resent it bitterly. Problems are rarely solved by running away from them.

God's command to Hagar was accompanied by a word of encouragement: "I will multiply your descendants exceedingly, so that they shall not be counted for multitude" (Gen. 16:10). That promise must have sounded familiar to Hagar, so similar is it to the promise Abram had received! Undoubtedly the story of the promise of the heritage and the land and other blessings had been recounted to her. The angel of the Lord continued to prophecy to her. "Behold, you are with child. [Well, that wasn't news.] And you shall bear a son. [That was news; while she suspected that to be the case, she wasn't sure.] You shall call his name Ishmael [which means 'God Hears'], because the LORD has heard your affliction." (Gen. 16:11).

Can you imagine how that must have sounded? This angel of the Lord God, the angel of Yahweh, the angel that represented the God of her master Abram and his wife Sarai, this God, of whom she had no doubt heard much, was speaking to her, a runaway Egyptian slave. Can you imagine how the angel's words must have comforted her?

The angel of the Lord then described the son she would bear . "He shall be a wild man; His hand shall be against every man, And every man's hand against him. And he shall dwell in the presence of his brethren" (v.12). (Otherwise, he's going to be a simply wonderful child!)

The God Who Sees Me

I think we can all agree that the angel's description of Hagar's son was not all that encouraging, but the point is that the God of her master knew her plight and spoke to her about her future. I'm impress with Hagar's response. We don't know much about her from the Scriptures; I would have liked to have known a lot more than the Old and New Testaments tells us. In the New Testament she was used by Paul to symbolize the Old Covenant as opposed to the New. (See Gal. 4:22-31.) Hers was the child of flesh, the child that Abraham produced when he was moving according to his own wisdom. Hers was the child of bondage. Paul's reference to Hagar is not terribly flattering, and I think there was more depth to her. She gave a name to the angel of the Lord who spoke to her, *You-Are-the-God-Who-Sees.* She named the Lord because there wasn't any name in her vocabulary sufficient to describe what she then knew to be true. She named him "El Roi"-that means "You are a God who sees me." That is no small revelation! Not only that, but she gave the place where the encounter happened another name, too. She called I Beer Lahai Roi-which means "the well of the Living God who sees me." What a legacy.

Many people believe that God started the universe in motion and then went away. They think of God as a first principle somewhere of philosophical idea. Bu Hagar recognized that God cared enough to give her direction and encouragement. If only more people could sees so clearly.

All the rest of her life, Hagar remembered the places of her meeting with God. I have in my own life some places like that, have you? Special places where the Lord came close, where He revealed a part of Himself, where He manifested His power, answered a particularly heartfelt prayer, or met a need supernaturally. God is with us all the time, of course, but these are places set apart.

It was characteristic of people in those day to make a little pile of stones wherever they had an encounter with the Lord God, or to build an altar. The first meaning of the word *altar* in the Scripture, remember, is "a place of meeting between God and man."

I once read the testimony of a woman who was raised in a strictly religious family. She was raised as a Roman Catholic, but it could have been any denomination. She was educated in the finest parochial schools and eventually became a num. all her life, she was told by parents and teachers that God was constantly watching her. As a small child, she was terrified by the prospect. She thought, *God sees me when I am old.* That line of thought has been used for many generations to control children. Many of you reading this may have had that thought implanted at an early age. This particular person, however, never outgrew the fear of that statement. Even when she became a well-educated adult and committed herself to serving God, she was not encouraged by the thought that she was seen by God.

Eventually she confided to one who was ministering to her, "It is always been a barrier to my relationship with God, the thought that He is seeing me when there were things I wanted to cover from His eyes." The person ministering to her was immediately given a gift of great wisdom from God. His reply was, "Oh my dear sister, what a tragedy that you were only told part of the truth! It is true God constantly sees you, but I've just got to tell you, it's because He loves you so much that He just can't bear to take His eyes off you!"

Whether God watches because He wants to record every little error and big sin we commit, or whether He watches because He loves us so much that He can't take His eyes off us, are altogether different perspectives. I prefer to think the latter, don't you? And this is the thought that Hagar somehow grasped.

You know, I don't think God has changed His ways of dealing with His people very much. Throughout Scripture we have evidence that the Lord knows our pain, that He has called us, that He sees us, that He knows us. We have His commands, and they are never without encouragement.

It's really a simple point. When in the pursuit of God's will we come to the place where we are unable to see how God could lead us come to the place where we are unable to see how God could lead us any further or how He could fulfill a promise to us, we must realize that our experience isn't enough. Our sight is not keen enough to understand His ways. It is then we need turn to Proverbs 3:5,6, "Trust in the LORD with all your heart, And lean not on your own understanding; in all your ways acknowledge Him, And He shall direct your paths."

God may not reveal His purpose how or when would like it, but when we don't see the end clearly we must move ahead because we feel the Lord is leading us. We must put our full trust in Him and not scramble around looking for ways to try to bring about what God intends to do in His time.

I wonder, did Abram get the lesson? Did Sarai? Hagar certainly did. Did you?

Prayer

Our heavenly Father, may we be a people who can learn from the experience of others. We pray that the truth You teach through the situation of our forefathers, may cast light on our path today and always.

Help us to turn back to You. Help us to know that you see us as we are, yet love us so much you can't take your eyes from us. Help us to know that you call us by name, that your commands to us are to be encouragement, your promises sure. Gibe us grace to yield to your timing, Lord; to live in your will for us, we ask it in the name of Jesus Christ.

Traveller's Journal

REFLECT

Do you have difficulty with the timing of events in your life? How can you yield more to God's timing?

Where have you come from? Where are you going?

Where have you come from? Where are you going?

Are you running away from God? BE honest with yourself.

Where are the Beer Lahi Roi's of your life? Where are those times and places of special mooting with God?

RECOMMIT

Knowing that you serve a God who sees you, who loves you so much that He can't take His eyes form you, recommit your life to walking more closely with Him. Try to see yourself throng God's eyes, and in your own words, write what He sees.

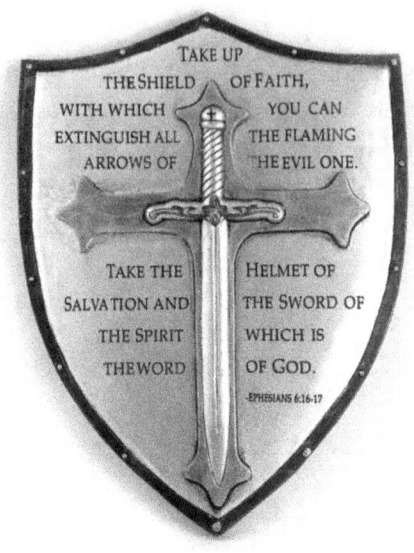

CHAPTER TWELVE

BACKSLIDING

Had I been the editor of Holy Scripture when it was being compiled. I am absolutely certain that I would have attempted to omit what has become Genesis 20. I must confess that I am tempted to omit any reference to this chapter from this book altogether, It's an embarrassment in the life of a man who is called the father of the faithful. Because he was not faithful in this instance.

However, the New Testament tells us the Old Testament was recorded for our sake, so that we, through understanding of the Sculptures, might have hope. We learn form the experience of God's people of other generations. Chapter 29. Then, address of practical matter: the sins of God's people sometimes become habits. The Bible never obscures the fact that God worked through instruments who were fragile, frail, and fallible.

David, for instance, was called "a man after God's own heart," How could God keep company with friends like that? David was an adulterer and a murderer, but he had a heart for God. When his sin was pointed out to him, he rented and asked that the joy of his salvation be restored to him, (See Psalm 51.) We do not that always learn from our experience, however. Sometimes our experiences do not provide us with the kind of instruction from which we can derive growth and then move on, beyond the experience. This is the case with Abraham.

We might surmise that Abraham had grown significantly in his faith twenty-five years after his trip to Egypt. WE might be mere inclined to excuse faithlessness in the early part of his walk with God; after all, he didn't have much experience with God's ways. He was not familiar with the faithfulness of God's provision, and so might have reason to doubt when a tough situation faced him. But after he had walked with God for so many years, we might not be so charitable in our judgment.

And Abraham journeyed from there to the South, and dwelt between Kadesh and Shur. And stayed in Gerar. Now Abraham said of his wife, "She is my sister" And Abimelech king of Gerar sent and took Sarah. (Gen. 20:1.2)

Gerar was on the coast near Gaza - in fact, it's part of the Gaza Strip – and was a part of the land known in those days as Philistia, from which the Philistines, bitter enemies of God's people, would come several hundred years down the road.

Again, Abraham and his wife agreed to work a deception, and again, she was invited to become a part of a king's household. By then Sarah was ninety years old. Was she so immensely attractive at ninety that she simply couldn't be resisted? It may have bin; she was pregnant. Not ling after she gave birth to the child of promise. Or perhaps the king merely wanted to align his house with the house of Abraham, by now a very wealthy and powerful Bedouin, and one way to do that was to take a woman from the entourage of another man and add her to his own, that may have been the motive. But whatever the reason, "God came to Abimelech in a dream by might, and said to him, 'Indeed you are a dead man because of the woman whom you gave taken, for she is a man's wife'" (Gen.20:3)

I am particularly interested in Abimelech as a character in this story. God was not a child of the covenant; he was not an inheritor of the promise of God. We don't know what he knew of the God who was here after to be called the Lord, God of Abraham. We may suppose that he was a pagan. We know that later generations of Philistines worshiped a god named Dagon, and he was a hideous god With that in mind, it's interesting to me that this pagan king, when awakened in the might, understood what was being said to him. He responded:

Lord will you slay a righteous nation also? Did he not say to me? ;"She is my sister? And she, even herself said. "He is my brother." In the integrity of my heart and innocence of my hands I have done this. (Genesis 20:4.5).

Abimelech was a man of honor, and he recognized that what he had done, he had done innocently. He did not know Sarah had conspired to deceive the people in Gerar.

And the Lord answered Abimelech:

Yes, I know that you did this in the integrity of your heart. For I also withheld you from sinning against Me; therefore I did not let you touch her. Now therefore, restore the man's wife; for he is a prophet, and he will pray for you and you shall live. But if you do not restore her, know that you shall surely die, you and all who are yours. (Gen. 20:6.7)

Early in the morning, Abimelech summoned the officials of his kingdom and explained to them what had happened. Can you imagine such a thing? The king was involved in a sordid mess, and he did not try to cover even the slightest detail! Not only am I amazed at that, but I am amazed at the response of the officials. Scripture records, "the men were very much afraid" (v.8).

And Abimelech called Abraham and said to him, "What have you done to us? How have I offended you, that you have brought on me and on my kingdom a great sin? You have done deeds to me that ought not to be done."(Gen. 20:9)

Isn't that astonishing? I doubt that anyone in the twentieth century would respond like that. We would say immediately, "I didn't know, so it's not my fault. "I am the victim of someone else's sin. "After all, I was lied to, you know. "We would protest our innocence before God and wouldn't admit to the slightest guilt. But not Abimelech and his officials! They somehow perceived that they dimly understood. They felt it, even if they had no intellectual basis for it.

Their response was striking because their sin was committed innocence. You may note that later on, in the book of Leviticus, one sacrifice devout Jews were expected to bring before the Lord was a sacrifice for sins committed innocently-sins they had committed but sins they were unaware they had committed.

There is a parallel in American jurisprudence, and it is recognized all over the world, not just in the United States: the difference between manslaughter, there is no intention to kill, and the death is ruled accidental.

Scripture recognizes that sin is sin, and sin is a violation of the will of God whether we knowingly violate it or not. If ignorance of the law is no excuse in a civil court, ignorance of spiritual is no excuse in God's courts. It is possible to commit a sin, and to commit it innocently, not even knowing it's sin, and to incur guilt.

Abimelech, a pagan king, understood that and perceived his guilt before the eyes of Abraham's God. And he called Abraham to account.

How terrible it was for Abraham to betray the god whom he served before the eyes of Egypt's Pharaoh and yet again in Philistia. (Might there be a connection between this fact and the fact that for many generations Egyptian and the Philistine forces wreaked havoc with the descendants of Abraham?)

Abraham betrayed his God. Abimelech could say for the rest of his life that he was not able to believe a word Abraham said about his God, because apparently God hadn't made any difference in Abraham's life.

Why? was the question. Abraham replied, "because I thought, surely the fear of God is not in this place; and they will kill me on account of my wife"(v.11). What a lame excuse. what an insult to the people of gerar. Abraham has persuaded himself that because God was not known in that place, he had to create a device to protect himself. In reality, the same fear had come over him as had afflicted him twenty-five years earlier. he had not grown measurably in all that time.

Abimelech, at this point, was far more righteous than our father Abraham. He was an honorable man. He may not have known much about the God Yahweh, but he loved Him, acknowledged

Him, and served Him at a distance. Abraham's argument was worthless.

Next? "But indeed she is truly my sister. She is the daughter of my father, but not the daughter of my mother; and she became my wife" (v.12). Did Abraham mean he hadn't lied? Sarah was his sister, well ….a half-sister. Why hadn't he told the rest of it? Abraham lied, not because of what he said, but because of what he didn't say.

Abraham's words were evil from the inception because of the intention of his heart. There is not such thing as little white lies in the eyes of our God. All lies are big black sins.

Did Abraham have another line to try? "And it came to pass, when God caused me to wander from my father's house that I said to her, 'This is your kindness that you should do for me: in every place, wherever we go, say of me, "He is my brother" (v.13).

Abraham was inserting his foot a bit deeper into his mouth. Abraham claimed that the lie was an agreement made with his wife thirty-five years earlier, when he had prepared to leave his father's land. Abraham had compromised her right from the beginning "Show me how much you love me, honey…" just between the two of them. A covenant of evil, a contract of deception.

Most of us, at one time or another, have contracted for evil with another. For example, a husband and a wife may agree to cheat on their income taxes. Or a company and an employee may agree to carry on a shady deal. "Only we know about it." We may lie to one another or to ourselves, because when we recognize something is wrong, we want to cover it up. We don't want to face it:

Well Lord, this is between You and me; You understand, it's a sort of struggle I have, Lord.

Lord, may husband will kill me if he sees this charge account-don't let him see the bill until I get it down to a reasonable level, okay?

I'll be righteous in all the important areas; you understand, don't you? Just go along with me on this one, all right?

The results of what we do under deceptive conditions are often painful. There may be a time lapse of twenty-five years between the sin and the consequence, but it always comes. The stage has been set. As for those little "look aside" conversations with the Lord, until they are settled and repented of, our lives are out of line with the will of God.

Not only are our lives affected by our sin, but other people's lives are affected as well. It's called "the ripple effect," because the circle of responsibility spreads out from a sin, just as the circles spread after a stone is cast into a puddle.

After all those years, Abraham could have repudiated the contract. Or Sarah could have said, "I really don't like to lie like that. After all, you are my husband. Are you ashamed of me? "Or Abraham could have Come to Sarah and said, as the head of the house hold, "You remember that agreement we made before we left Ur in the Chaldees? I realize that it was based on fear, and there's no faith in God in that. There is an intention to deceive, and it's wrong, because we're walking with and before a holy God, and He's calling us to be holy like Himself. So let's forget that, okay? I mean, God spared us once, let's repent of that and get on with being His people!" would that he had said something even remotely close to that.

If we are going to walk with god, we must break those contracts. We should not walk in contracts tainted by evil. We need to break them and take the consequences. The consequences will be less if we do it soon, more if we do it later! God will be with us. If we continue in deception, the consequences will come, but we will face them alone.

Back to Abimelech, who was an upright man. Then Abimelech took sheep, oxen, and male and female servants, and gave them to Abraham; and he restores Sarah his wife to him. (Does that sound familiar? Abraham acquire Hagar on the bonanza, and the wages of his sin have yet to be paid) And Abimelech said, 'See, my land is before you; dwell where it pleases you." (Genesis 20:14, 15)

Can you imagine yourself doing that? I can't. I might have responded as Pharaohs did, "Get out of here, we've had enough of you." Not Abimelech. He actually gave Abraham gifts. And Abraham saves face so that when Abraham uprooted his household once again, it looked the most natural of occurrences.

Abimelech's words to Sarah give no indication that he realized she was apart of the deception "I have given your brother a thousand. He didn't put the knife in and twist it, as we sometimes say. He took the gentle approach and covered their sin entirely. If you've been following this narrative with your own Bible, you will note that I left out completely the commentary on a part of what God said to Abimelech. I did this deliberately so that we could focus on the point separately. When in God's eyes, he was seen as the unfaithful one. Yet the Lord didn't take away the calling-God never does. A call is irrevocable. When we are called to serve the Lord, that divine call is never revoked (see Romans 11:29).We may be bad servants, or good ones, obedient or disobedient; but the call is not removed, even if we no longer move under it. Abraham was a Prophet even though he was enmeshed in deception, and the Lord upheld the call.

Who among us is worthy to serve the Lord? It's actually good for us to realize that we are not worthy! It keeps us in the proper place, in the proper mind-set before the Lord. Acknowledging our unworthiness was never intended to paralyze us into inaction, because the question of our worthiness does not count with God. Our yielding, our repentance, our openness, our teach-ability, and our mold-ability do count. God does His work through imperfect vessels, and He often has to keep reshaping us. If there could only be deserving ministers, God would have no servants at all!

I believe that the reason that the Holy Spirit wanted the little episode of Abraham's unfaithfulness included in Scripture was so that we can understand that men who have walked with God for many years can still fall away. We can, and grievously so, as the consequence of un-repented sin and unbroken agreements from our prior lives.

Or, perhaps the Lord wanted us to fully understand that His calling really is irreversible, and that even though Abraham failed Him, he was still a prophet, and that even though you and I fail Him, we are no less called to serve Him. Abraham's prayers were going to remove the blight of judgment from the house of Abimelech. Abraham could still be used of God in the midst of his disobedience-and perhaps in the process he was drawn a bit closer to the Lord.

Then again, perhaps the Lord God wanted us to understand that even outside the boundaries of our acquaintances, among those we think may not be of the faith, there are some who are obedient to Him. I love the phrase in The Book of Common Prayer when we pray for "those whose faith is known to you alone." Here is a man who may only have sensed the Lord, but who responded t Him with integrity. We, like Abraham, should never rush to judge that "the fear of God is not in this place."

Perhaps the Lord God of Abraham wanted us to understand more fully His perennial mercy and grace for those fallen in battle. God tends to pick them up, dust them off, mend them a bit, and send them back to the front lines. The church as the body of Christ, however, is a different matter. I have often heard it said that "the Christian army is the only one that shoots its own wounded."

Why is it that the Lord used the model of a pagan to show us how we should act? Abimelech's baling Abraham to save face is message for us. How often, when another falls away, we exploit the situation and broadcast it abroad-often inaccurately! How painful for us all, and even more so for those would be believers and see no love in us. Where is the witness of gentleness and compassion, of healing and reconciliation, that was given to us by Jesus?

If we are truly open, our deceptions and contracts for evil will be revealed to us through the Holy Spirit so that we can confess them, repent of them, and allow God to deal with them. Mercifully, God does not bring everything to us at once. We couldn't bear it! So for now, let's concentrate on the dishonesty in our lives, the lying spirit, the deceptive tongue, or whatever else is pointed out to us. Let's pray that God will enable us to cancel out and repudiate those contracts that we have entered into.

O God, whose glory it is always to have mercy, be gracious to all who have gone astray from your ways, and bring them again with penitent hearts and steadfast faith to embrace and hold fast the unchangeable truth of Your Word, Jesus Christ Your Son, who with You and the Holy Spirit lives and reigns, one God for ever and ever.

We pray that in Your mercy You minister to each one of us; breathe life upon the words we've read, that our hearts may be quickened, and our faith strengthened, our horizons enlarged, and our commitment deepened, and most of all, that our lives may be rendered more effective in being lived for Your glory. We pray in the awesome name of Jesus Christ. Amen.

Traveller's Journal

REFLECT

Have there been times in your life when you made the same sinful choice more than once?

Have there been times when the witness of an unbeliever was stronger in your life than that of a professing Christian?

Are there any "contract for evil" present in your life?

Are you quick to judge another's spiritual health?

RECOMMIT

To honesty and integrity in your dealings; to knowing your unworthiness of service, yet your worth as God's servant; to following the call He never revokes, to walk with Him.

CHAPTER THIRTEEN

TESTING AND TRIUMPH

For Abraham, the time had finally come. The promise which God had uttered years and years before laws about to be fulfilled. Abraham had fathered Ishmael, son of Hagar the slave. I wonder how Abraham felt when God said there was yet another child to come from him, that Ishmael was not the one through whom His promise would be fulfilled. Yet Abraham trusted God, even though years went by and no more was heard from the Lord. Abraham became eight-seven, eighty-eight, eighty-nine, then turned ninety. What's worse, his wife was eighty! Then he passed ninety-one, ninety-two, ninety-three, ninety-four - then ninety-five, ninety-six. God of heavens, Lord! Ninety-seven, ninety-eight and still no more word. Where had the Lord gone? Had He forgotten?

When Abraham was ninety-nine, the word of the Lord came to him again. He was told that the same time a year hence, his wife Sarah would bear a child. By that time, Abraham would be a centenarian, and Sarah would be ninety! The story is found in Genesis 21:12.

And the LORD visited Sarah as He had said, and the LORD did for Sarah as He had spoken. For Sarah conceived and bore Abraham a son in his old age, at the set time of which God had spoken to him.

There's just something about our Lord indeed He's God! Just when we think we've got Him nicely figured out, He delights in doing something totally unexpected. God never settles for being confined to the limits of our minds. He wants us to learn to wait for Him, to understand the fact that He knows what He's doing, to realize that His memory is just fine, thanks. He has not lost control of the universe.

One of the most difficult lessons to learn in walking with God is to discern His timing and to move in it! His word is sure, his promises, certain, but His time is not our time. (see Ecclesiastes 3:11)

It is amazing to watch the intricacy of the dancers' steps, all in perfect rhythm time, the same is with the Lord. Not a movement out of sync, not even a beat is missed – what a wonderful goal!

The dancers spend hours of concentrated rehearsal, getting each step just right, watching out for the persons next to them, keeping close watch on the directions they are give, and keeping their ears intent on the music.

I've already made the point, but I want to underscore it. **Training!** That's what it's all about. Abraham and Sarah had spent years in training to learn God's timing. He stumbled, fell, and made a bit of a mess with the show, but when it was time for the spotlight to be on him, he was ready.

Just in God's own appointed time, Isaac was born. Abraham gave the name *Isaac* to his son, which means "laughter." The likelihood of Isaac's arrival was no doubt something of a joke. God had promised Sarah that she would be the mother of nations. Kings of peoples would come from her. Abraham fell down and laughed. He asked the Lord, "Shall a child be born to a man who is one hundred years old? And shall Sarah, who is ninety years old, bear a child?" (Genesis 17:18). And Sarah also found it hilarious. "After I have grown old," she asked, "shall I have pleasure, my lord being old also?" (Genesis 18:12).

Finally, the promise of a heritage was fulfilled. "So the child grew and was weaned. And Abraham mad a great feast on the same day that Isaac was weaned" (Genesis 21:8). According to the practice of those times, Isaac would have been about three years old when he was weaned, the cause of great celebration. Isaac's weaning was no different, but it ended in sadness.

During the feasting, Sarah saw Ishmael, the son whom Hagar had borne to Abraham, testing Isaac. Sarah said to Abraham, "Cast out this bondwoman and her son, namely with Isaac" (v. 10). It likely was innocent play, but it awakened I Sarah a jealousy that had been smoldering beneath the surface for a long time. Her jealousy boiled over, and she demanded of her husband that Hagar and Ishmael leave the household. Sarah's demands distresses Abraham greatly, because he loved Ishmael intensely. He sought God, and God said to him:

Do not let it be displeasing in your sight because of the lad or because of your bondwoman. Whatever Sarah has said to you, listen to her voice; for in Isaac your seed shall be called. Yet I will also make a nation of the son of the bondwoman, because he is your seed. (Genesis 21:12,13)

Notice that the Lord did not support Sarah's attitude, but He did advise Abraham to pay attention to what she was saying. He reassured Abraham that He had a plan for Hagar and Ishmael as well as for Isaac, that He would make of Ishmael a great nation because he was Abraham's son also. So early the next morning, Abraham took some food and a skin of water and gave them to Hagar. He set them on her shoulder and set her off with the boy. She went on her way and wandered in the desert of Beersheba. When the water was gone, she put the boy under the bushes and went off and sat down nearby because she could not bear to watch her son die, and she sobbed.

Ishmael was not a young child at this point. He was fourteen years old when Isaac was born, and Isaac was then at least three, so Ishmael was at least seventeen. When Hagar and Ishmael left, they were given enough food and water to carry them to the next place. They were now provision less out to die. After all, God's promise was that Ishmael would be the father of a great nation, just as would Isaac. Abraham could take comfort in the fact that God had fulfilled His promise to him concerning Isaac, and had done so rather spectacularly. Abraham could trust God to work things out for his eldest son, too. Ishmael and Hagar likely took a wrong turn somewhere and found themselves in dire straits. Hagar could not watch her son die; what mother could? Ishmael would die before she would, because younger people require more water than their elders. Without water, Ishmael would die first.

And God heard the voice of the lad. Then the angel of God called to Hagar out of heaven, and said to her, "What ails you, Hagar? fear not, for God has heard the voice of the lad where he is. Arise, lift up the lad and hold him with our hand, for I will make him a great nation." Then God opened her eyes, and she was a well of water. And she went and filled the skin with water, and gave the lad to drink. (Gen. 21:17-19)God was with Ishmael as he grew up. He became an archer, and while he was in the desert of Paran, his mother got a wife for him from Egypt – her home country. The wilderness of Paran is directly east of Egypt in the Sinai area, and it is called Paran to this day. Only one other reference to Ishmael occurs. When Abraham died, his sons Isaac and Ishmael came together to bury their father. In that passage, the names of the sons of Ishmael are listed, in the order of their birth. If you count them, you will find that there are twelve sons, twelve tribal ruler. It recount that Ishmael lived a hundred and thirty-seven years and that his descendants lived in the area between Havilah and Shur, near the border of Egypt toward Assyria. (see Genesis 25:9-18). : They lived hostility towards all their borders" (v. 18).

The Test

Genesis 22 begins with, "Now it came to pass after these things that God tested Abraham." The King James Version says, "God did tempt Abraham." Some people have problems with that concept, especially when we think of the words of the Lord's Prayer, "And lead us not into temptation" (Matthew 6:13). Jesus was led into the wilderness to be tempted by Satan immediately following His baptism.

It seems clear that Jesus was led by the Spirit into the place of temptation – but it is also clear throughout Scripture that we are never to attribute temptation to God. "Let no one say when he is tempted, "I am tempted by God"; for God cannot be tempted by evil, nor does He Himself tempt anyone" (James 1:13).

The word *naah,* translate "tempt" in the Genesis verse, also means "test." There is a difference between temptation and testing. There is no question about it, god does not *tempt* us. Jesus was not led into the wilderness to be *tempted* by the evil one. The Scripture is clear, however, that God does, over and again, test us. Jesus was tested in the wilderness. From the moment of His baptism, he never again returned to the carpenter's bench. He began the ministry for which He had come into the world.

My brethren, count it all joy when you fall in into various trials, knowing that the testing of your faith produces patient. But let patience have its perfect work, that you may be perfect and complete, lacking nothing. (James 1:2-4)

No question about it, God wants to mature His people; and the way He does that is by bringing us into difficult circumstances. Had/been planning the way to spiritual maturity, I would have made us exempt trouble from the moment of our commitment to Christ onward. We could win more friends that way, and make lots more disciples. Saint Theresa of Avila is quoted as having said to be Lord, "If that's the way you treat your friends, no wonder you have so few!" But problem-free existence isn't God's way: He leads us to maturity through the valley of testing. Testing is His way for us; testing was so for Jesus. And two thousand years thousand years before Jesus, Abraham was severely tested by the Lord God.

Now it came to pass after these things that God tested Abraham, and said to him, "Abraham!" And he said, "Here I am." Then He said, "Take now your son, your only son Isaac, whom you love, and go to the land of Moriah, and offer him there as a burnt offering on one of the mountains which I shall tell you." (Genesis 22:1-2)

Can you imagine how that must have sounded to Abraham? It was the though the Lord were underscoring the fact that Isaac was the child especially promised for a very long time, the child for whom Abraham and waited twenty-five-years. Can you imagine what that child meant to him?

Isaac was a symbol of the fact that those who believed in God, accepted His promise, and acted upon it, would be called the children of the faithful One, and they would be received by the Father. Then came that dreadful demand. It seemed to countermand everything that Abraham had believed for more than a quarter of a century.

Technically, of course, Isaac wasn't his only son; Ishmael was born earlier. From God's point of view, however, Isaac was the son through whom God intended to fulfill His promise to Abraham.

Once during a study of this passage, a woman said to me, "I could never believe that God would ask anybody to do such a terrible thing!" I understood how she felt-who wouldn't? I had to reply to her that Abraham lived at a time when human sacrifice that surrounded him. Abraham didn't know that his God would not require him to offer his son as a burnt offering as others believed their gods did, which makes it striking when you read of his immediate response:

So Abraham rose early in the morning and saddled his donkey, and took two of his young men with him, and Isaac his son; and he split the wood for the burnt offering, and arose and went to the place of which God had told him. (Genesis 22:3)

He didn't wait! There is no evidence that Abraham argued that God or that he even tried to get out of obeying God's request. He prepared for the trip early in the morning. Perhaps he didn't tell Sarah about it; there is no record that he did. I wonder if she could have understood. Perhaps would have tried to persuade him not to go, and he knew that would have been a temptation to him, a test to see if he would resist the purpose of God.

Before Abraham and Isaac left, Abraham stopped to cut some wood to take with them. I wouldn't have done that. I'd have thought to myself, *When we get to the region of Moriah, perhaps there will be no wood for the sacrifice-it's very rocky there. Well, though! I mean, if there's a no wood for the sacrifice, there would be nothing to burn so we won't have to sacrifice. right, Lord?* But Abraham prepared to do what God called him to do. He took the wood with him.

I wonder what went through Abraham's mind as he made the three days' journey. Abraham never lost a moment's sleep, not the night before he left, nor any night during the journey, so secure was his faith in God.

Then on the third day Abraham lifted his eyes and saw the place afar off. And Abraham said to his young men. "Stay here with the donkey; the lad and I will go yonder and worship, and will come back to you."(Genesis 22:4)

Abraham didn't discuss the real purpose in going. Isaac certainly didn't know what the trip was about, neither did the servants. Abraham probably kept up a fairy jovial conversation, commenting about the heat and the weariness of the journey, the beauty of the mountains in the distance. When he saw the mountains before they arrived, he told the young men to wait. But notice: he said, "the lad and I . . . we will come back." How did Abraham know that?

By faith Abraham, when he was tested, offered up Isaac, and he who had received the promises offered up his only begotten son, of whom it was said, "In Isaac your seed shall be called," dead, from which he also received him in a figurative sense. (Hebrews 11:17-19)

For us, the veil has been lifted a bit. We can understand something of the mind of this man who was called the father of the faithful.

There was not way Abraham could have understood what the Father was about to do, and yet, h e obeyed. He obeyed because he so believed that God would keep his word that, if necessary, He would raise Isaac from the dead to do it. Abraham knew nothing about resurrection, as a concept or as an occurrence. it was yet two thousand years before Jesus was raised from the dead! Abraham believed god could do exactly what He said – even if he, Abraham, didn't understand how or why.

What kin of faith is it that can say to the Lord, *I don't understand what You are doing Lord, but I believe that You can fulfill Your covenant-not just with me, but with generations ye to born. So, if you tell me to offer my son as a burnt offering, that is exactly what I will do!*

So Abraham took the wood of the burnt offering and laid it on Isaac his son; and he took the fire in his hand, and a knife, and the two of them went together. But Isaac spoke to Abraham his father and said, "My father!" And he said, "Here I am, my son." Then he said, "Look, the fire and the wood, but where is the lamb for a burnt offering?" (Genesis 22:6.7)

I wonder how that struck Abraham. He knew that he was about to do, Isaac did not. Abraham had placed the wood on Isaac's back. He carried the wood up the mountain upon which he was to be sacrificed. Does this call to mind another Son, another Father, and another hill not more than a thousand yards away from where this took place?

Without any hesitation Abraham said, "My son, God will provide for Himself the lamb for a burnt offering" (v. 8). When they reached the top, Abraham and Isaac began to build an altar. They placed stone upon stone until they had an elevated place upon which to offer a sacrifice. Then came the moment, that terrible moment of testing.

But it wasn't so terrible. Abraham had made up his mind when the Lord God spoke to him in the middle of the night. He decided he would obey, rolled over, and went back to sleep. There had never been any question about it. So when the final time came, the decision had made earlier enabled him to move forward in obedience, "and he bound Isaac his son and laid him on the altar" (v.9).

I want to stop right here and talk about the faith of Isaac. Biblical scholars agree that Isaac was at least fifteen years old, and some say he was as old as thirty. In either case, he had the strength of a young man. His father was at least a hundred and fifteen years old, a very old man. It would have been possible for Isaac to break away and say, "Thanks for the talk, Father, but I will go in another direction from here!" Isaac could have resisted when his father tied his arms together. And I'm sure he could have removed himself from the altar without much difficulty. Abraham and Isaac were alone on the mountain; they had left the servants down at the foot. Think of the faith of the son, so committed to doing his father's will that in the moment of crisis, he asked a question, moved not a muscle, entertained not a thought in opposition.

Isaac was prepared to do whatever his father was the word of God, just as was another Son on another hill. Jesus certainly could have escaped the cross. In the garden of Gethsemane, when Peter in a moment of enthusiasm lopped off the ear of Malchus, the servant of the high priest, Jesus said, "Put your sword in its place . . . Or do you think that I cannot now pray to My Father, and He will provide Me with more than twelve legions of angels?" (Matt. 26:52, 52). But Jesus never did it. He certainly could have – and spectacular sight it would have been - but it would not have been in keeping with the Father's will.

Jesus had made up His mind years before, "I do not seek My will, but the will of the Father who sent me" (John 5:30). He determined to obey, and when the test came, the terrible test, He was able to pass it. "Though He was a son, yet He learned obedience by the things stand; and so was Isaac.

Isaac had no doubt, heard all his life the story of the faith walk of his father, the circumstances under which he was born, and the inheritance which would be his own. He had heard about the faithfulness and goodness of the God his father served. He had no doubts. He saw the strength of his father's faith and was willing to follow.

And Abraham stretched out his hand and took the knife to slay his son. But the Angel of the LORD called to him from heaven and said, "Abraham, Abraham!" So he said, "Here I am." And He said,

"Do not lay your hand on the lad, or do anything to him; for now I know that you fear God, since you have not withheld your son, your only son, from Me." Then Abraham lifted his eyes and looked, and there behind him was a ram caught in a thicket by its horns. So Abraham went and took the ram, and offered it up for a burnt offering instead of his son. And Abraham called the name of the place, The-Lord-Will-Provide; as it is said to this day, "In the Mount of the Lord it shall be provided." (Genesis 22:10-14).

I'd like to have you read it another way. "Father, we have the wood, we have the stones, but where is the sacrifice?" My son, God will provide *Himself* the Sacrifice" – because that is exactly what He did. No ram was caught in a thicket by its horns at Calvary, and Jesus didn't call for deliverance, because God provided Himself as the lamb. The mystery of God – Father, Son, and Holy Spirit-comprises there different forms, if you will, of the same substance. When Jesus went to the cross, God bled and died, just as when the Holy Spirit acts, God acts.

Abraham, I'm sure, was moved at the provision of the Lord, he said, "The Lord will provide." Then he named the mountain, and said, "In the Mount of the LORD it shall be provided."

Every so often on the radio, the Civil Defense Authority will break into the broadcast with the words, "This is a test. This is only a test." The words will be followed by a tone for a few moments while the system is tested. Then an announcement will follow stating that is was a test of the emergency broadcast system, and, he there been an emergency, instructions would have been given.

Similarly, God runs tests every so often. He tests to see if we're turned in for instruction, only He does not preface His tests by announcing them. It might not be a bad idea a train ourselves to think in times of difficulty. *This is a test. This is only a test.*

If we walk with God, He doesn't start with the big ones, Spiritual training is a gradual process, much like physical training. God trains His people on provision. He tries to teach us that nothing we exchange in obedience to the will of God is ever lost. He will ask more and more of us, but He will enable us to do whatever He asks.

God asked of Abraham the release of his first son, Ishmael, to an area outside of his fatherly provision. He obeyed and released him. God then asked of him the release of his dearly beloved son, Isaac, the one2 promised as his heritage. Abraham was prepared to slay him. NO wonder we say that our ancient ancestor, Abraham, is the father of the faithful. Abraham was trained by God in his walk through life, and wound up obsessed with a call and a purpose of God in his mid and in his heart.

God's message to us is a simple one in a difficult setting. When ever we are faced with a sacrifice, we may think we are losing the most precious thing in our lives. But God will be no man's debtor. He who gives much will receive much, Jesus said, "He who loses his life for My sake will find it" (Matthew 10:39)

Heavenly Father, we thank You for the great men and women in our heritage. Thank You for Abraham and his willingness that which was most precious to him; thank You for Isaac, whose perfect obedience made possible our great and miraculous provision. Lord, we thank You for the terrible time of testing of which we just red. We know that it was minor compared to another place, another time in which You offered Your Son as a living sacrifice for the whole of the world.

O Lord God, we bless You, and we bless Abraham. We thank you for our Lord Jesus, who took our place as the sacrificial lamb. Because of Him we can stand forgiven, cleansed, purified, redeemed. Because of Him we can stand before You with the Holy Spirit in our lives bearing witness that we are children of the promise and members of the family of God. We thank You that. We ask that You remind us of Your faithfulness to us again and again, and that those things which are ahead of us we will face together with You, to Your glory. In the most precious name of Jesus Christ. Amen.

Traveller's Journal

REFLECT

Do you often condition your response to God on the basis of your understanding of His ways and plans?

How often do you refuse to follow because ,it doesn't seem to make sense?

As you look back over your life, answer honestly: has God provided that which He required of you when the time of testing came?

RECOMMIT

As you look ahead to the tests that lie before you, realize that He's prepared you for them, and recommit to using that for which He has equipped to His glory.

Chapter Fourteen

Sarah, Our Mother

Abraham is the father of the Jewish people through his son Isaac. He also is the father of the Arabian through his son Ishmael (which is recognized in the Koran of the Muslim people). The New Testament tells us that all who have been baptized into Jesus Christ are Abraham's seed and heirs according to the covenant.

Listen to Me, you who follow after righteousness,/You who seek the LORD:/ Look to the rock from which you were hewn,/ And to the hole of the pit from which you were dug./ Look to Abraham your father,/*And to Sarah who bare you.* (Isa. 51:1-2, Emphasis mine)

Sarah is the mother of the Hebrew people and is greatly revered. In many ways, rabbinical traditional looks upon her as a model. In the books of Galatians although she is not named, there is reference to the two wives of Abraham; and those who were children of faith were seen as spiritual descendants of Sarah, the free woman.(See Gal.4:23)

The first biblical reference to Sarah is found in Genesis 11:29.It's a very clear statement, appearing in part of the genealogy of Abraham's father, Terah. "Then Abram and Nahor took wives: the name of Abram's wife was Sarai."

Sarai (Sarah) and Abram (Abraham) spent many years-over eighty- in close fellowship and love. The life they shared was not easy, and sometimes was extremely difficult. In spite of the circumstances in which they found themselves, however the life they lived together was continually under the call of God. The call was never withdrawn.

The following passage today seems out of step with the times, yet I believe it conveys eternal truths-not simply descriptive truths of historical facts, but normative truths. The passage speaks of matters as they ought to be, according to the will of God:

Wives, likewise, be submissive to your own husbands, that even if some do not obey the word, they, without a word, may be won by the conduct of their wives, when they observe your chaste conduct accompanied by fear.(1 Peter 3:1-2)

Those can be fighting words today! They sound to some ears as though women are put in a subservient position. But is that what God had in mind?

God's Order

God established certain orders. For instance, He established an order for the church. Jesus is the head of the church, and if we fail to recognize and live in line with that order, we forfeit the hand of God's blessing. Likewise, God established an order of the home. (See Eph.5:23) He established the husband as the head of the wife. That may seem as though the wife is relegated to a lower, inferior, stature ,but that is not the intention. God established a functional order. A family in which the husband acts as the head is a family in line with the purpose and plan of God. Any other order is spiritually dysfunctional.

The wife of an unbelieving husband is told to win her husband over without a word." wives are limited in what can be said to their husbands, even if the husbands are unbelievers or less advanced in the faith.

The passage continues:

Do not let your adornment be merely outward –arranging the hair, wearing gold, or putting on fine apparel –rather let it be the hidden person of the heart, with the incorruptible beauty of a gentle and quiet spirit, which is very precious in the sight of God.(1 Peter 3:3-4).

Nothing is intrinsically wrong with beautiful hairstyles, jewelry, or clothing, but the beauty women reflect should arise from a beautiful spirit. As which only calls attention to the external appearance, as good as that may be.

The passage goes on to say:

For in the manner, informer times, the holy women who trusted in God also adorned themselves, being submissive to their own husbands, as Sarah obeyed Abraham, calling him lord, whose daughters you are if you do good and are not afraid with any terror. (1 Peter 3:5-6)

Sarah was used as a model of a wife. She exemplified the right relationship between a husband and a wife. Let's find out why. I could say with a great deal of feeling, "Wives, be submitted to your husband. "The interesting thing is, my wife agrees that I am ultimately responsible. If things go badly, she can never say "I told you so" We have to learn that this passage means much more than it's apparent at first glance.

Much of the understanding of God's order rests upon the very clear teaching of the Scripture:

See then that you walk circumspectly, not as fools but as wise, redeeming the time, because the days are evil. Therefore do not be unwise, but understand what the will of the Lord is. (Ephesians 5:15-17)

What could be clearer? Understand – be careful – know how to live under God's leading.

Wives, submit to your own husbands, as to the Lord. For the husband is head of the wife, as also Christ is head of the church; and He is the Savior of the body. Therefore, just as the church is subject to Christ, so let the wives be to their own husbands in everything. (Ephesians. 5.22 – 24)

That's a tall order! in its complete context, however, the passage is preceded by these words, "submitting to one another in the fear of God" (v. 21).

Submission to one another and to the Lord creates a conducive environment wifely submission. To make sure that the message gets across, Paul added, "Husbands, love you wives, just as Christ also loved the church and gave Himself for her" (v. 25). What wife would mind submitting to a man who loved her as Christ loved the church?

So husbands ought to love their own wives as their own bodies; he who loves his wife loves himself. For no one ever hated his own flesh, but nourishes and cherishes it, just as the Lord does the church.....let each one of you in particular so love his own wife as himself, and let the wife see that she respects her husband. (Ephesians 5:28- 33).

I don't believe it's possible to take the commandment of the Lord concerning husbandly headship out of its context and seek to apply it universally. Verse 22 is often overworked and misapplied. In the context of a husband and a wife submitted to the Lord and to each other, the headship of the husband over the wife is functional and serviceable. Moreover, it has the blessing of God upon it. The burden of responsibility is on the husband. Where the entire relationship is in place and the husband sets the example, God's peace can be found in the home. Where the relationship is out of kilter, God's peace is absent.

We speak of this order in terms of the relationship between Christ and His church, but the description also applies to the marriage of Abraham and Sarah. The relationship between Sarah and Abraham was more than wife and husband, Sarah was also Abraham's half-sister, and since he was ten years older than she, he likely knew her from her birth.

Unfortunately, this double relationship became a source of great deception when Abram and Sarah went into Egypt, and again when they went into Gerar (Philistia). They used the same deception both times; they told but half the story, mentioning only Sarai's sisterly relationship to Abram. They had made the agreement for evil before they ever left the land of Ur of the Chaldees. What did that man do to that woman? He made her a partner in a lie. And she submitted to his wishes.

The fact that Sarah was barren was particularly unfortunate in the East in those days. Children were desired because they increased the size, wealth, and importance of a family group. Boys were especially desired, because when they married, their brides' dowries came into the family with them; When girls married, however, the fortunes of their families were decreased. A woman's inability to bear children was regarded as the reproach of God.

Abraham, Isaac, and Jacob were the three great patriarchs of the Hebrew race. It is striking that their wives – Sarah, Rebecca, and Rachel – were all sterile. All three were enabled to bear children eventually, but for a very long time they were unable to do so. Another common thread in their stories is that each woman agreed with impregnates her. God, however, brought them children through ways unmistakably His own.

The family of Abraham and his descendants was to be built on faith in God and His promises. God's provision, god's inheritance, repeated throughout three consecutive generations. Husbands led wives, in good times and bad. Husbands cared for wives, prayed for wives, and loved wives as they loved their own bodies. Starting with the example of Abraham and Sarah, Abraham's sons and their wives set the example Paul beautifully saw in harmony with Christ and the church.

Yes, Abraham got Sarah in some hot spots. Yes, Sarah was at times less than the submissive wife. (Remember how Sarah mistreated Hagar when Hagar was pregnant with Ishmael, even though it was all Sarah's idea? How she laughed in disbelief when she heard that she was going to bear a child at the age of ninety? How she cast Hagar and Ishmael out of the household in anger?) Sarah's and Abraham's relationship was not perfect; Sarah and Abraham were not perfect people. Why, then, are they models? They model what God can do in spite of our human frailty. The relationship between Abraham and Sarah lasted one hundred and twenty-seven years. Would you say they were secure in their marriage?

Sarah's submission to Abraham was based on her knowledge of who he was and her recognition of his submission to his God. She saw both his faithfulness and faithlessness to that God, and never said, "I told you so." Her security came from years of standing under Abraham's protection, that protection that was from the Almighty God, and knowing it to be sure, in spite of the heartbreak of the circumstances. "As Sarah obeyed Abraham, calling him lord, whose daughters you are if you do good ad are not afraid with any terror" (1 Peter 3: 6)

Sarah, our Mother

Think about Sarah the woman, the woman who followed Abraham out of Ur of the Chaldees without a question, not knowing where he was going and perhaps even hearing friends snicker cynically, "What a fool! Packing up and leaving and not even knowing where he's going!" It is hard to imagine a woman's faith in a man being so strong today, when men focus on career paths from kindergarten onward. Perhaps it would be easier to imagine Sarah's kind of faith if men today had a different kind of heritage, one like that which Abraham passed on to Isaac, who in turn passed it on to Jacob. The heritage of godliness and obedience to the plan of God and His revealed word, no matter what the circumstances, might enable more women not to give way to fear in their marriages. Paul said that a man cleanses his wife by " the washing of water through the word" (Ephesians 5:26). How? Through the written word, the Bible.By looking up all questions, by making God's word the common authority for married life, by turning in prayer together to the Author for guidance.

Think about Sarah the woman, the woman who willingly went along with her husband's deceptions, and went not once, but twice to the harems of wealthy, powerful men. She must have been a bit uncertain of her future, and she no doubt fervently prayed that, before the customary year's waiting period was over and she would be expected to be of service to the king in his bed, her beloved Abraham would somehow get her out.

Paul wrote that a husband's call to his wife, like Christ's call to the church, is to "present her to Himself.....not having spot or wrinkle or any such thing, but that she should be holy and without blemish"(Ephesians 5:27). Abraham had abdicated the protective, caring clause of his contract with Sarah. He had left her wide open for sexual infidelity, had, in fact, placed her in another man's bed out of concern for his own safety and provision.

Abraham reaped the disdain of the leaders with whom he had dealt deceptively, who, more honorable than he, returned his sister/wife to him without blemish. Where her husband failed, God did not.

There is a lesson in this. Even when it looks as if things are out of control, they are never irredeemable. God's protection was over Sarah in the harems just as it was in her husband's tent. His will and purposes were not thwarted. In fact, God even used those situations to provide for the family, to increase their substance. He redeems our mistakes! Abraham could have lost everything, including his honor. Make no mistake, he lost a precious opportunity to be a witness to the Lord god to the people he deceived; he sowed seeds that would be harvested in the future. But God used the opportunity to teach Abraham a private lesson about His saving grace.

Think of Sarah the woman, the woman who had to bear the whispered comments and the derisive laughter of the women in her household when her servant gave birth to Abraham's son. The fact that the practice was common did not alter the fact that God had favored Hagar, not Sarah. The pain of God's reproach must have seemed unbearable, for she drove Hagar form the household. Hagar returned to their household after her encounter with the angel of the Lord.

`Think of the pain Sarah must have suffered as she watched Ishmael grow, saw her husband grow to love the child, and saw Abraham bring him to the Lord, full of pride, offering him as the hoped for heir. Was she secretly glad when Abraham told her that god said Ishmael wasn't the one? When God again promised that she fouled bear the promised one? Or did she despairs that t it would ever happen and secretly doubt God's faithfulness as well as her husband's sanity?

Sarah had not heard the voice of the Lord herself. Hagar was one up on her in that area, too. God had dealt directly with Hagar. He had sent an angel to her with a prophecy that was auspiciously close to the one that Abraham had been given about their promised son's inheritance. What went trough her mind? Scripture does not record Sarah's inmost thoughts, but her laughter (the laughter that gave her miraculous son his name) indicates that, in spite of the circumstances, she understood that she and Abraham were "one flesh."

Sarah's love for husband included the knowledge that she was inextricably bound to him, for God's purpose, whether she thought he was right, or sane, or fair, or faithful to God, or faithful to her-whatever the circumstances. This was a marriage for God's convenience; not his. I wonder, how many women today could maintain even a portion of Sarah's unyielding commitment and love for her husband?

Think about Sarah the woman, the woman who held in her arms at long last the child of promise, who saw in her husband's eyes the joy of the faithfulness of God. Abraham treated Sarah as a queen, and likely even more so after Isaac was born. Yet Sarah asked Abraham to cast out his son Ishmael and his son's mother. Perhaps she had been angered by something Ishmael did. Or perhaps she reacted out of a mother's instinctive protectiveness of her offspring. Abraham had every right to refuse her request, and Sarah knew that Abraham would submit all his decisions to God before acting on them. Imagine her relief when she found that God said it was within His plan to have Ishmael go!

Might Abraham also have known that in honoring Sarah's request, he was identifying with her? Perhaps he knew the torment she was experiencing, and, motivated by love for her, asked the Lord's permission and grace to do something that was wrenchingly difficult-to let his son Ishmael go from his house, his care, his supervision, to commit Ishmael to the care of God.

Think about Sarah the woman, the woman who mothered Isaac, the child of promise, the woman whose son was taken to the mountain to be sacrificed, whose beloved son returned with his father with the amazing story of the ram caught by his horns, the substitute sacrifice,. Sarah, marveling at the faith of her husband and son, doubtlessly wept with joy and relief. In spite of the humanly impossible circumstances, God had had been faithful once again.

In Sarah's culture, the father and mother were seen as being God's representatives in the matter of authority over the children, yet she was not a part of this miracle until it was over. Did she come face to face in the God who had called her husband and had promised them much that would come along after she lived?

Could Sarah see the promise of salvation through the sacrifice of another Son, down through the years of the future when His mother would see her Son sacrifice, not spare? that Son would "give Himself up" in an image of God's design for marriage.

We speak often of "dying of self" in the Christian life, and it is nowhere more important than in the marriage relationship. Giving up one's self for a husband or a wife is much the same thing. Giving up ones' self is mutual submission; it is caring for the other's needs before one's own and not keeping score. It is a tough assignment. But the longer we do it, the more satisfying it is and the more our own needs are fulfilled. Selfishness simply has no place in marriage.

A Tribute of Tears

Sarah's death is recorded in Genesis 23

Sarah lived hundred and twenty-seven years; these were the years of the life of Sarah. So Sarah died in Kirjath Arba (that is, Hebron) in the land of Canaan, and Abraham came to mourn for Sarah and to weep for her (Genesis 23:1-2)

Abraham was not at home when Sarah died. He had vast flocks, and could have been twenty-seven miles away at Beersheba, or at another location; but when he heard the news he proceeded to Hebron.

He got down on the ground beside his dead wife and he wept. Abraham, the great patriarch, wept uncontrollably at the sight of his dead wife. There's no record of his having shed a tear when he left his family and friends in Ur of the Chaldees. Not a word about tears when he buried his father, Terah, in Haran, or when he said goodbye to his beloved son, Ishmael, or when he was told to sacrifice his child of promise, Isaac Yet he was not ashamed to weep at the sight of Sarah, a hundred and twenty –seven years his sister, more than eighty-years his wife, dead before him.

The Oriental custom of the day when one died was to set up a death wail to signal the tribe what had happened so that mourning would begin. Relatives and friends continued their mourning from the time of the death wail (described as a sharp, shrill, ear-piercing shriek) until the burial took place. That was the custom, and no doubt it was periodic wailing and grieving that met Abraham when he returned to his household.

But Abraham's grief was far more than custom dictated. I can well imagine what it meant to him to lose the only person on the face of the earth who could share those early memories of what life was like before they left Ur, of the family they had left behind. A large section of his life was gone. In fact, a large section of himself was gone. He lost the one person who had known him as he truly was, yet had never said, "I told you so,." He lost someone with whom he had shared growth and joy and shame and heartache. He lost a confidante, comforter, friend, and sister when Sarah died. He knew his loss was great, and he was not ashamed of his grief.

Abraham went to the Hitties and asked to buy a cave in which to bury his beloved: "I am a foreigner and a visitor among you. Give me property for a burial place among you, that I may bury my dead out of my sight" (Genesis 23:3). Although he had lived in the land for many, many years, he called himself a visitor. The New Testament author of the letter to the Hebrews said that Abraham regarded himself as a stranger and pilgrim in the land even after he came into the land of promise. (See Heb. 11:13). He never built a house; he always lived in tents. He recognized that the Land of Promise was not his final destination, "for he waited for the city which has foundations, whose builder and maker is God" (Heb. 11:10).

Abraham died before he reached the Land of Promise, but he saw it by faith. And because of that faith, God said, "I am not ashamed to be called his God"

An old gospel song illustrate the reality of what Abraham and Sarah experienced:

This world is not my home.

I'm just a passing through;

My treasures are laid up

Somewhere beyond the blue

The angels beckon me

From heaven's open door,

And I cant feel at home

In this world anymore

Abraham and Sarah lived a rich life, full of problems and pain and joy and wonder. They had no guarantees – save the word of a God they barely knew – when they started out. Were they so different from the way any couple are when they marry? I dare say that not one couple can claim that their marriage has been predictable, in anyway!

Christianity tells us that we are not to lay vast treasure in this world. This world is but an antechamber, a foyer, a front porch, if you will, to a vastly new kingdom. How deeply have we put down our roots in this world? Are we able to be pilgrims any longer?

How many wives, if called to leave family, friends, and family environments, would leave without hesitation to go to a distant place to serve God with their husbands? I don't mean to be missionaries to India or Africa or some exotic place. I mean to move to the inner city from the suburbs, to the country from the city, to the North from the South or relocating from the West to the East? How many wives are like Lot's wife, who turned back to look longingly at their past? Sarah looked forward, with her husband, to the promise she saw fulfilled only after she left this earth.

The people to whom Abraham spoke after Sarah died were honored. ***"You are a mighty prince among us; [in Hebrew, the words translate, "You are a prince of God"] bury your dead in the choicest of our burial places" (Genesis 23:6).***

Abraham said, "If it is your wish that I bury my dead out of my sight, hear me, and meet with Ephron the son of Zohar for me". (vs. 8).

The people interceded for Abraham, and Ephron was honored. He said, "No, my lord, here me: I give you the field and the cave that is in it; I give it to you in the presence of the sons of my people. I give it to you. Bury your dead!" (v.11).

But Abraham insisted,

"if you will give it, please here me. I will give you money for the field; take it from me and I will bury my dead there". And Ephron answered Abraham, saying to him, "My lord, listen to me, the land is worth four hundred shekels of silver..." and Abraham listened to Ephron; and Abraham weighed out the silver for Ephron which he had named in the hearing of the sons of Heth.... And after this, Abraham buried Sarah his wife in the cave of the field of Machpelah, before Mamre (that is, Hebron) in the land of Canaan. (Genesis 23:11-19).

Often when people die, they wish to be buried near their birthplace or childhood home. Abraham, however, didn't want to take Sarah back to Ur or to Haran or to any other place they had lived. Sarah's body could have been preserved for a journey by wrapping and with spices had it been desired. But Abraham chose to bury his wife in that cave in that field to lay claim to that whole country that had been promised to him, to Sarah, and to their descendants. That country was their home, and that was where they would be buried.

Abraham was buried in that same cave, beside his wife. Isaac also was buried there, and Rebekah. Jacob said when he went down to Egypt before he died, "I am to be gathered to my people; bury me with my fathers in the cave that is in the field of Ephron the Hittite, in the cave that is in the field of Machpelah" (Gen. 49:29,30). Today a vast mosque stands over the tombs of the great patriarchs and their wives in Hebron. After four thousand years, it is still holy ground.

Abraham lives on in the lives of those who share his faith. If we have the faith of Abraham, we are his children; if the same obedience, spirit, trust, and submissiveness as Sarah, her daughters.

Abraham and Sarah's story is our family album. Abraham and Sarah shared moments of excitement, of confusion, of calamity, of sadness of failure, and of triumph. Their life experiences were much the same as ours. Is God kindling your heart with a desire to share their faith?

Prayer

Father in heaven, we thank You for Your holy Word. We bless You today for Abraham and Sarah, our father and mother in the faith. We pray that You will instruct us from their lives, that we may not be foolish, but understand what Your will for us is. We pray that we may not give way to fear in fulfilling Your plans for us, but will be trust-filled and obedient.

We pray for the marriages of today, Lord – the ones that are beginning, the ones that are growing, the ones in trouble, those that are ending. Lord, You alone are most supreme, and supremely able to heal, to mend, to provide, to care for, to guide, to bless, and to restore the hand of blessing where it is needed.

Grant us ears to hear and mouths to rejoice, hearts to believe and wills to obey, that the world may see our good works but glorify You, our father in heaven, we pray in the awesome name of Jesus Christ. Amen.

Traveller's Journal

REFLECT

Is it comforting or disturbing to you to know that God has an intended order for marriage?

Have you experienced struggles similar to those experienced by Sarah? How has the Lord been present in them?

Could you, as a woman, be called Sarah's daughter?

RECOMMIT

To having your marriage for God's convenience, not your own, as much as you can.

DR.ABRAHAM PETERS

CHAPTER FIFTEEN

THE TRUST OF A TRUE BELIEVER

From the death of Sarah to the death of Abraham, only one major event is recorded. (actually, it is major incident and a small postscript. I'm saving that postscript for last, the last chapter).

Abraham was very old, his wife was dead, and he was concerned for his son, Isaac, who would inherit the covenant. He was particularly concerned that he provides a wife for his son. Genesis 24 tells the beautiful story of how Abraham provided a wife for Isaac.

It may seem strange that a father would provide a wife for his son, but that custom is still quite common in the Eastern cultures and in the Middle East, where Abraham's descendants live.

I spent one summer several years ago in West Africa, in the country of Liberia. On one occasion I spent a week about three hundred miles inland, in an interior place that was so remote they had not even heard of Africa! I was introduced by my guide to his grandfather, a man reputedly over a hundred years old. This man had over two hundred wives and children beyond counting. It is the custom in that part of the world, among the Ghia peoples of which this man was the chief, for the fathers to select wives for their sons. This was generally done when the sons were children, and boys and girls usually grew up knowing who they were to marry.

My interpreter and I spoke for a long time about the custom. He said two things that fascinated me. The first was that in his whole life he could only remember having disobeyed his father once. Once in his whole life! He said that it would not have occurred to him to have disobeyed his father, but on the one occasion that he did, it was important – he wanted to choose his own wife. He had become a Christian and wanted to choose a Christian wife. He had been married for about ten years at the time of my visit, and he said that his father still could not understand why he insisted on that choice.

The second thing I found fascinating was his statement, "There isn't anybody over here who would want to do it your way." He pointed out that among the seventeen hundred thousands Ghias, there are almost no single women. He also pointed out that divorce is virtually unknown in their culture. He said that knowing who they were going to marry made it possible for children to learn to love their intended spouses, and that's what happened most of the time. Since then, I've heard people from India and China say much the same thing. The absence of guesswork in the matter of marriage apparently has its advantages!

Abraham felt this responsibility toward Isaac keenly:

Now Abraham was old, well advanced in age; and the LORD had blessed Abraham in all things. So Abraham said to the oldest servant of his house, who ruled over all that he had, "....you shall go to my country and to my family, and take a wife for my son Isaac". And the servant said to him, "Perhaps the woman will not be willing to follow me to this land. Must I take your son back to the land from which you came?" But Abraham said to him, "Beware that you do not take my son back there. The Lord God of heaven….will send His angel before you, and you shall take a wife for my son from there. And if the woman is not willing to follow you, then you will be released from this oath" (Genesis 24:1-8).

Abraham called his chief servant to him who is Eliezer. Abraham asked the servant to promise that he would not select a wife for Isaac from among the women of the Canaanites, their neighbors. The servant posed a possible problem – what if the woman wasn't willing to follow him.

Abraham said, in effect, "Then you are absolved. You don't have to worry, though, because the God who called me into this land surely has a wife for him. He'll lead you, so you need not fear that. But, if for some reason, it doesn't work out, then you are absolved from your promise; but take my son Isaac back to the land from which I came".

Abraham was so concerned that his son not marry someone from the old culture because the Canaanites were pagans who knew nothing of the Lord God. He knew that if Isaac took a pagan wife it would be difficult, perhaps impossible, for Isaac to become the person that he was intended to be. Abraham trusted that God would complete the process He had begun. He had found God faithful in all ways, and so encouraged his servant who was to act on his behalf.

The Custom of the Day

A little bit of background on the marriage customs of the day might be helpful here. The new bride was selected by the bridegroom's parent because she would become a part of his clan. Sometimes the bride was consulted in the marriage agreement, sometimes not; in any case, her parents had the right to accept or reject the offer. The parents understood that love came after, not before, marriage. The parents chose according to the benefit the marriage would bring to the entire family, not just to the bridegroom (or the bride!).

If a young man had acquired sufficient means to make it possible for him to provide a marriage dowry, then his parents selected the girl and negotiations were begun. The father of the bridegroom called in a man to act as deputy. (Abraham's servant was his deputy). The deputy was fully informed as to the dowry the young man was willing to pay for his bride. Then, with the young man's father or some other male relative, the deputy went to the home of the young woman. (In Abraham's case, the deputy went with other servants). Once admitted to the prospective bride's home, the father of the bridegroom, if present, announced that the deputy would speak for his party. Then the bride's father would appoint a deputy to represent him.

Before the negotiations began, a drink or food would be offered to the visitors, but the visitors would refuse to partake until the mission was completed. The negotiations would then begin in earnest. Before they could be finished, there must have been consent for the hand of the young woman and agreement on the amount of dowry to be paid for her. When the agreement was made, the deputies rose, the congratulations were exchanged, and the repast was consumed as a seal of the covenant they entered into.

In the culture of Abraham's day, the family's efficiency was diminished when a woman left her family. Unmarried daughters would often tend their father's flocks, work in the field, or help out in other ways. When a woman married, she increased the efficiency of her husband's family and diminished that of her parents. The bridegroom, then, offered some sort of compensation. The dowry was often livestock, other goods, and money. If the bridegroom was unable to do that, he would offer his own service, as Jacob did for Rachel. (see Gen. 29:15-18).

Sometimes a part of the dowry would go to the bride herself. This was often in the form of coins that she would wear in her headgear, as provision should her husband divorce her. If the bride's father was able to do so, he also would provide her with other special gifts, such as servants, land, or livestock.

When the bride agreed, her relatives might escort her to the bridegroom's home. If they lived nearby, the bridegroom himself would go to escort her. If they lived far apart, she would be escorted by the deputy to the home of the bridegroom.

When Abraham's servant set out to find a bride for Isaac, he proceeded through the trackless wastes of Beersheba and Hebron where they were living, northward through Galilee, perhaps through the area now referred to as Syria, into the northwestern portion of Mesopotamia to a town by the name of Nahor, near Haran. "And he made his camels kneel down outside the city by a well of water at evening time, the time when women go out to draw water" (Genesis 24:11).

You may recall that Nahor and Haran were the names of Abraham's brothers. When the call came to Abraham to leave Ur of the Chaldees, Nahor and all of his family left, too. We know that Abraham brought his father Terah with him, and it is stated that his brother Haran died in Ur of the Chaldees before they left. It appears that Haran's family migrate with the clan of Abraham, proceeded northward, and followed the course of the Euphrates River to the northern regions before settling down. The towns were named Nahor and Haran, probably because a settlement grew up around the large family that first settled there.

The Task for Which He was sent

Abraham's servant took ten camels laden with gifts and went to Nahor. The bridegroom was obviously the son of a prosperous man. It was evening when the servant stopped at the spring just outside the village, about the time the women would come to draw water. *Then he prayed (v. 12).*

The servant could have been the one who might have been the heir himself. He could have been jealous; after all, he had been with Abraham a long time. But his sole intent was to fulfill the wishes of his master. "Then he said, 'O Lord God of my master Abraham, please give me success this day, and show kindness to my master Abraham" (v.12). Then he added:

> *Behold, here I stand by the well of water, and the daughters of the men of the city are coming out to draw water. Now let it be that the young woman to whom I say, "Please let down your pitcher that I may drink", and says, "Drink, and I will also give your camels a drink" – let her be the one You have appointed for Your servant Isaac. And by this I will know that You have shown kindness to my master." (Genesis 24:13,14).*

What extraordinary faith! We live in a day when all sorts of people imagine that God is the God of all the earth and all the people in it. That is true, if thinking of God as Creator only. He is the Creator of the whole earth, and every human being on the face of the earth is related to the Lord by virtue of creation. The relationship is sustained in some way because we all are created in His image.

But the Bible does not teach universal fatherhood. All men are not automatically brothers in the Lord. Some thirty years ago there was a phrase that went, "The Fatherhood of God, the brotherhood of man, and the neighborhood of Boston," That's wrong!

The Scripture draws a sharp distinction between those who belong to God and those who do not. Jesus said, "I know My sheep, and am known by them" (John 10:14). Others who do not know Him are not His sheep. They could be His sheep, and indeed, He wants them to be His sheep, but a believer and a nonbeliever are distinct from each other. The Spirit of God is a permanent, indwelling presence in a believer. Whatever other things a believer and a nonbeliever may have in common, at the great motivational source of their lives, there is a difference!

Abraham's servant prayed with borrowed faith. He prayed to the Lord God of his master, Abraham, and counted on God's goodness to Abraham to extend to him to act on Abraham's behalf. I think that is extraordinary! The servant had had no personal revelation, but he took the word of his master. His master's faith was good enough for him to begin with, but he was about to become a believer!

Before he had finished praying, a beautiful girl, Rebekah, came out with her pitcher on her shoulder. She went down to the well, filled her pitcher, and came up again:

And the servant ran to meet her and said, "Please let me drink a little water from your pitcher". So she said, "Drink, my Lord." Then she quickly let her pitcher down to her hand, and gave him a drink. And when she had finished giving him a drink, she said, "I will draw water for your camels also, until they had finished drinking" (Genesis 24:17-19).

Isn't that just like God? A man prayed on second-hand faith, and the very first person who came to the well met the conditions he had just set? Can you imagine how he felt? His heart must have been beating quickly when he heard those words. The servant stood there and watched as she watered the camels. As he looked at her, he no doubt was thinking, "What a beautiful girl she is. What an ideal bride for Isaac she will be!" what a faithful God his master served!

When Rebekah was finished, he asked whose daughter she was and if they could stay at her father's house. "I am a daughter of Bethuel, Milchah's son, whom she bore to Nahor," she said. "We have both straw and feed enough, and room to lodge" (vv. 24,25). The servant of Abraham knelt down and began to bless the Lord. Imagine! The Lord had brought him to the very family, the relatives of his master.

The servant gave her two bracelets and a ring for her nose, and she ran off to tell her family. She apparently left the servant standing at the spring and went to tell her mother and brother, Laban, everything that had transpired. The jewelry must have been distinctive and beautiful, for Laban ran to the spring and said to the man with the camels, "Come in, O blessed of the LORD! Why do you stand outside? For I have prepared the house, and a place for the camels" (v.31).

When Laban saw Abraham's servant for the first time, he recognized that the blessings of God rested on the servant. God's blessing was observable by others. The servant had just moved from a nonbeliever to a believer, and the blessing was obvious! It reminds me of Jesus' words on the Sermon on the Mount, "Let your light so shine before men, that they may see your good works and glorify your Father in heaven" (Matt. 5:16). And so it was with the servant of Abraham – he had seen how the Lord had blessed his master over the years, and was now personally dealing with God.

Then the man came to the house. And he unloaded the camels, and provided straw and feed for the camels, and water to wash his feet and the feet of the men who were with him. Food was set before him to eat, but he said, "I will not eat until I have told about my errand". (Gen. 24:32,33).

It was a sacred duty in that culture to offer hospitality. In fact, in Bedouin tribes, after a meal had been prepared, the head of the household would issue a call three times from a high spot to announce to any men in the are that they could come and partake of a meal. Desert men do not like to eat alone. Guests were believed to have been sent by God. And Abraham's servant certainly was, as Laban and his family were about to discover.

Laban's family had prepared a beautiful meal, but the servant was intent on the reason he had come, as a deputy for Abraham. He said, "I will not eat until I have told about my errand" (v.33). Then he told the story of his master, Abraham, and his promise not to take a wife from among the Canaanite people or from among the people whom Abraham had left behind but from among Abraham's own family. He told how he prayed at the well and how Rebekah came along and did the very thing that he had asked as a sign from the Lord.

After hearing the servant's story, Rebekah's father and brother said, "The thing comes from the LORD" (v.50). They knew something of the Lord God. They had heard of the call; their ancestor had come with Abraham out of Ur many years ago. Rebekah was Abraham's brother's granddaughter. In the two generations, the family had stepped away from the Chaldean paganism from which they had come, although they had not proceeded to the Land of Promise as Abraham had.

"Here is Rebekah before you; take her and go, and let her be your master's son's wife, as the LORD has spoken".... Then the servant brought out jewelry of silver, jewelry of gold, and clothing, and gave them to Rebekah. He also gave precious things to her brother and to her mother. (Gen. 24:51,53).

Early the next morning the servant of Abraham was ready to go when the brother and mother of Rebekah came to him and said "Let the young woman stay with us a few days, at least ten; after the she may go" (v 55). But he said, "Send me away so that I may go to my master" (v.56). The servant was so intent on accomplishing what he was sent to do that he cast all other concerns aside. Apparently the family decided to have a word with the bride-to be, and said they would have to ask Rebekah what she thought about the situation.(I'd say it was about time, wouldn't you?) They asked Rebekah if she would go with the servant, and she answered, "I will go"(v.58).

Isn't that amazing? In the short span of one day, a young woman was betrothed to a man, prepared to be married, and sent off by her family to join another household hundreds of miles away-and she was willing to go! Do you wonder why? God had put threat desire in her heart, and she had responded. She saw that God was in charge of these circumstances, and as He had moved in her heart, He would move in the heart of her husband-to-be. God can easily arrange circumstances in such a way that His providence can be discerned, His will made known, and His purpose accomplished.

Laban and her parents sent Rebekah off-probably never to see her again-with her nurse and her maids, They blessed her, saying, "Our sister, may you become/The mother of thousands of ten thousands;/And may your descendants possess/The gates of those who hate them" (Genesis 24:59). Rebekah's family knew that she would be marrying into the house of promise, that she would be marrying the very child of promise.

And Isaac went out to meditate in the field in the evening; and he lifted his eyes and looked, and there, there, the camels were coming. Then Rebekah lifted her eyes, and when she saw Isaac she dismounted from her camel ……. She took a veil and covered herself ……. And he took Rebekah and she became his wife, and he loved her, So Isaac was comforted after his mother's death. (Genesis 24:62-67)

The most important moment of the entire marriage festivity was that in which the bride entered her new home. Isaac took Rebekah to the tent of his mother, Sarah, and it is significant that they were married there, because that signified Rebekah's place as head of the household next to Isaac. Most likely, there was a great gathering of the clan to welcome Isaac's bride. Some of the older women may have had to duty of preparing the bride for the marriage, dressing her with special clothing and arranging her hair, the bride's hair would from this time on be concealed beneath a thick veil, and her face would be veiled in public. The marriage ceremony would become feast. Isaac was no doubt the most delighted man suited in every way to accomplish the mission God had in mind.

The story of Isaac and Rebekah is a four-thousand-year-old love story that speaks to us today. From Abraham, we learn of a father's concern for his son's well-being. That might marry the right person son from among those of the family of faith. From the servant, we learn of obedience, bathed in prayer, Lord, lead me to the one you have. Chosen.

Yesterday, Today, Forever!

When young people come to me, eager to be married, I explain the principles of God's idea for marriage and go through the ceremony line by line with them. Once a young woman came to me without her fiancé to discuss my officiating as her marriage. I asked her, "Is the young man you're contemplating marrying a Christian?"

She answered, "Well, no he's not, but you'd like him very much!"

"I'm sure I would", I answered, "but is he a believer?"

"Well, not really, but I know he will become one after we are married. Besides that, I really believe I'm being led of the Lord to marry him!"

I had to say to her, "No, you're not. That's deception! God will not lead you to violate His commandments".

I do not believe that a Christian is even, under any circumstances, led to marry a nonbeliever: "A wife is bound by law as long as her husband lives; but if her husband dies, she is at liberty to be married to whom she wishes, only in the Lord" (1 Corinthians

7:39). Also, "Do not be unequally yoked together with unbelievers. For what fellowship has righteousness with lawlessness? (1 Cor. 6:14).

The young woman said to me, "Yes, but I know a lot of unbelievers who are wonderful people!"

"So do I", I admitted.

"And I know a lot of believers who are creeps!"

"And so do I", I replied, "but I am not talking about that. I am simply saying that at the root of their being, there is an absolute and total distinction, a foundational difference between those who know and love the Lord and recognize the voice of the shepherd and follow Him, and those who do not."

"But he's very well educated...."

Yes, but you can be an educated sinner. Your base of operation is in opposition to the Lord. We're talking about something much deeper than the surface of a person's life. We're dealing with change at the roots!"

"Nobody's perfect", she said.

"Believers are not perfect by any stretch of the imagination, but they follow the Lord who knows the perfect plan for them. That's not true of an unbeliever. Would you want to marry a person who was not able to hear the plan of the Lord, who was unable to follow the path to God's best for you?" I eventually had to say to her, "I cannot marry you because I will not, cannot, bless what God will not bless. Do you understand?"

I don't know if she did or didn't understand. I didn't see her again. I don't know if she married the young man, and if she did, how they are doing. On a number of occasions I have recommended that a couple be married by a justice of the peace, which is honorable if two unbelievers are uniting or an unbeliever and a believer. But I can't sanction a marriage that God won't.

Scripture addresses other questions regarding marriage. *What happens if neither one is a Christian believer when married, and then one is converted?* Well, the problem is the same, but it assumes a different dimension. If the unbelieving partner is willing to remain in the marriage, the believer is not to seek in any way to depart from the marriage. If the unbeliever seeks to break the marriage, then the believer is not under law in that manner. (See 1 Cor. 7:12-15).

What if I make the wrong decision? If the wrong decision has been made and only now understood, there is good news. God is a God who is able to mend broken things, and He can redeem situations that are not as he would have them. If the heart is set to do right, even if the marriage is a disaster, God can redeem that situation so that good will come out of it. It takes faith for me to say these things to you, but it's true, it's absolutely true.

On a human level, it would be possible for any one of us to marry perhaps a thousand different people or more, and we could probably build some sort of life with any of them. But I also believe that the God who directs our lives has selected somebody for us. I believe that if it is in the will and purpose of God for us to be married, He has somebody in mind! The principle is that we are to avoid unequal yoking. We are to marry only within the family of faith, if we are believers. Each of us is to marry the person God has chosen, just as Isaac married Rebecca.

If you are a person with this dilemma, you can commit the whole situation to the Lord! You can pray that God will guide you and keep you from making the wrong decision. If you have children who are not yet married, you can make this a matter for prayer as well. Pray for your son-in-law, or daughter-in-law, even if your child is yet an infant. Pray that God will lead your child and your child's future partner together. I believe that the God who has bound us into a covenant family will indeed provide the answer.

Do you dare to believe that God is able to take your life, your marriage, your family, and work through them in a way that will manifest His blessing and His purpose?

Abraham, thank you for your concern.

Servant, friend, and deputy, thank you for your obedience.

Isaac, thank you for your experience and for reminding us that our God is behind all the circumstances of life and wants to work in all circumstances.

Father, we thank You or the wonder of Your love for us. We thank You for the example of love of Abraham for You and for his son, for the love of his servant for his master, and for the love of Isaac for his father, and for Rebekah.

We thank You for the amazing story of Your purposes being worked out in spite of time and distance; and for the great joy that is ours when we are in line with Your will. Grant that we may increase in obedience and understanding, in faith and strength. We ask it in the precious name of Jesus Christ. Amen.

Traveller's Journal

REFLECT

If you are a parent: what would you look for in your child's mate?

If you are yet to marry: what would you look for in your own mate?

Do you trust that choice to God in daily prayer?

Is your faith in God's guidance second-hand, or your own?

How has He worked on your behalf, and on behalf of those you love?

RECOMMIT

To seeking the guidance of God in all of the matters in life.

God misses no opportunity to make His divine plans and purpose known – remember the servant of Abraham.

THE FOOTPRINTS OF FAITH

CHAPTER SIXTEEN

THE END OF THE JOURNEY

We have come to the end of our journey, walking with the Lord through the personhood of Abraham. All earthly lives come to an end, and Abraham died. I mentioned in the last chapter that between the death of Sarah and the death of Sarah and the death of Abraham there was a major incident (the passing of the heritage to Isaac) and a small postscript.

The postscript? "Abraham again took a wife" (Genesis 25:1). Dare I call that event a postscript? There is really no way to know whether Abraham did this after the death of Sarah, she is only mentioned afterwards.

Her name was Keturah. And she bored him Zimran, Jokshan, Medan, Midian, Ishbak, and Shuah. [six sons]. Jokshan begot Sheba and Dedan. And the sons of Dedan were Asshurim, Letushim and Leummin. And the sons of Midian were Ephah, Epher, Hanoch, Abidah, and Eldaah. All these were the children of Keturah. (Genesis 25:1-4).

Interstingly, Keturah, the name of Abraham's "new" wife, means "the perfumed one". We know nothing about Keturah's background or her life. We know only about her offspring. She bore Abraham six sons, and some of the grandsons were named, along with some of the tribes that proceeded from Abraham and Keturah. Their son Midian was the father of the Midianites, who have an important part to play in the Old Testamnet. The Midianites were the enemies of Israel. Gideon, one of the judges, fought agains and defeated the Midianites.

We need to know about Keturah and her offspring because many Arabian nations proceeded from her union with Abraham. The land of Midian is what we today call Saudi Arabia. Mecca, which is the world headquarters of the Islamic faith, is home to a tribe of people who are known by the name Keturah, and they trace their origins to the wife of Abraham.

Abraham had three distinct lines of descendants:

(1) Hagar's son Ishmael, his eldest, who fathered twelve sons that headed twelve major tribes of Arabia:

(2) Keturah's six sons, who also became his Arabian descendants; and

(3) Sarah's son Isaac, who was the child of promise given by the Lord to Abraham.

But of all the descendants of Abraham, the covenant was to be established through Isaac, the son of Sarah, and not through the sons of Hagar and Keturah.

And Abraham gave all that he had to Isaac. But Abraham gave gifts to the sons of the concubines which Abraham had; and while he was still living he sent them eastward, away from Isaac his son, to the country of the east. (Genesis 25:5-6).

While Abraham was still living, he gave gifts to the sons of his concubines. He gave to them out of his vast possessions. He was a very wealthy man, greatly blessed by the Lord, and well able to provide for all of his sons. Abraham gave the sons of Keturah gifts and then sent them away from his son Isaac to the lands of the east, as he had earlier sent Hagar and Ishmael away. Abraham did not want any but Isaac to have any claim on the land of Canaan. Abraham saw to it while he was living that they would be separated.

The Lord originally had told to Abraham that he would be a father of many nations. (See. Gen. 17:5). Not just one, but many nations. There would be a multiplicity of nations, and Ishmael himself was father of twelve, even as Jacob, son of Isaac, would be father of the twelve tribes of Israel. The sons of Keturah settled in the east side of Canaan, and the sons of Ishmael settled in what we today call the Sinai Peninsula east of Egypt.

These were Ishmael's sons, and these are the names of the twelve tribal rulers according to their settlements and camps. Altogether, Ishmael lived a hundred and thirty-seven years. He breathed his last and died, and he was gathered to his people. His descendants settled in the area from Havilah to Shur, near the border of Egypt, as you go toward Assur. And they lived in hostility toward all their brothers. (Genesis 25:16-18).

The prophetic description of Ishmael before his birth declared that he would be, among other things, "a wild man" and that his hand would be "against every man". (See Genesis 16:12). At his death, that prophecy was echoed in its fulfillment.

The Arab peoples of the world all trace their identity to Abraham, and the Islamic people all trace their origins back to him as well. The fact that the OPEC nations can't get together is symptomatic of their heritage! Not too many years ago, a group of Arab states controlled the flow of oil into the non-OPEC states. Those Arabs states had the power to paralyze absolutely the western world, and we could do nothing about it. We rationed gas and stayed in line for great periods of time, and we were horrified to find ourselves at their mercy.

It was a difficult time, but it wasn't a long siege; the sheiks eventually began arguing among themselves, and their stronghold was broken. They couldn't "get their act together" – and they never could, at any time in history. If they ever could, they could siphon off the resources of the western world and virtually hold it hostage. Abdel Nasser tried to establish what he called the United Arab Republic, but it never got off the ground. It wasn't united, for one thing, and it wasn't a republic, for the other. Their only common denominator was that they were Arabs. And four thousand years of history have shown that they eventually will lift their hands against one another.

Scripture reveals that those sons of Abraham were going to constitute a mighty force on the face of the earth, and prophecy has been fulfilled. They are a vast multitude of peoples, and they are all out of sync with their brothers.

Abraham fairly and lovingly provided for the offspring he produced. There was no question of his love for his sons. Yet Abraham must have wanted to separate Isaac from his other sons to protect the covenant according to God's instruction. It may well be that he would have wanted the covenant to include all of his sons to protect the covenant according to God's instructions. It may well be that he would have wanted the covenant to include all of his sons; we know that Ishmael was rejected and that Abraham understood that his rejection was the sovereign purpose of God being worked out.

This is the sun of the years of Abraham's life which he lived: one hundred and seventy-five years. Then Abraham, breathed his last and died in a good old age, gathered to his people. (Genesis 25:7-8).

The phrase *gathered to his people* means simply that Abraham died. Another expression that means the same is *slept with his forefathers*. Both expressions are figures of speech.

And his sons Isaac and Ishmael buried him in the cave of Machpelah, which is before Mamre, in the field of Ephron the son of Zohar the Hittite, the field which Abraham purchased from the sons of Heth. There Abraham was buried, and Sarah his wife. And it come to pass, after the death of Abraham, that God blessed his son Isaac. And Isaac dwelt at Beer Lahai Roi. (Genesis 25:9-11).

What happens at funerals is interesting. People who don't get along in life can come together for a few peaceful hours at funerals. I've seen it happen scores of times. Families who are divided for one reason or another put aside their differences to pay their last respects for one of their kin. It was the same principle with Isaac and Ishmael.

Think of the tension that might possibly have been there! Ishmael was the firstborn son, and he had every reason – in the world's terms, that is – to believe he would inherit everything from his father. When Isaac was weaned, Ishmael and his mother were sent away, permanently. There is no reference to any further contact between Abraham and his son Ishmael or to any between Isaac and Ishmael during those years. I'm not suggesting that there was any antagonism; we don't know for sure. Scripture specifies only that Ishmael would live in hostility.

A View of the Church

Another difference among Abraham's offspring has profound importance for the church. In the book of Galatians, Paul addressed the jealousy that had arisen among the Jews as more and more Gentiles were converted to faith in Christ. The very first Christians were Jews who accepted Jesus as the Messiah, and they were dominant for a short period of time. Very quickly, though, more Gentiles were being converted than Jews.

The question arose in the church: "Do people have to become Jews before they become Christians?" some said yes and some said no. Those who said yes said that men had to be circumcised, and this edict was presented to all Gentiles who were being converted. Paul, however, said that circumcision was not necessary for Gentiles, that the New Covenant was not dependent upon the Old Covenant. A crisis of faith arose, and the first council of the church was held. The record of this meeting is found in Acts 15.

Some men who came down form Judea to Antioch taught that unless circumcision was performed, believers could not be saved. This teaching brought Paul and Barnabas into sharp dispute with them. The decision ultimately was made in favor of what Paul proclaimed, that Gentiles did not have to enter the Old Covenant rites in order to become a Christian and that salvation does not come by fulfilling a set of laws.

Paul wrote in Galatians 4:21:

Tell me, you who desire to be under the law, do you not hear the law? For it is written that Abraham had two sons: the one by a bondwoman, the other by a freewoman. But he who was of the bondwoman was born according to the flesh, and he of the freewoman through promise.

There is nothing mysterious about the birth of Ishmael. He was conceived by the physical union of Abraham and the bondwoman, Hagar. The son of the freewoman, Sarah, was born as the result of an act of God in fulfillment of His promise. The apostle maintained that these could be taken figuratively, for the women symbolize two covenants: one made with Abraham (the flesh), the other made through Jesus (the promise).

The covenant with Abraham was confirmed from Mount Sinai, and it bore children who were destined to be slaves. Figuratively speaking, Hagar stands for mount Sinai, in Arabia, and corresponds to the city of Jerusalem, because she was in slavery with her children, "But the Jerusalem above is free, which is the mother of us all" (Galatians 4:26).

Paul used the two children and their mothers to illustrate a profound truth: that there are two kinds of religion, one of human effort, the other of grace and promise.

Now we, brethren, as Isaac was, are children of promise. But, as he was born according to the flesh then persecuted him who was born according to the Spirit, even so it is now. Nevertheless what does the Scripture say? "Cast out the bondwoman and her son, for the son of the bondwoman shall not be heir with the son of the freewoman. So then, brethren, we are not children of the bondwoman but of the free. (Galatians 4:28-31).

Hagar, Abraham's concubine, represented his attempt to operate on the basis of his own understanding. Sarah, his wife, simply depended upon the gift of God. They represent the two covenants. The Old Covenant was of works, and the New of grace. Paul said that the great tragedy is (and I can echo it today) that people want to rely on the things they can do to establish a relationship with God, and so are like children of Hagar. Paul wanted us to know that we are saved by grace, received through faith in what God has done, does, and can do, alone. Man's effort to control God didn't work for Abraham, and it doesn't work for the people in churches today.

In liturgical churches the tendency is to trust in the ceremony. Some churches teach that grace of God is received simply by receiving the sacraments. And that's not true. Paul said that we can eat and drink damnation to ourselves by receiving the Eucharistic elements and not perceiving the Lord who called us to them. (See 1 Corinthians 11:29)

Worship is not form; it is not automatic. We don't worship simply by sitting through a church service. Scripture says that worship is offering ourselves as living sacrifices to the Lord. (See Romans 12:1). Whatever we do in our worship services, we have to keep in mind the reality that lies behind the form. God deals with us through our response to Him in faith, even if we don't fully understand. Paul used Abraham's wives to illustrate that point, and it is relevant to our churches today.

The Legacy of Abraham

Abraham was buried with Sarah in the cave he had purchased, the only property he wanted to own. Isaac and Rebekah also would be buried there, and Jacob, too, would join them in that same cave at their lives' end. In Hebron today, a vast, fortress like building stands over the cave of Machphelah. It is a Moslem mosque, but also contains a Jewish segment and a Christian segment. Once when I was in Israel with my brother, we rented a car and drove out to Hebron. We happened to be there at a time when three services were going on at the same time in Abraham's tomb. Muslims were in the main area; a small group of Jews were in another area; and some Christians were there to worship, also. How this spoke to me of the heritage of this man! Gathered at his burial place were representative of the three great monotheistic faiths of the world. This man, who lived four thousand years ago, had exercised an immense influence on the human race, far greater than he could have thought when he first heard the call of God in Ur of the Chaldees.

Two aspects of Abraham's walk with God impress me; that he was a servant of God and that he was a friend of God.

Abraham was the servant of God. In Genesis 26:24, the Lord spoke to Isaac, Abraham's son:

And the LORD appeared to him the same night and said, "I am the God of your father Abraham; do not fear, for I am with you. I will bless you and multiply your descendants for My servant Abraham's sake".

God spoke to Abraham as His servant, and Abraham saw himself as the servant of the Lord. It is characteristic of a servant to be obedient to his master; and obedience is a great virtue, with many consequences. God honored Abraham for his obedience.

In the New Testament, Paul called himself a slave of Jesus. (See Romans 1:1). Another term used in some translations in "bondslave", and sometimes this is translated to "underrower". The term underwater refers to the lowest slave in the slave galley in a ship. Underowers were absolutely worthless, in their own eyes and in the eyes of those who drove them, often to their deaths.

Neither you nor I would aspire to be slave or a servant. We would far rather be masters than slaves. After all, who would want to constantly take orders from others? To be controlled by others? Paul wanted this, and he identified himself as much. (See. Rom. 1:1)

It is a paradox that when we serve the Lord Jesus Christ we have the exhilarating feeling of being absolutely, totally free. That is what Jesus meant when He said, "He who finds his life will lose it, and he who loses his life for My sale will find it" (Matt. 10:39).

When Jesus met with His disciples to keep the Passover, the usual household servant – whose duty it was to wash the feet of the travelers – were not present. It was certain that the disciples were not about to do it. After all, they were the Lord's right-hand men! Such a lowly duty was clearly beneath their dignity. Imagine how they must have felt when, without a word, Jesus got up, took off His raiment, girded Himself with a cloth, took a basin of water, and bent to wash their feet. What shame, that they would not do what their Master knew was needed.

When He finished, He girded Himself again, took His place, and said, "You call Me Teacher and Lord, and you say well, for so I am" (John 13:13). And then He drew the inevitable conclusion, "If I then, your Lord and Teacher, have washed your feet, you also ought to wash one another's feet" (John 13:14)

Jesus was talking about an attitude of servant hood. Nobody was willing to do the dirty work, but everybody wanted to be part of the prayers, teaching, healings and miracles.

When I was a boy, I used to play "King of the Mountain" – and I was good at it, too. The mountain could be a pile of snow, a great rock, a mound of dirt, a sand dune, anything. The king would have to get to the top of the heap and beat off all newcomers. I didn't realize when I was playing that game so successfully that I was acting out on a minor scale the whole human enterprise. Our world tells us that the position on top of things is the desired position, not the one on the bottom. We didn't need to be taught the never-mind-who-you-step-on-to-get-there philosophy, we just did it! Once on top, we had to hold the territory. So it wasn't just getting there that was important, it was staying there. Our decisions on the top affected those climbing up and those on the bottom, too.

Jesus said:

Yet it shall not be so among you; but whoever desires to become great among you, let him be your servant. And whoever desires to be first among you, let him be your slave – just as the Son of Man did not come to be served, but to serve, and to give His life a ransom for many (Matthew 20:26-28).

The posture of supremacy does not make a favorable impression on the world or on the church. If we could hear each of Abraham's children say more consistently, "I am a servant of the Lord," the impact would be tremendous!

Abraham was the friend of God. King Jehoshaphat Prayed:

O LORD God of our fathers, are You not God in heaven, and do You not rule over all the kingdoms of the nations, and in Your hand is there not power and might, so that no one is able to withstand You? Are You not our God, who drove out the inhabitants of this land before Your people Israel, and gave it to the descendants of *Abraham Your friend forever?* (2 Chronicles 20:6-7, emphasis mine).

And the Lord said:

But you, Israel, are My servant, Jacob whom I have chosen, The descendants of Abraham My friend (Isa. 41:8, emphasis mine).

Imagine being called a friend of God! I can more imagine being called a servant of God, but a friend? You know the old saying that you can tell a person by the friends he keeps. The Old Testament prophets said, "Can two walk together, unless they are agreed?" (Amos 3:3). And Jesus said,:You are My friends if you do whatever I command you" (John 15:14)

Servants have to obey; friends choose to agree. Friends want to please those who befriend them, and that's the attitude of the New Covenant. The Old Covenant, is contrast, was a series of do-this-or-else- laws. It is easier to do that which we want to do; it is altogether different with that which we have to do. Under the New Covenant, we can respond as we yield to the Spirit, who inclines our hearts to do God wants.

Abraham walked with God and obeyed Him. He was His servant, but he was also His friend. Abraham is "the father of all those who believe" (Romans 4:11). A vast number of people claim Abraham as their father – the Jews, the Arabs, his linear descendants of flesh and blood, and those children of his spirit, the children of faith.

And he (Abraham) received the sign of circumcision, a seal of righteousness of the faith which he had while still uncircumcised, that righteousness might be imputed to them also. (Romans 4:11). Abraham is the father of Gentiles who did not receive the covenantal sign, the father of the Jews who were circumcised, and the father of those who believe, trust, and have faith in the Lord God.

And [he is] the father of circumcision to those who not only are of the circumcision, but who also walk in the steps of the faith which our father Abraham had while still uncircumcised. (Romans 4:12).

To unbelievers who claimed to be Abraham's children, Jesus said, "You are of your father the devil, and the desires of your father you want to do" (John 8:44). If Abraham's children, those people would be people of faith, because Abraham believed and obeyed. Abraham is the father only of those who walk in his footsteps.

Therefore it is of faith that it might be according to grace, so that the promise might be sure to all the seed, not only to those who are of the law, but also to those who are of the faith of Abraham, who is the father of us all (as it is written, "I have made you a father of many nations") in the presence of Him whom he believed. (Romans 4:16-17)

Are you a child of Abraham? Walk in his footsteps. Don't claim descent through a sacramental sign. You could be baptized, confirmed, even ordained, and not be His servant. You could be born again and baptized in the Spirit, and not be His friend.

Have you named God's people as your people? Do you feel at home in the family of God? Do you feel as if it's a place where you can give of yourself and be accepted, as well as take in all that is offered?

Have you understood the scenes as we walked with our father, Abraham, through the family album? God has called us to be His faithful people, His servants, His friends, and His children.

Prayer

Heavenly Father, thank You for taking us, different people though we are, through our common heritage. Thank You for Abraham, the rock from which we were cut, the quarry from which we were hewn, and for Sarah, our mother. Help us to sense somehow the oneness of the vast family of faith that is our inheritance. Help us to sense that we belong to one another, and teach us not to despise other members of the family or to say to them, "I have no need of you". We pray for Your family, Lord, all over the world. We know that family is not called by the name of any denomination, or nation, or race. We pray that You would give us the grace to transcend all human labels and man-made divisions and sense that, at the very depths of our hearts, we are one and we belong together with all who know and love You, all who have heard Your call into covenant and have responded in faith.

We pray that You will bind the company of all Your faithful people into the kind of fellowship where we may strengthen and mutually encourage one another in our common walk with You. We ask it in the precious name of Jesus Christ. Amen.

Traveller's Journal

REFLECT

Are you a child of the bondwoman or a child of the freewoman in terms of your worship of God?

Could you be called a servant of God? How about an underrower?

Could you be called God's friend?

RECOMMIT

To walking in the footsteps of our father, Abraham.

DR.ABRAHAM PETERS

Epilogue

Hebrews 11 Encountering the hall of fame of faithAnd their Life Lessons:

[1] Now faith is the substance of things hoped for, the evidence of things not seen.

The definition of faith given in this verse, and exemplified in the various instances following, undoubtedly includes justifying faith, but not directly as justifying. For faith justifies only as it refers to, and depends on, Christ. But here is no mention of him as the object of faith; and in several of the instances that follow, no notice is taken of him or his salvation, but only of temporal blessings obtained by faith. And yet they may all be considered as evidences of the power of justifying faith in Christ, and of its extensive exercise in a course of steady obedience amidst difficulties and dangers of every kind.

Now faith is the subsistence of things hoped for, the evidence or conviction of things not seen — Things hoped for are not so extensive as things not seen. The former are only things future and joyful to us ; the latter are either future, past, or present, and those either good or evil, whether to us or others. The subsistence of things hoped for - Giving a kind of present subsistence to the good things which God has promised: the divine supernatural evidence exhibited to, the conviction hereby produced in, a believer of things not seen, whether past, future, or spiritual; particularly of God and the things of God.

Verse 2 For by it the elders obtained a good report.

By it the elders — Our forefathers. This chapter is a kind of summary of the Old Testament, in which the apostle comprises the designs, labours, sojournings, expectations, temptations, martyrdoms of the ancients. The former of them had a long exercise of their patience; the latter suffered shorter but sharper trials.

Obtained a good testimony — A most comprehensive word. God gave a testimony, not only of them but to them: and they received his testimony as if it had been the things themselves of which he testified, Hebrews 11:4,5,39. Hence they also gave testimony to others, and others testified of them.

Verse 3 Through faith we understand that the worlds were framed by the word of God, so that things which are seen were not made of things which do appear.

By faith we understand that the worlds — Heaven and earth and all things in them, visible and invisible.

Where made — Formed, fashioned, and finished.

By the word — The sole command of God, without any instrument or preceding matter. And as creation is the foundation and specimen of the whole divine economy, so faith in the creation is the foundation and specimen of all faith.

So that things which are seen — As the sun, earth, stars.

Were made of things which do not appear — Out of the dark, unapparent chaos, Genesis 1:2. And this very chaos was created by the divine power; for before it was thus created it had no existence in nature.

Verse 4 By faith Abel offered unto God a more excellent sacrifice than Cain, by which he obtained witness that he was righteous, God testifying of his gifts: and by it he being dead yet speaketh.

By faith — In the future Redeemer.

Abel offered a more excellent sacrifice — The firstlings of his flock, implying both a confession of what his own sins deserved, and a desire of sharing in the great atonement.

Than Cain — Whose offering testified no such faith, but a bare acknowledgment of God the Creator. By which faith he obtained both righteousness and a testimony of it: God testifying - Visibly that his gifts were accepted; probably by sending fire from heaven to consume his sacrifice, a token that justice seized on the sacrifice instead of the sinner who offered it.

And by it — By this faith.

Being dead, he yet speaketh — That a sinner is accepted only through faith in the great sacrifice.

Verse 5 By faith Enoch was translated that he should not see death; and was not found, because God had translated him: for before his translation he had this testimony, that he pleased God.

Enoch was not any longer found among men, though perhaps they sought for him as they did for Elijah, 2 Kings 2:17.

He had this testimony — From God in his own conscience.

Verse 6 But without faith it is impossible to please him: for he that cometh to God must believe that he is, and that he is a rewarder of them that diligently seek him.

But without faith — Even some divine faith in God, it is impossible to please him.

For he that cometh to God — in prayer, or another act of worship, must believe that he is.

Verse 7 By faith Noah, being warned of God of things not seen as yet, moved with fear, prepared an ark to the saving of his house; by the which he condemned the world, and became heir of the righteousness which is by faith.

Noah being warned of things not seen as yet — Of the future deluge. Moved with fear, prepared an ark, by which open testimony he condemned the world - Who neither believed nor feared.

Verse 8 By faith Abraham, when he was called to go out into a place which he should after receive for an inheritance, obeyed; and he went out, not knowing whither he went.

Genesis 12:1,4,5

Verse 9 By faith he sojourned in the land of promise, as in a strange country, dwelling in tabernacles with Isaac and Jacob, the heirs with him of the same promise:

By faith he sojourned in the land of promise — The promise was made before, Genesis 12:7.

Dwelling in tents — As a sojourner With Isaac and Jacob - Who by the same manner of living showed the same faith Jacob was born fifteen years before the death of Abraham.

The joint heirs of the same promise — Having all the same interest therein. Isaac did not receive this inheritance from Abraham, nor Jacob from Isaac, but all of them from God. Genesis 17:8

Verse 10 For he looked for a city which hath foundations, whose builder and maker is God.

He looked for a city which hath foundations — Whereas a tent has none.

Whose builder and former is God — Of which God is the sole contriver, former, and finisher.

Verse 11 Through faith also Sara herself received strength to conceive seed, and was delivered of a child when she was past age, because she judged him faithful who had promised.

Sarah also herself — Though at first she laughed at the promise, Genesis 18:12. Genesis 21:2.

Verse 12 Therefore sprang there even of one, and him as good as dead, so many as the stars of the sky in multitude, and as the sand which is by the sea shore innumerable.

As it were dead — Till his strength was supernaturally restored, which continued for many years after.

Verse 13 These all died in faith, not having received the promises, but having seen them afar off, and were persuaded of them, and embraced them, and confessed that they were strangers and pilgrims on the earth.

All these — - Mentioned Hebrews 11:7-11.

Died in faith — In death faith acts most vigorously.

Not having received the promises — The promised blessings.

Embraced — As one does a dear friend when he meets him.

Verse 14 For they that say such things declare plainly that they seek a country.

They who speak thus show plainly that they seek their own country — That they keep in view, and long for, their native home.

Verse 15 And truly, if they had been mindful of that country from whence they came out, they might have had opportunity to have returned.

If they had been mindful of - Their earthly country, Ur of the Chaldeans, they might have easily returned.

Verse 16 But now they desire a better country, that is, an heavenly: wherefore God is not ashamed to be called their God: for he hath prepared for them a city.

But they desire a better country, that is, an heavenly — This is a full convincing proof that the patriarchs had a revelation and a promise of eternal glory in heaven. Therefore God is not ashamed to be called their God: seeing he hath prepared for them a city - Worthy of God to give.

Verse 17 By faith Abraham, when he was tried, offered up Isaac: and he that had received the promises offered up his only begotten son,

By faith Abraham — When God made that glorious trial of him.

Offered up Isaac — The will being accepted as if he had actually done it.

Yea, he that had received the promises — Particularly that grand promise, "In Isaac shall thy seed be called." Offered up - This very son; the only one he had by Sarah. Genesis 22:1,etc.

Verse 18 Of whom it was said, That in Isaac shall thy seed be called:

In Isaac shall thy seed be called — From him shall the blessed seed spring. Genesis 21:12.

Verse 19 Accounting that God was able to raise him up, even from the dead; from whence also he received him in a figure.

Accounting that God was able even to raise him from the dead — Though there had not been any instance of this in the world.

From whence also — To speak in a figurative way.

He did receive him — Afterwards, snatched from the jaws of death.

Verse 20 By faith Isaac blessed Jacob and Esau concerning things to come.

Blessed — Genesis 27:27,39; prophetically foretold the particular blessings they should partake of.

Jacob and Esau — Preferring the elder before the younger.

Verse 21 By faith Jacob, when he was a dying, blessed both the sons of Joseph; and worshipped, leaning upon the top of his staff.

Jacob when dying — That is, when near death. Bowing down on the top of his staff - As he sat on the side of his bed. Genesis 48:16; Genesis 47:31

Verse 22 By faith Joseph, when he died, made mention of the departing of the children of Israel; and gave commandment concerning his bones.

Concerning his bones — To be carried into the land of promise.

Verse 23 By faith Moses, when he was born, was hid three months of his parents, because they saw he was a proper child; and they were not afraid of the king's commandment.

They saw — Doubtless with a divine presage of things to come.

Verse 24 By faith Moses, when he was come to years, refused to be called the son of Pharaoh's daughter;

Refused to be called — Any longer.

Verse 26 Esteeming the reproach of Christ greater riches than the treasures in Egypt: for he had respect unto the recompense of the reward.

The reproach of Christ — That which he bore for believing in the Messiah to come, and acting accordingly.

For he looked off — From all those perishing treasures, and beyond all those temporal hardships Unto the recompense of reward - Not to an inheritance in Canaan; he had no warrant from God to look for this, nor did he ever attain it; but what his believing ancestors looked for,-a future state of happiness in heaven.

Verse 27 By faith he forsook Egypt, not fearing the wrath of the king: for he endured, as seeing him who is invisible.

By faith he left Egypt — Taking all the Israelites with him. Not then fearing the wrath of the king - As he did many years before, Exodus 2:14. Exodus 14:15, etc.

Verse 28 Through faith he kept the Passover, and the sprinkling of blood, lest he that destroyed the firstborn should touch them.

The pouring out of the blood — Of the paschal lamb, which was sprinkled on the door-posts, lest the destroying angel should touch the Israelites. Exodus 12:12-18.

Verse 29 By faith they passed through the Red sea as by dry land: which the Egyptians assaying to do were drowned.

They — Moses, Aaron, and the Israelites.

Passed the Red Sea — It washed the borders of Edom, which signifies red. Thus far the examples are cited from Genesis and Exodus; those that follow are from the former and the latter Prophets.

Verse 30 By faith the walls of Jericho fell down, after they were compassed about seven days.

By the faith of Joshua.

Verse 31 By faith the harlot Rahab perished not with them that believed not, when she had received the spies with peace.

Rahab — Though formerly one not of the fairest character.

Verse 32 And what shall I more say? for the time would fail me to tell of Gedeon, and of Barak, and of Samson, and of Jephthae; of David also, and Samuel, and of the prophets:

After Samuel, the prophets are properly mentioned. David also was a prophet; but he was a king too.

The prophets — Elijah, Elisha, etc., including likewise the believers who lived with them.

Verses 33-34

[33] Who through faith subdued kingdoms, wrought righteousness, obtained promises, stopped the mouths of lions, [34] Quenched the violence of fire, escaped the edge of the sword, out of weakness

were made strong, waxed valiant in fight, turned to flight the armies of the aliens.

David, in particular, subdued kingdoms. Samuel (not excluding the rest) wrought righteousness. The prophets, in general, obtained promises, both for themselves, and to deliver to others. Prophets also stopped the mouths of lions, as Daniel; and quenched the violence of fire, as Shadrach, Meshach, and Abednego. To these examples, whence the nature of faith clearly appears, those more ancient ones are subjoined, (by a transposition, and in an inverted order,) which receive light from these. Jephthah escaped the edge of the sword; Samson out of weakness was made strong; Barak became valiant in fight; Gideon put to flight armies of the aliens. Faith animates to the most heroic enterprises, both civil and military. Faith overcomes all impediments effects the greatest things; attains to the very best; and inverts, by its miraculous power the very course of nature. 2 Samuel 8:1,etc.; 1 Samuel 8:9,etc.; 1 Samuel 13:3,etc.; Daniel 6:22; Daniel 3:27; Judges 12:3; Judges 15:19,etc.; Judges 16:28,etc.; Judges 4:14,etc.; Judges 7:21.

Verse 35 Women received their dead raised to life again: and others were tortured, not accepting deliverance; that they might obtain a better resurrection:

Women — Naturally weak.

Received their dead — Children.

Others were tortured — From those who acted great things the apostle rises higher, to those who showed the power of faith by suffering.

Not accepting deliverance — On sinful terms.

That they might obtain a better resurrection — An higher reward, seeing the greater their sufferings the greater would be their glory. 1 Kings 17:22; 2 Kings 4:35

Verse 36 And others had trial of cruel mockings and scourgings, yea, moreover of bonds and imprisonment:

And others — The apostle seems here to pass on to recent examples.

Verse 37 They were stoned, they were sawn asunder, were tempted, were slain with the sword: they wandered about in sheepskins and goatskins; being destitute, afflicted, tormented;

They were sawn asunder — As, according to the tradition of the Jews, Isaiah was by Manasseh.

Were tempted — Torments and death are mentioned alternately. Every way; by threatenings, reproaches, tortures, the variety of which cannot be expressed; and again by promises and allurements.

Verse 38 (Of whom the world was not worthy:) they wandered in deserts, and in mountains, and in dens and caves of the earth.

Of whom the world was not worthy — It did not deserve so great a blessing.

They wandered — Being driven out from men.

Verse 39 And these all, having obtained a good report through faith, received not the promise:

And all these — Though they obtained a good testimony, Hebrews 11:2, yet did not receive the great promise, the heavenly inheritance.

Verse 40 God having provided some better thing for us, that they without us should not be made perfect.

God having provided some better thing for us — Namely, everlasting glory.

That they might not be perfected without us — That is, that we might all be perfected together in heaven.

THE LIST OF KINDS OF FAITH IDENTIFIED IN THE NEW TESTAMENT

1. Great Faith - Matthew 8:10-28

2. Weak Faith - Romans 14:1

3. Little Faith - Luke 12:28

4. Saving Faith - Ephesians 2:8

5. Healing Faith - Mark 10:52

6. Dead Faith - James 2:17, 26

7. Strong Faith - Romans 4:20-21

8. Rich Faith - James 2:5

9. Mustard Seed Faith - Matthew 17:20

10. Overcoming Faith - 1 John 5:4

11. Growing Faith - 2 Thessalonians 1:3

12. Creative Faith - Hebrews 11:3

13. Praying Faith - James 5:14-15

14. Tried Faith - 1 Peter 1:7

15. Measure of Faith - Romans 12:3

16. Justifying Faith - Romans 5:1

17. Perfect Faith - James 2:22

18. Word of Faith - Romans 10:8

19. Purifying Faith - Acts 15:8-9

20. Sanctifying Faith - Acts 26:18

THE FOOTPRINTS OF FAITH

21. Spirit of Faith - 2 Corinthians 4:13

22. Walk of Faith - 2 Corinthians 5:7

23. Shield of Faith - Ephesians 6:16

24. Breastplate of Faith - 1 Thessalonians 5:8

25. Unity of Faith - Ephesians 4:13

26. Steadfast Faith - Colossians 2:5

27. Gift of Faith - 1 Corinthians 12:9

28. Unfeigned Faith - 2 Timothy 1:5

29. No Faith - Matthew 4:40

30. Visible Faith - Matthew 9:2

31. Unfailing Faith - Luke 22:32

32. Full of Faith - Acts 6:5

33. Door of Faith - Acts 14:27

34. Faith that is spoken about - Romans 1:8

35. Mutual Faith - Romans 1:12

36. Faith to Faith - Romans 1:17

37. Living by Faith - Romans 1:17

38. Law of Faith - Romans 3:27

39. Faith that gives one access - Romans 5:2

40. Speaking Faith - Romans 10:6

41. Standing Faith - Romans 11:20

42. House of Faith - Galatians 6:10

43. One Faith - Ephesians 4:5

44. Grounded Faith - Colossians 1:23

45. Work of Faith - 1 Thessalonians 1:3

46. First Faith - 1. Timothy 5:12

47. Fight of Faith - 2 Timothy 1:5

48. Keeping Faith - 2 Timothy 4:7

49. Common Faith - Titus 1:4

50. Sound Faith - Titus 2:2

51. Effectual Faith - Philippians 1:6

52. Rich Faith - James 2:12

53. Precious Faith - 2 Peter 1:1

54. Holy Faith - Jude 20

A TO Z BIBLICAL REFERENCES ABOUT THE LIFE OF ABRAHAM

FINGER-TIP FACTS CONCERNING HIS LIFE

I. **Events During His Early Years: From birth to age 86 (Gen. 11-16)**

   1. He was born and raised in Ur of the Chaldees, a city located in the land of Mesopotamia (Gen. 11:27-29; Acts 7:2-4).

   2. Prior to his conversion, Abram was a worshiper of idols (Josh. 24:2).

   3. God appeared to him, and Abram became a believer (Acts 7:2).

   4. He was commanded by God to leave Mesopotamia for a new land that God had promised to show him (Gen. 12:1; Acts 7:3).

   5. He receives a seven-fold promise from God (Gen. 12:2-3).

   6. He departs from Haran at age 75 (Gen. 12:4).

   7. He arrives in Canaan, is promised the land by God, and builds an altar at Bethel (Gen. 12:5-9).

   8. He goes to Egypt during a famine in Canaan, and lies about his wife Sarai (Gen. 12:10-20).

   9. He returns to Bethel and again worships God (Gen. 13:4).

10. He separates from his nephew Lot after an argument over land grazing rights (Gen. 13:5-13).

11. God again promises to give him the land of Canaan (Gen. 13:14-17).

12. He moves to Hebron and builds an altar to God (Gen. 13:18).

13. He rescues his nephew Lot (now living in Sodom) who had been taken prisoner by a Mesopotamian king named Chedorlaomer (Gen. 14:1-17).

14. He meets, gives tithes to, and is blessed by Melchizedek, king of Salem (Gen. 14:18-24).

15. He is promised a son and to become the father of a great nation (Gen. 15:1-5).

16. He believes God and is declared righteous due to his faith (Gen. 15:6).

17. He enters into a blood covenant with God (Gen. 15:7-11).

18. In a dream God reveals to him that his descendants would serve in a foreign land for 400 years, but then depart with great substance (Gen. 15:12-17).

19. He is now given the boundaries of the land (Gen. 15:18-21).

20. At the advice of his barren wife Sarai, he marries Hagar, her Egyptian handmaid with the hope that he could father a son through her (Gen. 16:1-3).

21. Soon after conception, and following an argument, Hagar is sent to the desert by an angry Sarai (Gen. 16:4-6).

22. Hagar is ministered to by the angel of the Lord, promised a son whose name would be called Ishmael, and sent back to Sarai (Gen. 16:7-14).

23. Hagar gives birth to Ishmael when Abram was 86 (Gen. 16:15-16).

II. **Events During His Latter Years: From 86 to 175 (Gen. 17-25)**

2. God appears to Abram when he was 99 years old and changes his name to Abraham (Gen. 17:1-5).

3. He again is promised both seed and soil (Gen. 17:6-8).

4. God now institutes the ceremony of circumcision (Gen. 17:9-14).

5. Sarai's name is now changed to Sarah (Gen. 17:15-16).

6. God promises to bless Ishmael and reassures Abraham that Sarah would give birth to a baby boy who would be called Isaac (Gen. 17:17-22).

7. Abraham circumcises himself and all the males in his camp (Gen. 17:23-27).

8. Abraham is visited by the Lord and two angels, who again reassure him of Isaac's birth, now to occur in less than a year (Gen. 18:1-15).

9. God tells him Sodom would soon be destroyed (Gen. 18:16-22).

10. God grants Abraham's request to spare the city if but ten righteous people could be found living in it (Gen. 18:23-33).

11. Abraham later views the smoke of this burning city, destroyed by God for its immorality (Gen. 19:27-29).

12. He moves to Philistia and, as he had once done in Egypt, lies about his wife (Gen. 20:1-2).

13. Later he prays for and accepts gifts from the Philistine king (Gen. 20:3-18).

14. Isaac is born when Abraham was 100 years old (Gen. 21:1-8).

15. At God's command Abraham separates from both Hagar and Ishmael (Gen. 21:9-21).

16. He enters into a special agreement with a Philistine king at Beer-sheba (Gen. 21:22-34).

17. He offers up Isaac on Mt. Moriah at God's command (Gen. 22:1-10).

18. He is ordered to kill a ram in place of Isaac (Gen. 22:11-13).

19. He calls the name of that place Jehovah-jireh (Gen. 22:14).

20. The Abrahamic Covenant is now reconfirmed (Gen. 22:15-19).

21. He learns concerning the births of his brother Nahor's children including a daughter named Rebekah (Gen. 22:20-24).

22. Sarah dies at age 127 (Gen. 23:1-2).

23. Abraham buys the cave of Machpelah from a Hittite ruler to bury her in. (Gen. 23:3-20).

24. Abraham sends his servant to Mesopotamia to fetch a bride for Isaac (Gen. 24:1-67).

25. Abraham marries Keturah and fathers six sons through her (Gen. 25:1-6).

26. He dies at the age of 175 (Gen. 25:7-11).

DR. ABRAHAM PETERS

A BIBLICAL REFLECTION ON HIS LIFE

I. His Names and Titles

    A. He is called *"the friend of God"* (2 Chron. 20:7; Isa. 41:8; James 2:23).

    B. He is the acknowledged *"father of the Hebrew nation"* (Psa. 47:9; 105:6; Isa. 41:8; 51:2)

    A. The abode of departed believers prior to Calvary was named after him, known as *"Abraham's bosom"* (Luke 16:22). From this abode Abraham himself carried on a conversation with a rich man who had died unsaved (Luke 16:24-31).

        1. The man, being tormented by flames, asked Abraham for relief.

        2. Abraham told him this could not be done.

        3. The man then asked Abraham to send Lazarus (a poor beggar who had died saved) back to earth that he might witness to the rich man's five lost brothers.

        4. Again, Abraham refused, pointing out that they had had ample opportunity to hear the prophets.

        5. If his brothers did not heed their message, they would not listen even if someone were to be raised from the dead.

II. His Universal Influence

A. He was referred to by John the Baptist to rebuke the unbelieving Pharisees and Sadducees (Matt. 3:7-9).

B. Abraham was often referred to by Christ.

1. In distinguishing between Abraham's physical and spiritual seed (Matt. 8:11-12; Luke 13:28-29; John 8:39).

2. To prove that God is the God of the living and not of the dead (Matt. 22:32).

3. To contrast himself with Abraham—*"Jesus said unto them, Verily, verily, I say unto you, Before Abraham was, I am"* (John 8:58).

4. To testify that Abraham enjoyed the blessings of the preincarnate Christ—*"Your father Abraham rejoiced to see my day: and he saw it, and was glad"* (John 8:56).

C. Peter mentioned Abraham on two occasions during his sermon at the Jerusalem gate called Beautiful.

1. "The God of Abraham, and of Isaac, and of Jacob, the God of our fathers, hath glorified his Son Jesus; whom ye delivered up, and denied him in the presence of Pilate, when he was determined to let him go" (Acts 3:13).

2. *"Ye are the children of the prophets, and of the covenant which God made with our fathers, saying unto Abraham, And in thy seed shall all the kindreds of the earth be blessed"* (Acts 3:25).

B. Stephen referred to Abraham on five occasions during his defense before the Jewish high priest (Acts 7:2, 8, 16-17, 32). Stephen pointed out the following:

1. The God of glory had appeared to Abraham in Mesopotamia.

2. God gave him the seal of circumcision.

3. Abraham had purchased the cave of Machpelah as a burial ground.

4. God had promised Abraham that he would someday deliver his descendants from Egyptian bondage.

5. God invoked the name of Abraham during his call to Moses.

C. Paul mentioned Abraham.

1. During his first recorded sermon (Acts 13:26).

2. To illustrate four great truths

a. The meaning of and need for justification (Rom. 4:1-3, 11-12, 16; Gal. 3:16-18)

b. The true identity of Abraham's spiritual seed,

namely, saved Jews and Gentiles, and not merely physical Jews (Rom. 4:11-12, 16; Gal. 3:6-9, 14, 29)

    c.   The sovereignty of God (Rom. 9:6-9)

    d.   The wisdom of God (Rom. 11:1)

F. God himself on three occasions reminded various individuals that he was Abraham's God.

    1.   He reminded Isaac (Gen. 26:24).

    2.   He reminded Jacob (Gen. 28:13).

    3.   He reminded Moses (Exod. 3:6).

G. At least 10 individuals referred to Abraham in their prayers or admonitions.

    1.   Jacob (Gen. 32:9-12)

    2.   Moses (Exod. 32:13)

    3.   David (1 Chron. 16:15)

    4.   Elijah (1 Kings 18:36)

    5.   Jehoshaphat (2 Chron. 29:7)

    6.   Hezekiah (2 Chron. 30:6)

    7.   The Levites in Nehemiah's time (Neh. 9:7)

    8.   Micah (Mic. 7:20)

9. Mary (luke 1:55)

10. Zechariah (Luke 1:73)

III. His Enduring Legacy

    A. God often spared Israel and delivered that nation because of his covenant with Abraham. This occurred:

        1. In the days of the Egyptian captivity (Exod. 2:24)

        2. During the Exodus (Psa. 105:42)

        3. During the reign of King Jehoash (2 Kings 13:22-25)

    B. At least 18 events from Abraham's life are mentioned in the New Testament:

        1. His early life in Mesopotamia (Acts 7:2)

        2. His belief (Acts 7:2; Rom. 4:3; Gal. 3:6; James 2:23)

        3. His receiving of the Abrahamic Covenant (Luke 1:73; Acts 3:25; Heb. 6:13-14)

        4. His call to Canaan (Heb. 11:8)

        5. His sojourn in Haran [Charran, KJV] (Acts 7:4)

        6. His nomadic life in Canaan (Heb. 11:9)

        7. His victory over Chedorlaomer (Heb. 7:1)

        8. His meeting with Melchizedek (Heb. 7:1)

        9. His (and Sarah's) faith in God's promise concerning the birth of

Isaac (Rom. 4:18-21; Heb. 11:11)

10. His circumcision (Acts 7:8; Rom. 4:11)

11. His marriage to Hagar and the birth of Ishmael (Gal. 4:22-24)

12. His meeting with God, just prior to Isaac's birth (Rom. 9:9)

13. His circumcising of Isaac (Acts 7:8)

14. His offering up of Isaac (Heb. 11:17; James 2:21)

15. His belief that, if necessary, God would raise up Isaac from the dead (Heb. 11:19)

16. His submissive wife, Sarah (1 Peter 3:6)

17. His purchase of a sepulcher for Sarah (Acts 7:16)

18. His anticipation of that heavenly city (Heb. 11:10)

DR. ABRAHAM PETERS

PERSONAL THOUGHTS ABOUT HIS LIFE

How Abraham could have reflected on his life:

I still miss Sarah. Let's see, how long has she been gone? I was 137 when she died at age 127. On my next birthday I'll be 175. Nearly 40 years. That's a long time to be separated from someone you love. I can still vividly remember when she and I packed up and left Ur a century ago! What a handsome couple we were back then. Of course all our friends and relatives thought we were crazy! They told us it was bad enough to leave the comfort and safety of city life, but to head out for an unknown land at the command of some invisible God, well, that was sheer insanity! I wonder how Ishmael is doing these days? As I remember, he'll be 88 on his next birthday. The last report I heard was that he had married an Egyptian girl and had fathered 12 sons. That's good! I hope the best for him. My heart still grieves when I think back on those events which made it necessary for us to go our separate ways. Keturah has been a good wife to me, certainly a fruitful one, giving birth to six healthy sons. But it is Isaac of course, the heir of the covenant, the miracle son, who is the source of my joy and comfort.

Again my thoughts turn to Sarah. So much has happened since leaving Ur. God's righteousness has been imputed to the both of us. Her barren womb bore us our beloved Isaac. Each of our names has been changed for the good. From our seed the Messiah Himself will someday come. No, old girl, our friends, not us, were wrong. You probably did on occasion miss the comfort and safety of big city life. I know I still do at times. But not to worry, beloved daughter of the covenant, for we both look for *"a city which hath foundations, whose builder and maker is God."*

SPIRITUAL LESSONS GLEANED FROM HIS LIFE

1. The believer's relationship to the world is never the same after his conversion (Gen. 12:1-3).

2. I am never to depend upon Egypt (a type of the world) in time of trouble (Gen. 12:10).

3. Lying always increases, but never decreases, our problems (Gen. 12:13).

4. My sin can affect unsaved people (Gen. 12:17; 20:18).

5. Righteousness is only imputed by faith (Gen. 15:6).

6. Never substitute God's revealed plan for one of your own (Gen. 12:2; 16:2-3).

7. The purest kind of faith is accepting from God those terrible things you cannot possibly understand (Gen. 22:1-2, 15-18; Heb. 11:17-19).

8. Make every attempt to see that your children marry believers (Gen. 24:1-4).

9. Anticipate the "sweet by and by" while living in the "nasty now and now!" (Heb. 11:10).

DR.ABRAHAM PETERS

A STATISTICAL SUMMARY OVERVIEWING HIS LIFE

Father: Terah (Gen. 11:26)

Spouses: Sarah, Hagar, and Keturah (Gen. 11:29; 16:3; 25:1)

Sons: From Hagar: Ishmael (Gen. 16:15-16). From Sarah: Isaac (Gen. 21:2-3). From Keturah: Zimran, Jokshan, Medan, Midian, Ishbak, and Shuah (Gen. 25:2)

Brothers: Nahor and Haran (Gen. 11:26) Sisters: Half sister was Sarah (Gen. 20:12) First mention: Gen. 11:26

Final mention: 1 Peter 3:6

Meaning of his name: "Father of a multitude" Frequency of his name: Referred to 307 times

Biblical books mentioning him: 27 books (Genesis, Exodus, Leviticus, Numbers, Deuteronomy, Joshua, 1 Kings, 2 Kings, 1 Chronicles, 2 Chronicles, Nehemiah, Psalms, Isaiah, Jeremiah, Ezekiel, Micah, Matthew, Mark, Luke, John, Acts, Romans, 2 Corinthians, Galatians, Hebrews, James, 1 Peter)

Occupation: Patriarch

Place of birth: Ur of the Chaldees (Gen. 11:31)

Place of death: Near Hebron in Canaan (Gen. 23:19; 25:9) Age at death: 175 (Gen. 25:7)

Important fact about his life: He was the father of the Hebrew nation and the ultimate role model for faith (Gen. 12:1-3; 1 Chron. 1:34; 2:1-2; Heb. 11:8-10).

DEDICATION

This book is dedicated In loving memory of my Son, Dominion and my Father Archdeacon Peter F. A. of blessed memory.

DR. ABRAHAM PETERS

ACKNOWLEDGEMENT

A very special gratitude I give to my beloved wife, wonderful woman of God and covenant partner in the ministry Reverend, Teresa Yvonne H Peters, who has always been a constant encourager, prophetess, inspiration and strong supports. I am also very grateful to all other family members. Many thanks to our friends, to mention a few, Lady Gloria Gooden and Mrs. Kathleen Earl, for being a blessing to our ministry.

A million thanks to the family of Enrique, Nancy, Henry and Japheth Moran, your demonstration of love to God and faithfully walking in obedience of faith is exemplary. I am ever grateful for your family for all your love, devotion and dedication to our Lord God. Praying that our Father God continually bless you all immensely!

To all who have helped in the technical process of publishing this Book, I am ever grateful for your labor of love and excellence. To everyone who's searching for answers in their walk of faith and who will come in contact with this book, I can assure you that this is one book inspired by the Holy Spirit and definitely will be worth reading, studying and keeping in your reference library for training and equipping of every Christian minister.

Above all, I would like to express my deepest profound appreciation to my ABBA Father Jehovah GOD Almighty for our redemption through His only begotten Son, our Lord Jesus Christ and the inspiration of His Holy Spirit for the success of this book. To GOD be all the glory. Amen.

ABOUT THE AUTHOR DR. ABRAHAM PETERS

Dr. Abraham Peters is Apostle and Prophet, a multi-gifted preacher, leadership mentor, distinguished author, erudite educator, consultant and counselor who addresses critical Issues affecting the full range of Human, Social and Spiritual development. The central theme of his message is Leadership development by discovery of personal destiny and purpose and building capacity through intensive training of trainers and the maximization of individual potential by transforming follower into efficient and effective leaders; with the focal mission of reviving the saints and rescuing sinners, by taking God's word as the shinning torch of the gospel light unto the darkness in every communities and countries around the world, in the spirit of love and excellence.

He believes that fulfilling God's purpose and Improving your life requires more than inspirational words, religious and motivational concepts, that too many books give you great ideas but don't show you how to apply them. What you need and what Dr. Abraham provides are proven practical steps for actions that work, each designed to help you solve a specific life challenge or problem. He writes books for a variety of people hungry for spiritual growth, positive change and willing to take action to make it happen, men and women who want better relationships, stronger confidence, positive habits, and deeper faith walk with God, for improved social emotional intelligence. What makes Dr. Abraham Peters' books different is his ability to explain complex ideas and strategies in a very simple, accessible way that you can implement right away.

Dr. Abraham Peters' commitment to teaching the complete Word of God continues to make him a sought-after speaker and writer. His passion for reaching the lost and encouraging believers in their faith is demonstrated through his faithful communication of sound Biblical truths. He has earned degrees as Doctor of Epidemiologist and Public Global Health Consultant, in ministry he is licensed as Ordained Minister with Doctor of Divinity in Theology degrees. He is the Presiding Bishop of Winners' Power House, The All Nations House of Prayer Prophetic Ministries International.

Dr. Abraham Peters functioning in the role of an Apostle/Prophet and is sounding a clear voice in this season that it is time for God's people to wake up from their sleep and slumber through the Great Awakening Prophetic Prayer and Praise Fire Conferences. He has and continues to minister in Churches and Conferences. He has published several Books noted for their crisp simplicity, Biblical balanced, spiritually healthy and practical principles. He enjoys spending time with his Family.

You can Connect with Dr. Abraham Peters on Facebook Like Page (@Dr. Abraham Peters), Twitter (@ApostleAbPeters), YouTube (@Abraham Peters) and on Instagram (@ApostleDr Ab-Peters). E-Mail: abrahampeters@rocketmail.com

www.ingramcontent.com/pod-product-compliance
Lightning Source LLC
Chambersburg PA
CBHW052015070526
44584CB00016B/1761